Rights sold to:
Critica (Barcelona)

La Nouvelle Agence
7, rue Corneille
75006 Paris

FROM SLAVE TO PHARAOH

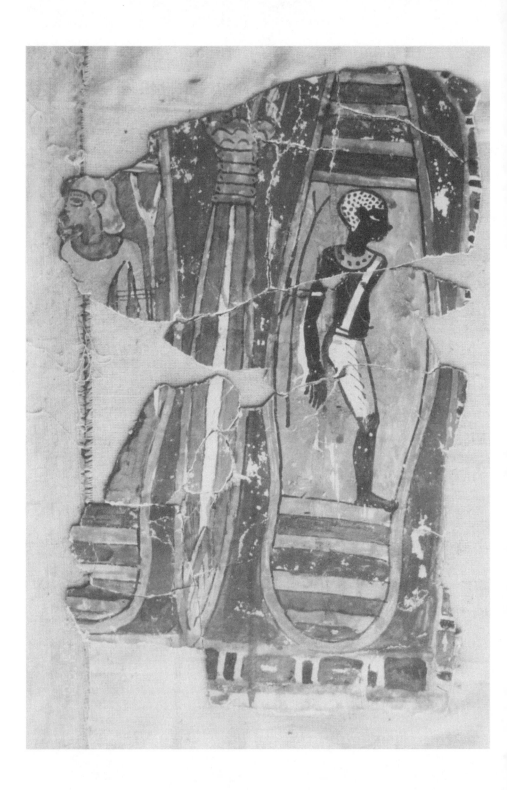

DONALD B. REDFORD

FROM SLAVE TO PHARAOH
THE BLACK EXPERIENCE
OF ANCIENT EGYPT

THE JOHNS HOPKINS UNIVERSITY PRESS
BALTIMORE AND LONDON

© 2004 The Johns Hopkins University Press
All rights reserved. Published 2004
Printed in the United States of America on acid-free paper
2 4 6 8 9 7 5 3 1

The Johns Hopkins University Press
2715 North Charles Street
Baltimore, Maryland 21218-4363
www.press.jhu.edu

Frontispiece: Nubian and Asiatic, traditional enemies of Egypt, bound under the sandals of a mummy, in a traditional pejorative device. Thebes, Late Period.

Library of Congress Cataloging-in-Publication Data
Redford, Donald B.
From slave to pharaoh : the black experience of ancient Egypt / Donald B. Redford.
p.   cm.
Includes bibliographical references and index.
ISBN 0-8018-7814-4 (hardcover : alk. paper)
1. Egypt—History—To 332 B.C. 2. Nubia—History. 3. Blacks—Egypt—History. I. Title.
DT83.R4 2004
932′.015—dc21

A catalog record for this book is available from the British Library.

CONTENTS

CONTENTS

ILLUSTRATIONS

MAPS

FIGURES

PREFACE

The present work is *not* a history of Nubia and the Sudan in antiquity, still less a history of Egypto-Nubian relations up to the seventh century B.C. The advent of complex society in the Nile Valley and the possible role and interaction of Nubia in the process of the development of the state are, similarly, not the burden of the inquiry, however fascinating speculation on these topics might be. A disquisition on the efflorescence of historical cultures in Nubia, such as the A-group or the C-group, is the preserve of the archaeologist and the historian of the subcataract Nile Valley and is really not germane to the topic at hand. Begun with an eye on the achievements of the Twenty-fifth Dynasty in Egypt, *From Slave to Pharaoh* has expanded into a general overview of the Nubian and Kushite experience of the expansionist power of Egypt and its culture up to 671 B.C. The fundamental questions that lead into, and inform, the discussion are those that have suggested themselves from time to time to all who reflect on ethnic relations in northeastern Africa: How were the dark-skinned Nubians and Sudanese blacks perceived and treated by the Egyptians? Did the several communities in the Nile Valley separate from one another in the conceit of spatial and spiritual boundaries? If they did so, why did one community, that of imperial Egypt, consider extensive tracts beyond its boundary to be its own legitimate sphere of influence? And how did the Nubian and Sudanese inhabitants of these tracts react to the loss of self-determination that inevitably followed their being swallowed up in such a sphere of influence? Following this discussion is a description of the imposition of more regularized, imperial structures, first at Kerma, then in Egypt proper; and the long, checkered history of the relationship between the communities is then traced against the backdrop of empire up to 671 B.C. This date was chosen as a stopping point because, with the rise of Saïs, the focus shifts dramatically to the north and one is obliged to pursue new or modified themes.

The investigation of these themes in the years between 671 and 332 B.C. will be the subject of a forthcoming publication by the author.

Studies somewhat related to the purpose of the present work center upon what an earlier generation might have termed "race relations" between Mediterranean and Nilotic peoples. Sadly, these have in some cases degenerated into acrimonious wrangling over who owes what to whom in a cultural sphere and the ingratitude in failing to acknowledge the alleged debt. Although the more extreme positions of Eurocentrists and Afrocentrists alike have now been abandoned, neither they nor their more sober counterparts show much inclination to adopt a dispassionate empirical approach. What I have tried to do is to allow the Egyptian texts to speak for themselves, whether or not their statements appear to us moderns to be "politically correct." It matters not a whit whether the ancients bolster or destroy our prejudiced positions: listening to their voices is the first thing we ought to do. Perhaps their words will have the salutary effect of marginalizing some prejudices and rendering them of no real moment.

A number of people contributed to the completion of the manuscript. Thanks are especially due to my wife, Susan, who is responsible for the graphics, and to Linda Wilding, who typed and edited the text. I should like also to acknowledge the excavation staff who, between the years 1975 and 1990, helped excavate the Twenty-fifth and Twenty-sixth Dynasty villas in East Karnak. Parts of Chapter 14 anticipate an unpublished paper on domestic architecture at Thebes in the Late Period.

FROM SLAVE TO PHARAOH

INTRODUCTION

Despite its course through inimical terrain and its periodic interruption by cataracts (see map 1), the Nile constitutes one of the truly great and most easily negotiated transit corridors in the world. It also provides security and a guarantee of life. A community living along its banks is sheltered from hostile incursions from almost any point of the compass. Although it is a simple matter to keep in touch with people on the other side of the cataract, one need not fear them, for it is extremely difficult to bring major force to bear across such a natural obstacle. The permanence of the food stocks seems a heaven-sent blessing: an abundance of fish, fowl, and game eliminates the need to wander in search of them and provides for a continuum in human settlement over millennia.

From the time of the desiccation of the erstwhile savannah terrain in the eastern Sahara and the enforced movement of human groups towards the Nile (c. 50,000 B.P.), the evidence militates in favor of the continuity and longevity of ethnic groups in northeastern Africa from the mid-Sudan to the Mediterranean. The old notion of waves of "races" flowing up the Nile Valley, effecting cultural change and improvement, is now known to be as erroneous as it was simplistic.[1] New ideas need not come by means of invasion: occasionally they are indigenous and may parallel similar discoveries elsewhere which are wholly unrelated. Already towards the close of the last glaciation in Europe, for example (c. 14,000–12,000 B.P.), the communities in Lower Nubia which go under the label "Qadan" culture were experimenting with harvesting grasses and possibly artificial cultivation.[2] This early trial of agriculture—the knowledge appears not to have survived—does not alter the fact that quite independently in the Mediterranean woodlands of the Levant similar domestication of cereals and animals was taking place;[3] and it was awareness of these experiments which eventually stimulated similar attempts in the Lower Nile and Delta.

1

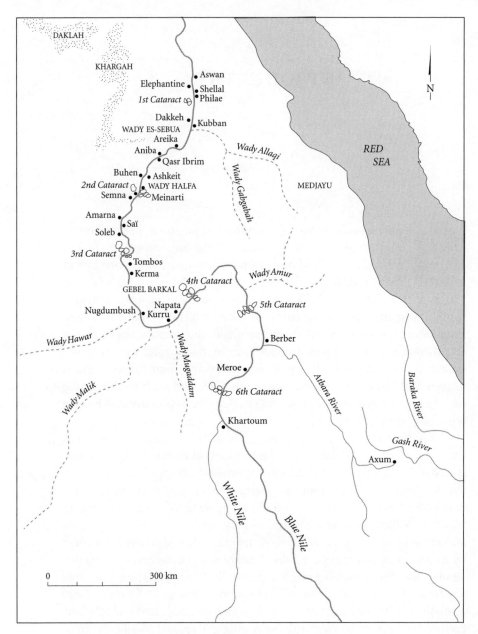

Map 1. Nubia, Kush, and Sudan.

Human societies invite comparative "grading" on the basis of intellectual achievement, technology, sophistication in art, and organizational complexity. This is both inevitable and invidious. But it is nonetheless true that at certain times and places energy and imagination appear to concentrate and to be stimulated in a limited number of centers, around which other communities revolve as "lesser breeds without the law" (in the perception of the "center" of course!). Regionality and the parochialism that attends it had already set in by 20,000 B.P. in northeastern Africa.[4] Lower Nubia, Dongola, and the region of Khartoum gradually evolved their own individual and distinct culture sequence, related to but clearly different from the culture sequences in Egypt proper north of the First Cataract. Although they shared an artistic tradition with Egypt and imported commodities from and were stimulated by the ceramic styles of the north,[5] the prehistoric Nubians were disadvantaged by the reduced agricultural potential of the river valley south of Aswan. With surer food stocks and easier access to international transit corridors, the inhabitants of the Nile Valley between Aswan and the Mediterranean looked as though they had been especially favored by the Fates. This feeling, a subconscious rationalization of climatological and geographical determinants, must have appeared to have been confirmed when, during the last quarter of the fourth millennium B.C., a new phenomenon was born at the apex of the Delta, namely, a political regime that we today would call a "monarchy." Moreover, this new system of governance claimed a *territorium* embracing not merely a circuit described by one day's march from the "center" but the entire length of the Nile Valley, where a single ethnic and linguistic group resided! This was shortly to turn Aswan and the cataract region of Elephantine into the Nubian frontier for all time.[6] North of this point lay Egypt, Egyptianness, and organization; south, foreign land, foreignness, and disorder.[7]

If the content of the last sentence reflects how the Egyptians thought of Nubia—and it does, as we shall see—it did not exactly correspond to reality in the years immediately preceding and following 3000 B.C., for the inhabitants of Lower Nubia in the second half of the fourth millennium had established themselves and their culture in a series of independent chiefdoms of some sophistication.[8] This culture, known as A-group,[9] comprised a series of relatively small communities, each occupying a limited stretch of arable land on the Nile and relying still on hunting and fishing,[10] but it now found itself lying athwart an important transit corridor by which sub-Saharan products came north. The new Egypt and its rulers craved these products, and for a while A-group graves yield evidence of trade with the north.

But the pharaonic regime must shortly have been impressed by its own power and the relative ease and economy of taking what it wanted by main force. Several rulers of the First Dynasty have left their names or rock drawings (or both) indicating bellicose activity in either Lower Nubia or the southeastern desert;[11] and annalistic labels and ivories from Protodynastic Egypt confirm the warlike stance contemporary kings had adopted towards the south.[12] Shortly they were to realize also that Nubia could provide substantial quantities of manpower, and these rulers would raid the south for slaves.[13]

For Nubia the result of this unhappy confrontation was disastrous. The promising culture of the A-group peoples was swept away, and Lower Nubia suffered a setback in its ongoing development from which it was not to recover for one thousand years. The die was cast. Now Egypt found itself a dominant—and domineering!—culture, the only one of its kind in northeastern Africa, facing adjacent peoples who could not read or write; had no "Perfect God" to rule them; could not erect colossal monuments; had no surpassing goldsmiths, coppersmiths, sculptors, or joiners; knew no advanced techniques of agriculture; and still lived in huts. How could an Egyptian help but feel superior? More to the point: How could an Egyptian help not feeling contempt?

EGYPTIANS AND NUBIANS

uman interaction between communities operates on many levels. Although conventional attitudes and propaganda do not necessarily characterize each one, at root lies an intensely personal identification of the individual which thrives on hostility, for one must not only, for purposes of safety and power, define and belong to the "kin" group, the "us," but must also identify, isolate, and confront all who do not belong to the group, the "them." Moreover, the criteria on which the judgment is made as to who does or does not belong are not imposed consciously from the top: the aversion springs spontaneously and unconsciously in the human psyche and is always based initially on observable traits such as color, language, costume, and social practice. The Id cannot tolerate differences in another human being, for they constitute a threat. The individual perceives a need to hate as well as to love, and a state seeks only to control and channel both emotions.

Even before the appearance of the "state," whatever that is, the human community had begun consciously to create a rationalizing mythology to explain the existence of "them" (as well as "us"). Eventually the great archetypal myths (which all have their roots in parochial communities of agricultural subsistence) provided a moral basis for the individual's working out of his or her love and hatred. If and when a complex society is born with a political and economic "center" and a supporting "periphery," the former simply gives a voice to the base instincts of the latter: it does not change them.[1]

The spontaneous xenophobia that results is well attested by the ancient Egyptian experience. Egyptians were well aware of color differences.[2] They perceived themselves as a russet hue, whereas Asiatics were of a paler yellowish color (see fig. 1). Southerners are depicted as darker (chocolate brown or black) than Egyptians and Asiatics (see Frontispiece);[3] the very name *Nḥsi*, "Nubian," originally meant "bronzed/

Fig. 1. Anatolian blondes and Nubian blacks, representing the northern and southern extremities of Egypt's New Kingdom empire. Thebes, throne dais of Nefertity, fourteenth century B.C.

burnt," in the same vein as the Greek ΑἰθίοΨ.[4] Egyptians were also well aware of the existence of Sudanese blacks (see fig. 2).[5] That they spoke a tongue markedly different from Egyptian was self-evident. Egyptian partook of the "words of God,"[6] and every Egyptian longed to hear it even when abroad.[7] In contrast, foreign languages were pure gibberish, and those who spoke them, especially Nubians, were "gibberers."[8] Costume provided clear differences: foreigners wore "shoulder-knots," "kilts," "skins," and the like, or wore feathers, or refrained from shaving; they also handled the bow and throw stick.[9]

The obvious alien nature of foreign society drew from Egyptians a wide variety of reactions, but all were more or less hostile. They ranged from mere curiosity (rare), through fear, contempt, and revulsion, to a will to annihilate. Foreigners were those who knew "not how they should live . . . hungry and living like wild game."[10] They were given to rapine and cattle rustling[11] and were cowardly, timorous, and deceitful: "The Nubian has but to hear (a sound) and he falls at a voice, it is merely answering him that makes him retreat; if one is aggressive against him, he turns tail, retreat and he becomes more aggressive. They are certainly not people to be respected: they are craven wretches. My majesty has seen them—it is no lie!"[12]

Even at the best of times Nubians were irresponsible and lazy but dangerous because of their ability in black magic. Amenophis II advised his southern viceroy (c. 1425 B.C.): "Don't be at all lenient with Nubia! Beware of their people and their magicians![13] See to the labour-taxes of the

Fig. 2. Upper-class Nubian gentry. Thebes, tomb of Ramesses III, twelfth century B.C.

peasants which you shall bring in order to give it to the (appropriate) officer; if there is no officer of yours, let it be reported to His Majesty. Otherwise, one will have to listen to (the following): 'an axe of electrum with fixtures of bronze is missing, and the stout quarter-staff is in a water hole, and the other one is in the marsh(??)!' Don't listen to their words and don't meddle in their affairs!"[14] Kush is usually said to be "weak/ vile";[15] the Nubians are "doomed" from the outset. Any appearance by the king on an expedition south of the First Cataract usually carries with it the explicit purpose "to overthrow vile Kush."[16]

On the battlefields Nubians fell into a well-crafted and much used framework of pejoration. They were "the god's abomination,"[17] fit only to be "tenants" of Egypt. Lurid rhetoric described their defeat: "[My Majesty] made [a great slaughter among them], (both) men and women, the valleys being (filled) with the flayed and the mountains with the transfixed";[18] "the Nubian grows limp, choked in his grasp . . . none of them survives, the Nubian troglodytes fall to his slaughter cast aside throughout their territories, their entrails flood their valleys the mouths of which were smeared red as with a cloudburst of driving rain. The carrions were overhead, a host of birds pecking and carrying away."[19]

This fundamental attitude towards foreigners differed little from theater to theater: Asiatics, Libyans, Nubians *mutatis mutandis* excited the same pejoratives and scorn. The Egyptian worldview was too far-reaching to exempt them. Pharaoh ruled all that the sun-disk encircled, Egyptian and foreigners: any act or omission on the part of the latter in their own interests was labeled "rebellion" or "uprising" in Egyptian rhetoric.[20]

The Nubians belonged to the *ḫ3st*, as did non-Egyptian peoples in general, and that denoted their essential otherness, for *ḫ3st* signified the hilly desert terrain in diametric contradistinction to the alluvial flood plain of the Nile. Nothing grows there,[21] it is the domain of the sterile Seth,[22] it is raw and undeveloped.[23] Too often it is associated with "Chaos,"[24] but there is nothing "chaotic" (in the sense of lacking order, unpredictable) about it. The desert is "antilife," inimical to humans, but neither amorphous, nor infinite, nor disorganized. It is in the Egyptian mind associated with a moral, not a primordial, plane: *ḫ3st* displays sheer malevolence.[25] Those humans who originate there and represent this essential characteristic, therefore, must be restrained; their proper position is prostrate and bound beneath the feet of Pharaoh.

At the level of personal contact the conventional attitude just described was modified somewhat. Within Egypt, or territory held by Egypt, Nubians displayed varying degrees of acculturation, and one cannot generalize over three millennia of ancient history. In the Nubian districts controlled by Egypt under the empire, it was very much the "thing to do" for chiefs to mimic Egyptian ways and become proper Egyptian gentlemen.[26] The rank and file of the Nubian tribesmen, on the other hand, could expect only tight control by Egyptian overseers or intimidation by the Egyptian army.[27] Expatriate Nubians located inside Egypt lived for the most part in separate cantons,[28] though intermarriage and assimilation were not unheard of and may even have been the norm at certain times. In the First Intermediate Period we find Nubians living side by side with Egyptians in towns of Upper Egypt, some transcribing their names in hieroglyphic script and setting up mortuary stelae.[29] Nubian residents of Egyptian communities were able to employ the organs of the law just like natives.[30] Within Egypt they found certain occupations reserved for them by common consent: paramilitary police[31] with a reputation for tough treatment of the civilian population,[32]

Fig. 3. Brutalizing a captive Nubian. Saqqara, tomb of Ḥoremḥeb, fourteenth century B.C.

certain minor functions at court such as fan bearer,[33] lesser priesthoods,[34] and, in the Eighteenth Dynasty, tutorships.[35]

It cannot be denied, however, that adverse discrimination is attested in our sources. Foreigners, or even residents born in Egypt of foreign extraction, were not necessarily accepted as Egyptians:[36] acclimation of Egyptian language and culture was the basic ingredient of "Egyptianness." A decree of Pepy I (c. 2325 B.C.) prohibits Nubians from harvesting (on lands belonging to the pyramid towns of Snofru) or from entering the temple.[37] Nubians employed in the infrastructure of the state might suffer neglect or deprivation or endure haranguing.[38] A poignant document from the twenty-seventh year of Thutmose III (c. 1477 B.C.) implies that discrimination at law, segregation at the palace gate, and even beating could be expected by foreigners resident in Egypt.[39] And a vivid scene from the Memphite tomb of Ḥoremḥeb (c. 1350 B.C.) actually depicts the beating of a Nubian prisoner (see fig. 3). And all foreigners, of course, including Nubians, were normally prohibited from entering the sanctuaries of the gods and excluded from the mysteries.[40]

When individual Egyptians found themselves in autonomous communities of Nubians and wrote of their experiences, the xenophobia described earlier is conspicuous by its absence. Those Egyptian freebooters who sought their fortunes in the independent kingdom of Kush in the seventeenth and sixteenth centuries recount their adventures in a matter-of-fact way free of pejoratives, either formulaic or original. "I am the doughty servant of the ruler of Kush," says one Ka; "I washed my feet in the waters of Kush in the service of the Ruler Nedjeḥ-ḳen(?), and I came back [therefrom] safe and endowed(?) <with> chattels." "I was the doughty commandant of Buhen," says Seped-ḥer. "No other commandant ever did what I did: I built the Temple of Horus lord of Buhen to the satisfaction of the Ruler of Kush."[41] Clearly the prospect of adventure, and more particularly the acquisition of wealth, exerted an overriding attraction on these expatriates. On his side the ruler of Kush required warriors and builders, and so the interests of Egyptian and Nubian coincided. Promoting hatred now served no useful purpose: inflammatory propaganda therefore died.

It would be interesting to know how the Nubians reacted to the racial attitudes Egypt manifested towards them, and in particular whether they shared a similar xenophobic aversion to all Egyptians. Unfortunately, such knowledge will always be difficult to acquire. It is very doubtful whether the Nubians and Kushites of the third and second millennia ever developed their own script, so that the vast majority remained illiterate and cannot speak to us over the centuries. It will forever be unknown whether the little Nubian princesses brought to Pharaoh's court in the Eighteenth Dynasty silently cursed Egypt and its people or whether, like Aïda, they breathed a tearful "O patria mia!" in remembering their homeland. Of those few who, through acclimation, attempted to write in Egyptian, most passed themselves off as "People of the Black Land," natives of Egypt and loyal subjects of Pharaoh. One should never underestimate the overwhelming and irresistible attraction of the way of life of the triumphant imperial culture, whether Egyptian, Hellenic, Roman, or British. Something more than a grudging admiration had overcome Nubian chiefs such as Heḳa-nefer or Ruya: they had "realized" that to be Egyptian meant to be an Übermensch. In a supreme irony of history, when finally Kush emerged from its dark age in the eighth century B.C. and began to erect memorials in the Egyptian language, the clear contempt it entertained towards Egyptians was born of the firm belief that Kush alone was the preserver and promoter of the pure Egyptian way of life.

THE PROBLEM OF FRONTIERS

gypt enjoys the protection of a series of well-defined natural frontiers that enhance the meaning of *boundary* in the consciousness of anyone resident in the land.[1] Rugged deserts east and west demarcate the limits of life with the sureness and abruptness of a single line, and the treacherous Mediterranean and the shelving beaches of the Delta prevent passage as effectively as a physical wall. In the south, though the land is transected by the Nile, one of the easiest transit corridors in the world, a series of five rapids (cataracts) distributed over nearly a thousand miles of valley makes passage in either direction extremely difficult. Within the floodplain and Delta the sharp demarcation of plots of ground by waterways undoubtedly contributed to the late semantic shift of *t3š* to mean "district" (i.e., a tract defined by a *t3š*).

The overriding importance of "boundary," in the thinking of Egyptians, is underscored by the centrality of real estate disputes in times of economic decline or outright civil war. The first act of reform following any period of intestine strife was the resurveying of landed property throughout the entire country and the creation or revising of the land cadaster.[2] The result in times of prosperity was the existence in various archives[3] of "inventories of hundreds of thousands of farm-lands, 'islands,' high-ground and all (types of) fields,"[4] all marked by boundary stelae sometimes qualified as "His Majesty's decree-stela, certified by survey."[5] To move such boundary stelae was a moral outrage roundly condemned in wisdom literature,[6] and owners sometimes called down a hail of curses on the heads of those who might be tempted.

THE RESTRICTIVE BOUNDARY

To the Egyptian, "boundary" implied the security that accompanied permanence and stability, and no stability could be enjoyed if there was flux.

To abide in one place, permanent and unchanging, meant happiness, peace, and conformity to *ma⟨at*. Within the boundary the sedentary agricultural community, whose members never moved away, symbolized civilization as it had come from the hand of the creator. The members of the extended family,[7] working the soil in their ancestral town, reflected the ethical values pleasing to god and king. And moving from their ancestral home was the farthest thing from their minds. "Be stout-hearted! Embrace your children, kiss your wife and see to your house! That's better than anything! . . . Thrive at home and be buried (there)!"[8]

Beyond the boundary malevolence reigned. Out there the bedu eked out their miserable existence, constantly on the move, unable to settle, always fighting.[9] The boundary marked the separation between the sedentary, god-ordained community of Egyptians and the lawless, doomed wanderers of the desert. As a line of demarcation a watch had to be placed on it and fortifications built. Above all, unauthorized incursions of the wanderers to settle in the "home counties" could not be tolerated: strong points were set up on the frontier to bar the way to would-be settlers and monitor the movements of seasonal migrants. The latter were allowed to cross on certain days and traders to carry their goods to Egyptian markets;[10] but neither were allowed to stay beyond the duration of their immediate mission. The southern boundary stela of the late Middle Kingdom (mid–nineteenth century B.C.) set on record the regulation and published it for all to see: "Boundary made in regnal year 8 under the Majesty of the King of Upper and Lower Egypt Kha-kau-re, given life forever and ever! in order to prevent any Nubian from crossing it on water or land in a *k3i*-vessel, or any livestock of the Nubians; except for the Nubian who may come to trade in Aḳen or on a mission. They are to be treated favorably in every way, but no Nubian *k3i*-vessel is to be allowed to pass by Ḥeḥ going northwards forever!"[11] Surveillance of the border required implacable resolve, constancy, and vigilance: it was not a task for the lazy or timorous. The same king, Senwosret III, sternly admonished his successors in this regard: "Now as for any son of mine who shall strengthen this boundary which My Majesty has made, he *is* my son, he was born to My Majesty—how fine is a son that champions his father and strengthens the boundary of him that begat him!—But as for him who shall lose it and not fight for it, he is not *my* son, he certainly wasn't born to me!"[12]

If the boundary was intended to restrict movement from the outside to the "interior," it was also meant to filter goods coming into Egypt, or, perhaps more accurately, to see that the best goods were allowed to pass and directed to their proper destination. The title "overseer of the restricted(?) entry-point(s) of Upper Egypt"[13] indicates supervision of what was coming into Egypt either across the cataract or via the wadies leading into Upper Egypt from the western desert.[14] Much of this imported material was classified as confidential, and local governors were proud to have been confided in by the royal administration: "I was privy"—an oft-repeated boast—"to anything confidential which was brought from the restricted(?) foreign entry-point from the southern foreign lands."[15]

THE DEFENDED BOUNDARY IN THE DELTA

Egypt enjoys natural and defensible frontiers bestowed on it by its geographical setting. The deserts east and west of the Nile were virtually impassable. Only three wadies through the eastern desert offered themselves as transit corridors, but all three were used and controlled by the Egyptians themselves: the Wady Araba, in the north opposite the Fayum, provided easy access to the coast of the Red Sea and the Sinai beyond; the Wady Hammamat proffered the diorite quarries and the shortest route to the Red Sea and Pwēnet; and the Wady Mia gave access to the gold mines. If bedu occasionally slipped through to the Nile Valley, they came in small, manageable groups. The western desert, though dotted with oases and a major north-south route, yields limited access to the Nile: entry through the Fayum, Asyut, or Abydos never appealed to large hostile groups bent on plunder or conquest.

The three points of entry through which foreigners were to be expected lay on the sides of the Delta and at Elephantine at the First Cataract. The prospect of upwards of nine major Nile mouths on the Mediterranean coast might have cheered the heart of some unsuspecting Asiatic or Greek mariners, but in fact they each proved notoriously difficult to negotiate by Bronze or Iron Age sailing vessels. All the Egyptians had to do was to "man" the Delta mouths with garrisons and build well-sited watchtowers, and few hostile fleets had any chance of penetrating Lower Egypt by sea. The land routes along the North African coast are narrowly confined by the Sahara and Sinai Deserts and debouch into the Delta at single, not multiple, access points. At the best of times one or two strategically placed forts were sufficient to block the entry of any undesirable body of visitors for an indefinite period of time. Although for the Old and Middle Kingdoms no archaeological remains of such forts have been recovered, the titles of fortress commandants from these periods conclusively prove their sometime presence. To judge by the forts of Nubia in the Middle Kingdom and representations in tomb paintings and reliefs, these forts must have been substantial affairs with thick walls and towers of mud brick, embellished with merlons, glacis, and (at times) moats. In times of political weakness and "downsizing" when commandants and garrisons were withdrawn, the unwatched border suffered nought but the incursions of small groups of bedu, intent on watering their flocks.

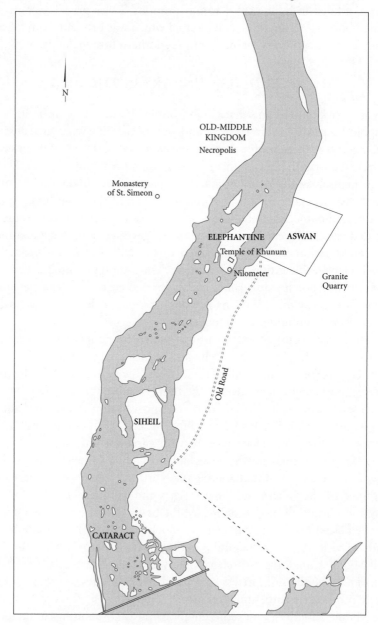

Fig. 4. Elephantine and the First Cataract region.

THE SOUTHERN FRONTIER

Despite the Twelfth Dynasty's accomplishment in pushing Egypt's political border to Semna at the Second Cataract, an extension perpetuated in the modern state's boundary, Egypt in fact terminated at the First Cataract (see fig. 4).[16] Here the Egyptian language and the native Egyptian culture found their most southerly exponents in the communities of Aswan and Elephantine. Few in number and isolated in what is essentially an oasis on the Nile, the inhabitants of the cataract region were rustics speaking a dialect almost unintelligible in the north. Tradition had it that the noise of the cataract rendered them hard of hearing. Like most of the townships of the "Head of the South," they lacked the resources or the political clout to command the best artisans, and the result was, for the most part, tombs and shrines of mediocre and provincial workmanship. Only when the king lent the necessary skilled workers and material did buildings of first-rate quality arise.

Elephantine's remoteness and lack of resources conferred on its local leaders a second-class status vis-à-vis their counterparts farther north (see fig. 5a). Most, if not all, of them were $ḥ3ty-ᶜ$, a royal functionary who held office-cum-estate at the king's pleasure. Very few achieved the quasi-baronial status of "Great Chief of the Township," like their colleagues in the

Fig. 5a. Staircase approach and facades of Old Kingdom tombs at Qubbet el-Hawa. Elephantine, twenty-third century B.C.

Fig. 5b. Outcrops of granite, First Cataract.

Fig. 5c. Scene of the mortuary meal in the tomb of the mayor of Elephantine, Nubkhaure-nakht (Sirenpowet II), prepared by his son Onkhu. Qubbet el-Hawa, nineteenth century B.C.

second, fourth, and sixth townships of Upper Egypt. They worked for the king, sometimes supervising the quarrying of granite (see fig. 5b) or more often leading commercial expeditions. Passing by on expedition into Nubia, the king might fete the town and send the local governor a meal from his own table.[17] The gift of three hundred northern chattels and a tomb constructed at the king's expense was something to boast about;[18] and when invited to attend the royal jubilee, a governor might launch into ecstatic transports of hyperbole.[19] A robust male who dallied with the ladies,[20] Governor Sirenpowet bragged of not having to perform *proskynesis* to any magistrate of greater rank than he, by royal authorization (see fig. 5c).[21] At times when the central administration was concerned about the south, Elephantine found itself courted by the government; but remoteness had its compensations, and wayward governors might indulge in corrupt practices with only a slight risk of being hauled into the "Broad Hall of Horus."[22]

But life was hard on the rocky island. The food base was restricted by the limited amount of arable land, and the community subsisted through

Fig. 6. Inscriptions on the rocks of the island of Siheil, First Cataract. New Kingdom.

infusions of food from farther north and by fishing. And fishermen did not look forward solely to the quiet life of the angler: on them fell the task of keeping the navigable channel through the cataract clean and dredged.[23] Doubtless the local population eagerly awaited expeditionary forces en route to Nubia or quarrying expeditions bound for the nearby granite quarries, for then a demand for services would result in remuneration. The same anticipation must have attended the return of troops from a Nubian campaign, when dignitaries from the court gathered at the cataract to greet the victorious pharaoh (see fig. 6).

NUBIA
EGYPT'S PRIMARY SPHERE OF INFLUENCE

Throughout all its ancient history Egypt oriented itself upriver: south would have been "up" on any pharaonic map large enough to include northeastern Africa. The word for "west," *imntt,* was derived from the Afro-Asiatic root for "right hand," and the verb "to go forward (by ship)" meant "to sail south." The "forward part" of every township was located on its southern side, and the "forward part of the earth" denoted the southern extremity of Nubia. The latter, then, constituted Egypt's field of vision and, certainly in the Old Kingdom, the main focus of its interests.

THE MANPOWER RESOURCES OF THE SOUTH

The outward expansion of the warlike Horuses of the First Dynasty was apparently not continued in the Second Dynasty. For unknown reasons, in both the Sudan and Asia Egypt seems to have suspended its efforts to implant a *domestic* authority among peoples who did not speak Egyptian. The one exception was the barren stretch of the Nile between Silsileh and Aswan, the upper part of which was always remembered as "the Land of the Bow," that is, Nubia. But this may have been but sparsely settled in the early third millennium, and in any case the natural frontier of the cataract beckoned, a more secure barrier than Silsileh.

Now Egypt's interests were restricted to the resources of the region south of the cataract, and its overall policy was modified to ensure access and acquisition. The high cartouches of the king might glower over the cataract[1] and fortified blockhouses might watch the frontier,[2] but a much more effective way of realizing goals was to mount an armed "march-about," a veritable pharaonic *chevauchée.*[3] This was bound to produce booty, if not goods and slaves acquired through trade (if the locals proved sufficiently intimidated), and consequently would more than

19

pay for itself. The evidence that has survived suggests that expeditions were mounted on a grand scale. The annals for Snofru's thirteenth or fourteenth year record in part "hacking up the land of the Nubian: bringing living captives, 7,000; cattle, 200,000."[4] On the rocks of Lower Nubia are found two graffiti that date from not long after Snofru's reign: "royal chargé-d'affaires[5] for the 17th Upper Egyptian township Kha-bau-bat: his arrival with an army of 20,000; the hacking up of Wawat," and "the royal chargé-d'affaires for the northern district of the 'East' Zau-ib; seizing 17,000 Nubians."[6] The immediate result of such bondage en masse must have been the depopulation of Lower Nubia (which does in fact show up in the archaeological record).[7] Pictorial depictions of such captives are more difficult to produce,[8] although they turn up pictured in domestic service as (generically) nḥsyw "Nubians,"[9] ḫ3styw "foreigners,"[10] or -ʿw "kilt-(wearers)." The last, wrongly translated as "interpreters" in the older literature,[11] are in fact paramilitary units, used as auxiliaries or perhaps police, as were the Medjay in the New Kingdom.

Nubians were highly regarded as fighters, and this reputation was to survive the reality. Already in the Old Kingdom the recruitment of an Egyptian host bears eloquent testimony to the value placed on them as auxiliary troops. When Weny, the governor of Upper Egypt, was commissioned by Pepy I (c. 2350 B.C.) to command a punitive expedition against the inhabitants of Palestine, he levied troops not only from Upper and Lower Egypt but also "Nubians of Irtjet,[12] Nubians of Medja,[13] Nubians of Yam,[14] Nubians of Wawat and Nubians of Kaw."[15] During the First Intermediate Period, when Egyptian influence over Nubia weakened perceptibly, Nubians still sought employment in Egyptian military units. Nomarchs of Upper Egypt were by no means averse to attracting Nubians into their small municipal militias.[16]

THE PRODUCTS OF THE SOUTH

From remote prehistoric times the inhabitants of the Nile Valley and Delta north of the First Cataract had been aware that the source of a large number of desirable tropical products lay not in Egypt but in the lands of the Sudan, if not farther south. For the Predynastic Period only chance finds in archaeological contexts provide the rather spotty evidence on what Nilotic communities were able to procure from the south; but with the invention of writing a more complete record becomes available. Then it is apparent that acquisition of goods from Africa in bulk could be effected only by individuals commanding transport, manpower, and supplies, and this meant the king. Such products acquired through either coercion or trade went to Memphis and into the royal stores, where they were termed "royal luxury products."[17]

It is less clear that much of the material Egypt craved from Nubia did not originate there but was intercepted by the Egyptians, or traded for, as it came north from a source much farther south. The majority is of a tropical nature, unavailable north of the First Cataract. Two of the commonest items, from the Old Kingdom through classical times, were ivory[18] (tusks or manufactured) and ebony.[19] In more detailed lists of the New Kingdom both emanated from the more remote Kush,[20] and ebony seems to have been three times more plentiful than ivory.[21] Panther skins are nearly as common (less often the living animal).[22] Myrrh, incense,[23] and various aromatic woods[24] are frequently mentioned, as well as gums, resins, and spices.[25] Of precious metals gold tops the list,[26] and although the Egyptians knew of its presence in the south at an early date, the extensive working of the mines dates from the New Kingdom. Other precious metals, semiprecious stones, or minerals include electrum,[27] red jasper,[28] ochre,[29] malachite,[30] haematite and amethyst,[31] gems,[32] and eye paint.[33] Nubia was not particularly noted as a source of building materials, but diorite was quarried,[34] and wood of the dom palm was used for shipbuilding.[35] Strangely perhaps, for a country that today looks so barren, Nubia in antiquity offered livestock,[36] wild game,[37] birds,[38] and exotic animals[39] (undoubtedly brought north from sub-Saharan locales). It also produced a harvest that was not entirely disregarded by the Egyptians.[40]

POLICING AND MILITARY TRAINING

It is only to be expected that Egypt should, shortly after the inauguration of the state, have come to view the vast tracts of the Sudanese south as a great cornucopia, pouring its riches in a northerly direction. To tap them, all that was required was an expedition and a modicum of cooperation by the local inhabitants. That cooperation might be fostered, if not ensured, by a certain amount of pressure attendant upon a show of force. The titles of Egyptian officers which reflect service south of the First Cataract hint subtly at such pressure: "seal-bearer of the King of Lower Egypt, courtier, lector priest, overseer of aliens . . . governor of the foreign lands for his lord in Yam, Irdjet, and Wawat, . . . who sets the fear of Horus [among the southern foreign lands . . .][41] . . . who pacifies the southern foreign lands."[42] If the local inhabitants construed cooperation as intimidation and resisted, the Egyptians would have to resort to coercion, and this meant military action.

The excuses for action were usually paper-thin and always accompanied by much self-righteous posturing. Trespassing, brigandage, and cattle rustling provided legitimate reasons for calling out the militia, but all too often we are told no more than that such-and-such a Nubian tribe was plotting rebellion. The topos in contemporary propaganda of the arriving messenger with the bad news[43] goes on to describe the king's irritation rapidly escalating into rage: "What is vile Irem that they should transgress during the reign of My Majesty? It is my father Amun-re that shall bring about their downfall through My Majesty's slaughter, that I may so deter another foreign land that may act in a similar fashion against My Majesty![44] . . . As I live, as Re loves me . . . ! I shall certainly not let any of their males (remain) alive! I shall lay devastation among them!"[45]

The subsequent punitive action hardly varied (see fig. 7). Two examples recorded by a vizier (twentieth century B.C.) and a viceroy (fifteenth century B.C.) demonstrate the nature and outcome of such hostilities. "I slaughtered," says vizier Antefoker, "the Nubians on several occasions in Wawat. Then I went south in might slaughtering the Nubian in his (own) land, and I came north uprooting the harvest and cutting down the remainder of its trees, and their houses were set on fire—just as is done to anyone who rebels against the king!"[46] Viceroy Merimose recalls a surprise attack against the small enclave of Ibhat:

> After ⌈some days⌉ [had passed . . .] came the corn harvest and the doomed inhabitants of Ibhat, each one went down to his neighboring plot. Then they mustered [the garrison] of Pharaoh l.p.h. which was under the command of the viceroy. Then the squadrons were assembled and the commanders assigned, each man being with his town beginning at the fort of Baky and ending with the fort of Taroy, making 52 *itr* of sailing.
>
> The mighty arm of Nebmare got them in a single day, in a single hour! . . . Ibhat, the great ones wailed aloud in their midst, for the fierce-eyed lion, the Ruler had slain them by the command of Amun the precious father. He it was that led him in valor and victory!
>
> Tally of the plunder brought to H.M. from the land of vile Ibhat: living Neḥsyu, 150; warriors, 110; female Neḥsyu, 250; servants of the Neḥsyu, 55; their children, 175; total, living, 740; hands thereof, 312; grand total with the living, 1,052.

Numbers of killed and captured are paltry, showing the smallness of the native enclaves involved and belying the threat claimed by the propaganda: 70,[47] 1,052,[48] 434+,[49] 225.[50] The object of the exercise involved

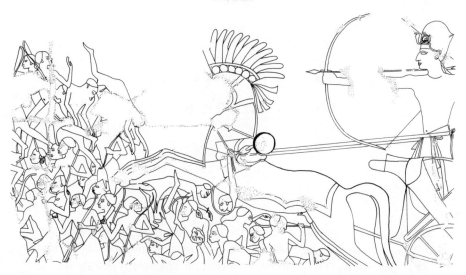

Fig. 7. Ramesses II charges into a throng of fleeing Nubians. Gerf Hussein, Nubia, thirteenth century B.C.

only partly the booty and chattels brought back to Egypt: of far greater importance was the deterrent value of wiping out whole villages, destroying their economic base, and mutilating or impaling the survivors. In the process, of course, the army was blooded: excuses for training with "live ammunition" could always be found in Nubia. So routine did the obligatory raid into Nubia become that some texts and reliefs were set up in *anticipation,* and the figures for casualties and captives never filled in![51]

"PLOTTING IN THEIR VALLEYS"
THE UNRULY TRIBESMEN

By the last quarter of the third millennium B.C., northeastern Africa and the Levant were experiencing major changes on all fronts. The prosperous period of large towns in Palestine, labeled EB III in archaeological nomenclature, ended in the abandonment or destruction of these settlements and the absence of sedentary society thenceforth for several centuries.[1] At the same time, northeastern Africa began to suffer a diminution of rainfall and a 30 percent decline in the volume of Nile discharge.[2] Finally, on the southern frontier the Nubian tribesmen were no longer content to remain quiescent in the face of Egyptian demands on their possessions and commercial relations.

THE C-GROUP PEOPLE

In a modification of the practice of the Fourth and Fifth Dynasty kings, who had assigned southern operations to governors from Middle and Lower Egypt, the Sixth Dynasty kings were content to have commerce and surveillance in the hands of the magnates of Elephantine.[3] Whether or not this was in part an effort to economize, it had the effect of making the "march lords" of the southern frontier responsible for the region with which they were most familiar. They were obliged to repair to the Memphite residence for the commission of Pharaoh and for supplies: thereafter a number of routes offered themselves as access corridors to Nubia (see map 2). There was "the road of Elephantine," by which was intended the Nile route on the west bank leading from Gebel Tingar directly south of the First Cataract;[4] but, although seemingly the most appropriate for an inhabitant of Elephantine, this road was not often used. The cost of traversing the six hundred miles between Memphis and Elephantine, with the harbor tolls levied at every jetty to which the flotilla put in,[5] would probably have increased the total expenditure; and the time and effort ex-

24

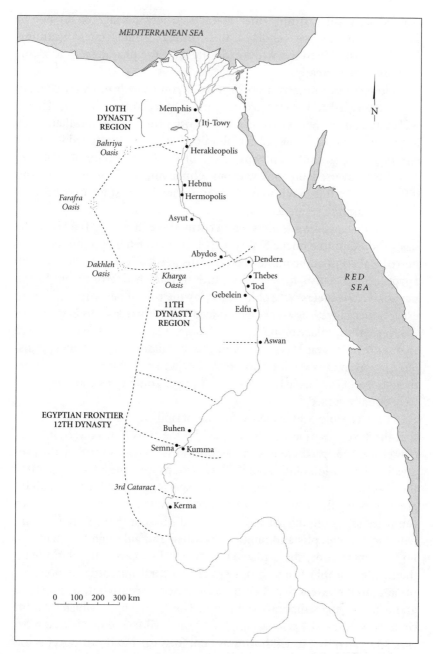

MEDITERRANEAN SEA

N

10TH
DYNASTY
REGION

Memphis
• Itj-Towy

*Bahriya
Oasis*

• Herakleopolis

*Farafra
Oasis*

• Hebnu
• Hermopolis

Asyut •

Abydos •

*Dakhleh
Oasis*

*Kharga
Oasis*

• Dendera
• Thebes
• Tod
Gebelein •

Edfu •

11TH
DYNASTY
REGION

• Aswan

RED
SEA

EGYPTIAN FRONTIER
12TH DYNASTY

Buhen •

Semna • Kumma

3rd Cataract

• Kerma

0   100   200   300 km

Map 2. Regimes and transit corridors in northeast Africa, c. 2300–1700 B.C.

pended in getting around the cataracts, where portage could not be avoided, would have rendered this "direct" route time-consuming. Whereas cost-effectiveness counted little with the pharaohs, time saving exercised them greatly.

A longer but strangely more negotiable route lay through the chain of oases (Bahriya-Farafra-Dakhleh-Khargeh-Dush) and regained the Nile in Nubia at Tomâs.[6] Several starting points offer themselves, but that which gives on to an oasis route at Manfalūt north of Asyut is attested in the biography of Kharkhuf.[7] This precursor of the later "Route of 40 Days" could be traversed on foot with accompanying pack animals without difficulty,[8] and this may also be the route whereby livestock were brought to the Memphite residence.[9]

But the expedition leaders who ventured south during the Sixth Dynasty did not find a docile Nubia. Expeditions to fetch building stone required warships, and commercial caravans needed the protection of both Egyptian and native forces.[10] Intestine warfare had broken out,[11] and Egyptian caravaneers were obliged to play the role of peacemaker.[12] In an exceptional move,[13] Merenre felt obliged himself to repair to Elephantine to receive the homage of the chiefs of Nubia.[14] Large armies were required to put down Wawat,[15] and chieftains, their children, and retainers transferred to Memphis.[16] Chieftains, retainers, and even Egyptians who were thought to harbor nefarious designs but who could not be apprehended were ritually cursed.[17]

The archaeological evidence for the period suggests that the turmoil that the texts describe was occasioned by the arrival in Lower Nubia of new ethnic groups, driven from the southwestern desert through the progressive dessication of the area.[18] These groups were the advance guard of the "C-group" people, as archaeologists have long called them, a main ingredient being the tribe of the Medjay (modern Beja).[19] For more than six centuries following the collapse of the Old Kingdom they were to dominate the demography and politics of Nubia; and although they have left no written records, the artifactual remains they have left behind lends them a clear profile. Primarily they were a pastoral and cattle-rearing people and, to the extent that their flocks and herds required it, seasonal migrants occupying temporary campsites. The animal upon which their life centered was the *Bos primigenius,* the horned wild ox of northeastern Africa, so treated that its left horn was bent forward and downward (as it is today).[20] Most domiciles were presumably in the form of wattle huts, but as time passed, houses with rounded corners and stone orthostats are also attested.[21] The shallow graves of the C-group were often surrounded by a low circle of crude sandstone approaching a meter in height, with bucrania in close association.[22] Usually the body lay in a flexed position on the right side, with head to the east facing west, and sometimes sheep were sacrificed and placed at the foot of the corpse.[23] In some few cases leather garments are in evidence.[24] Grave goods show the C-group people using local materials but also enjoying trade with Egypt and African localities to the south.[25]

A sketchy though nonetheless vivid picture of the Neḥsyu and Medjay/C-group society is provided by the Execration Texts, which have survived from the close of the Old Kingdom and the Twelfth and Thirteenth Dynasties.[26] The Egyptians clearly knew these people very well indeed. Districts and clans were ruled by "(foreign) chieftains"[27] whose names, parentage,[28] and even nicknames are given. In the majority of cases the names are at home in the language family to which "Nubian" belonged; but in a few significant cases Egyptian names are borne![29] Such names as Tety-ʿonkh and Unas-ʿonkh suggest an erstwhile status as *fœderatus* vis-à-vis Egypt,[30] and the application of an Egyptian nickname[31] must mean that the individual in question enjoyed frequent contact with Egyptians. Sometimes a chief's wife is singled out[32] and occasionally a female chieftain.[33] A chief disposes of "strong men, runners, associates and allies,"[34] as well as "henchmen," and these forces may even be termed "his army."[35] The main concern in employing the curse formula is that those named "may rebel, may conspire, may intend to conspire, may fight, may intend to fight"; and the hope, therefore, conveyed in a (prospective) participial form, is that they be "smitten (ones)."[36]

The Execration Texts published by Posener add an interesting qualification to the name of the Nubian to be cursed.[37] After the indication of the proper(?) matrilineal descent ("born of his mother"), the scribe interposes before the concluding words "and his army" the qualification "to whom was said." In two cases[38] the added word is a noun, scil. "calf" (A11), "bull born of ⌈ ... ⌉" (A1), justifying our rendering "who is called 'calf'/'bull.'" In four cases an interrogative clause follows, and the translations must be: (A7) "to whom was said: 'are you recalcitrant?'"; (A8) "to whom was said: 'are you a [...]?'"; (A9) "to whom was said (f.): 'have [you(?)][39] not slaughtered?'"; (A10) "of whom was said: 'is there a loyal follower of his?'" Clearly this phrase adds information, of interest to Egypt, regarding known aliases of the Nubian chiefs, their stance towards Egypt, their warlike habits, and the degree of local support they enjoyed. The use of second-person suffixes and the interrogative makes it very tempting to reconstruct as a *Sitz im Leben* a formal interrogation by Egyptian authorities.

27

EGYPT ESTABLISHES A FRONTIER

The weakening and collapse of the authority of the "residence" following Pepy II's death terminated the centuries-long ability of the royal regime to send for and acquire at will whatever goods and services were desired from south of the First Cataract. Left to their own devices, the Nubian communities thrived,[40] and, as we have seen, some of their members filtered north to seek their fortunes in Middle and Upper Egypt. Although the kings of Herakleopolis who had retrieved the political situation in the north were nominally acknowledged throughout Egypt, they lacked the power or the inclination to stem the entry of these freebooters. Even within the bounds of Egypt they were virtually powerless south of Abydos, where the seven southernmost townships from Hu to Elephantine lapsed into an anarchy from which even a royal commissioner could not rescue them.[41]

The rise in Thebes of the family of Montuhotep "the great,"[42] "the ancestor,"[43] brought about a unification of the seven townships. Very soon the family head, the baron of Thebes, is found to have arrogated to himself the titles "Great Baron of the Southland" and "superintendent of the restricted foreign entry-point, pillar of the south."[44] The takeover of the valley as far as the First Cataract was paralleled by the extension of Theban hegemony as far as U.E. VII. The rebellious enclave, now heartened by its own claim to sovereignty—it was to be remembered as the "Eleventh Dynasty"—set about to tighten its control over this 180 miles of valley and to resist Herakleopolitan attempts to restore the authority of the north. Elephantine was firmly held by the rebel king Antef II, who was shrewd enough to realize not only the strategic importance of the cataract but also the value of the granite quarries. The stone was much in demand in the north, and Antef may have used it in bargaining with Herakleopolis.[45] Antef II honored Elephantine by building the *ku*-chapel of the local hero and saint Ḥeqa-ib, who had lived two centuries earlier.[46] Contemporary texts claim that Theban influence extended beyond Elephantine and into the vastness of the western desert: Tjetji the treasurer states that his suzerains, Antef II and III, were in receipt of "benevolences" from Upper and Lower Egypt as well as from "the chiefs who are upon the desert."[47]

The inevitable reassertion of direct control of Nubia began about this time but took many generations to accomplish. Antef II boasted, "Any army I sailed [against, I effected its slaughter(?) . . .] at a single stroke [. . .] I seized its[48] chiefs and its armies."[49] Two generations later, after the long war with Herakleopolis terminated in a Theban victory, Neb-hepet-re Montuhotep I was able to strike both north and south beyond the traditional boundaries. "Let us go north!" said he to his army, "after we have crushed the foreign lands . . . I have given you all its[50] sealed treasures, everything you might desire!" The army(?) responds: "[The foreign chiefs(?) come] to you doing obeisance and kissing you all over. May you sleep with composure, the South and the foreign lands ⌈beneath⌉ [your feet . . .]." Montuḥotep continues: "[. . .] the enemies who were in it. I annexed it to Upper Egypt . . . I attained the shores of the Great Sea (= the Mediterranean) . . . having instilled Elephantine with strength; [the foreign chiefs(?) came with arms] respectfully bent, and took the divine oath, each one of them upon his head, with neck-crushing tribute [on their backs . . .]."[51] Montuḥotep was even able to use Nubia as a recruiting ground for troops, so successfully had he imposed his own personal paramountcy upon the inhabitants.[52] The victor in the short-lived civil war that followed ten years after Montuḥotep's death inaugurated a regime wholly committed to completing the annexation of the land between the First and Second Cataracts: Amenemhet, founder of the Twelfth Dynasty, and his successors hammered Nubia, using the periodic razzia as the means of inculcating respect for Egypt and reducing the inhabitants to abject servitude and robbing the C-group people of their status of independent intermediaries on the trade routes to Africa.[53] Settlement quickly followed, as three fortress towns were built at Aniba, Kubban, and Buhen, a harbinger of things to come.

No more fitting memorial can be found to the Twelfth Dynasty's resolve to dominate the land between the first two cataracts than the forts erected between Serra East and Semna South.[54] Built late in the dynasty, these were sited with a view to taking complete advantage of the defensive possibilities of the terrain. Usually located on high spurs of rock close to the Nile, the forts were surrounded by massive walls of mud brick and equipped with outworks to protect the river approach. Size varied considerably: Semna al-Sharq was only 50 × 60 meters, whereas Buhen attained 1,000 × 130 meters. The number of people who could live in these confined spaces was probably small (twenty-five families in the case of Uronarti),[55] but this small number appears to have been sufficient to do the job.

But what was the job? The sophistication in military architecture is striking: moats, glacis, berms, towers, arrow slots—all bespeak a concern that can hardly be squared with the threat from a population of cattle herders! Sappers, siege ladders, and rams, in anticipation of which these features were developed, were unknown to the C-group or Neḫsyu.[56] It is tempting to view this fortress architecture as exemplifying the same kind of conspicuous "energy waste" as the mortuary complexes of the Old

Fig. 8. Wrestling training and siege warfare. Beni Hassan, Middle Egypt, Middle Kingdom.

Kingdom, a celebration of power and the divine link, wholly divorced from practical need.[57] Textual evidence, however, suggests that the forts did indeed fulfill a military purpose primarily (see fig. 8). The forts' names—"Repelling the Medjay," "Curbing the Deserts," "Subduing the Bow-people"[58]—leave no doubt about the expected function. But the sealings and inscriptions retrieved from the forts tell of a much broader purpose.[59] The forts were manned by a variety of military and paramilitary personnel, including generals, commanders of alien auxiliaries,[60] archers, police,[61] and (most common) retainers;[62] but there were many more "civil" officials both resident and passing through. Among the former were a variety of district officials and scribes, labor officials, construction engineers, stewards of "manpower registration,"[63] prospectors,[64] and officials connected with gold production.[65] Many more officials were to be found in transit, representing every major department of the government, as well as commercial agents for temples.[66] Quarrying expeditions of appreciable size penetrated the hills: in Amenemhet II's fourth year, a team of 20 chamberlains, 50 lapidaries, 200 stonecutters, 1,006 workers, and 1,000 asses passed by Toshke in quest of stone.[67] A state flotilla of ships sailed up and down the river, touching at every fort, and a regular service of couriers kept the garrisons in touch with Egypt. As with the northern border facing Asia, the southern march was inspected at regular intervals by a military patrol led by a general or (occasionally) a civil official.[68]

FROM CHIEFDOM TO STATE
AND BACK AGAIN
THE FINAL CONQUEST OF KUSH

The extraordinary effort expended by the pharaonic government of the Twelfth Dynasty to occupy and hold Nubia cannot be entirely explained by the attraction of natural resources: a certain degree of apprehension is attested in the preoccupation with military concerns. It has been noted that many of the forts at the Second Cataract are so sited as to maximize their potential for confronting and intercepting a large-scale movement from farther south.[1] Did the Egyptians really have anything to fear? And whence did they expect such a movement to come?

Certainly the hymns to Senwosret III (c. 1850 B.C.) betray a certain anxiety but also relief at a threat overcome by that king's annexation of the Second Cataract:[2] "Hail to thee O Khakaure, our Horus, divine of forms, protector of the land, who extends his frontiers and subdues the foreigners with his great crown; . . . who slays the Bow-people without striking a blow, who lets fly the arrow without drawing the bow; fear of whom has smitten the Troglodytes in their (own) land, terror of whom has slain the Nine Bows, whose slaughter has killed thousands of the Bow-people who had attacked his frontiers . . . His Majesty's tongue is the restraint of the Southland, his 'paroles' are what puts the savages to flight; a unique and rejuvenating one [fighting] for his frontiers, who does not weary his serfs, who lets the patricians recline in the sun—his levies sleep for his heart is their protector."[3]

The sequel, however, shows that a threat remained, and it took the form of an incipient state of native inspiration.[4]

THE KINGDOM OF KUSH

Approximately 130 miles south of the self-proclaimed border of Senwosret III at Semna-Kumma lies the large site of Kerma, just beyond

the Third Cataract on the Nile. Excavations by G. A. Reisner in the first
two decades of the twentieth century, now continued by the French, have
demonstrated that from the Twelfth Dynasty[5] until the early New Kingdom Kerma was the political and cultural hub of a distinct African community, with remote cultural connections to the C-group, stretching
from the Second Cataract to somewhere south of Nugdumbush[6] in the
Dongola.[7] Both temporal and spatial limits suggest that the "Kerma culture" was what contemporary Egyptians referred to as Kush and their Old
Kingdom ancestors as Yam/Irem.[8]

Considerations of strategic defense and maximum food production
influenced the choice of site and terrain.[9] Situated on the east bank,
Kerma enjoyed the protection of a cataract and a long buffer of arid valley
against the Egyptian presence to the north. The wide floodplain on which
it was built offered a food source that could make the community largely
self-sustaining.

The result, especially after the decline of Egyptian power around 1750
B.C., was the rise of what has been called "the first city" in Sudanese history,
more than sixty acres in extent, with perhaps two thousand inhabitants.
Mud-brick walls ten meters high reinforced by stone and a ditch provided
protection for inhabitants and the rural population of the surrounding
countryside.[10] The variation in size and appointments of the mud-brick
houses as well as the graves suggests a stratified society with differentiation
of occupation and gradations of power and income. Occupying prime location and dominating the city in size were temple, audience hall, and palace. The first comprised a massif of brickwork, about eighteen meters high,
pierced by a staircase and perhaps surmounted by a shrine. The vast circular audience hall and the "un-Egyptian" plan of the palace suggest room use
based on a purely native tradition. Also of native derivation was the importance of cattle and sheep in the life of the community: space was provided
for livestock within the city, and burials were frequently accompanied by
the sacrifice of sheep and the installation of bucrania.

The political structure of Kerma, certainly at the apogee of its power in
the seventeenth and sixteenth centuries B.C., seems to have evolved beyond a paramount chiefdom. What the power wielders in Kerma would
have called themselves,[11] or whether their polity would have qualified for
"statehood" in our nomenclature,[12] is unknown and perhaps irrelevant.
We are fortunate to possess a few scattered allusions to the head of the
Kushite community (undoubtedly the power holder at Kerma) by Egyptians in his employ and a king of the Fifteenth Dynasty. The former use
the term $ḥḳ3$,[13] the common word for tribal chief or state ruler alike.[14]
Apophis, the Fifteenth Dynasty—Hyksos—king, also employs $ḥḳ3$ in a

letter he is reputed to have sent to Kush,[15] and whether the piece is genuine, paraphrased, or fabricated, it reflects the perception of the times: the Kushite ruler "accedes" to the throne[16]—that is, there is a monarchic succession; he can be termed "son" in the quasi-"feudal" nuance of the diplomatic jargon of the Middle Bronze Age; it is expected that he will correspond (and presumably in Egyptian!) with other rulers who consider themselves "kings"; he is considered valuable as an ally with whom a treaty can be made. All this militates in favor of the thesis that contemporaries would have classed Kush/Kerma as a monarchic state rather than a chiefdom.[17]

In fact, the burial arrangements at Kerma bear out such a thesis.[18] The rulers were buried in "barbaric splendour" in circular tumuli more than eighty-five meters in diameter and three to four meters in height. The corpse was laid upon a bed of costly material equipped with a head rest and sometimes covered with an ox hide. Silver crowns, weapons, sandals, fans, and edibles accompanied the deceased on his last journey, and hundreds of servants went to their deaths as human sacrifices to his future well-being.

All this bespeaks a vibrant native culture, promoting its own forms with little essential influence from outside. Apart from pharaonic Egypt, Kerma represents the earliest autochthonous efflorescence of high culture on the African continent.

THE CONFRONTATION WITH EGYPT

It was Kerma's good fortune to realize its full potential when Egypt had begun to suffer political decline. Following the death of Amenemhet IV (c. 1786 B.C.) for reasons not clearly known, the royal office entered upon a century of progressive weakening.[19] The house of Amenemhet collapsed and was succeeded by a line of short-lived kinglets occupying about twenty-five years, unrelated to the Twelfth Dynasty or to one another. The anarchy towards which Egypt gives the appearance of slipping was averted about 1760 B.C. by the assumption of power of a Sobekhotpe II, who inaugurated a period of nine short reigns—the longest was only eleven years!—which partially retrieved the situation. But an enervated administration inside Egypt could scarcely bode well for the security of an annexed province lying far to the south!

Kush must have sensed its opportunity. A continued Egyptian presence is attested in the Nubian forts until about 1720 B.C., if not later,[20] and Nubian chieftains continue to present themselves at court;[21] but thereafter our evidence virtually ceases, and darkness closes in. Fragmentary texts suggest hostility: a broken stela in the British Museum[22] from the reign of Sobekḥotpe IV (last quarter of the eighteenth century B.C.) mentions "[Wa]wat," the "[...] whom he has smitten," and a "great miracle." Many of the Egyptian forts in Lower Nubia were found to have been burned,[23] and it is most tempting to single out the forces of Kerma as responsible. Two seventeenth-century inscriptions from Karnak even allude to Thebes itself as under threat of attack by foreigners,[24] but whether Nubian or Hyksos is difficult to decide. Consonant with a Kushite expansion north of the Second Cataract and an abandonment of the area by Egypt are the numerous Egyptian artifacts including statuary found at Kerma in conjunction with the royal burials. This context is clearly secondary for all such objects, and the conclusion must be that they had been brought off by the Kushites as booty from Egyptian locations farther north.[25] Kushite pressure on the townships of Upper Egypt could only be expected to increase with the Hyksos conquest of Lower Egypt towards the middle of the seventeenth century B.C. These West Semitic–speaking invaders put to flight the last vestige of the Middle Kingdom regime and obliged it to withdraw south to Thebes. Thus, further deprived of territory, the surviving "free" Egyptian authority (albeit subverted de facto to the Hyksos) was obliged to witness the tripartite division of northeastern Africa, over which a century earlier its ancestors had exercised complete control. Kerma, with a jurisdiction probably as far north as a point close to the First Cataract, was totally independent; the Hyksos, after some skirmishing farther south, had raised their frontier at Kusae in the fourteenth township of Upper Egypt.

These were halcyon days for Kush. Not only was its triumph celebrated in the display of captured trophies, but even its erstwhile masters now came seeking to serve it.[26] Pretensions to imperial status meant adopting the trappings of the only imperial power Kush had known, namely, Egypt. Construction techniques reminiscent of those employed in Egypt make their appearance;[27] the temple is fronted by a pylon,[28] and Egyptian devices such as the solar disk and the *djed* form part of architectural decoration.[29] As the Kamose stela II clearly shows, Kush controlled the oasis routes whereby trade with the Hyksos could bypass Thebes; and numerous Hyksos sealings, daggers, and Tel el-Yehudiya juglets[30] in Nubian sites and at Kerma attest to the strength of this commerce.[31]

THE EIGHTEENTH DYNASTY CONQUEST

Early in the sixteenth century B.C. the weak and discredited descendants of the Thirteenth Dynasty,[32] holed up at Thebes for more than sixty years, disappeared, and a new family, Dynasty 17, assumed leadership in the Thebaid. Although the circumstances remain obscure, it is a fairly safe assumption that the new regime was Nubian in origin,[33] for in the reversal of national fortunes in the seventeenth and sixteenth centuries B.C., not only had Egyptian adventurers entered the service of the king of Kush, but Nubians had also drifted north of the First Cataract as auxiliaries of the small Theban enclave. In the archaeological record, roughly contemporary with the inception of the Seventeenth Dynasty, a peculiar type of Nubian cemetery appears in Nubia and Upper Egypt, examples of which extend from the Third Cataract on the Nile as far north as Deir Rifeh. The interments are made in shallow circular or oval pits, dubbed "pan-graves" by early excavators, and the grave goods comprise pottery and weapons solely of Nubian derivation.[34] The Seventeenth Dynasty has left inscriptional evidence of the use of Medjay as scouts and ancillary troops in its war against the Hyksos;[35] and it is most tempting to identify the occupants of the pan-grave burying grounds as Medjay "mercenaries."[36] If this be the case, it may indicate a community of interest between Egypt and the Medjay of the eastern desert fostered by the antipathy of each community to Kerma/Kush farther south.

The war of liberation launched by the Seventeenth Dynasty was designed to rid the Nile Valley and Delta of non-Egyptian occupation and was thus aimed as much at Kerma as it was at Avaris. As far as we know, the first blow was struck by Kamose, third king of the dynasty, in his first or second year. An "official" record of the campaign has yet to be recovered, passing allusions in nonroyal stelae being our sole source to date. That the expedition preceded Kamose's attack on Avaris follows from Apophis's statement in his letter to the Kushite ruler written, in Kamose's third year, to relieve pressure on his Delta stronghold:[37] "Do you see what Egypt has done to me? The ruler who is in it, Kamose-the-mighty-given-life!, is pushing me off my land! I have not attacked him in any way comparable to what he has done to you!" A drummer boy in Kamose's forces recalls passing the king's third regnal year drumming every day: that is to say, the year was occupied by constant conflict on the battlefield.[38] Another individual was a "brave warrior" of Kamose's who was rewarded with forty-six chattels, presumably captives he was allowed to keep.[39] Although the expedition is claimed to have reached a point as far south as Miu, which would have meant passing clean through the *territorium* of Kerma itself,[40] few, if any, of the intervening deserts were permanently secured for Egypt. Buhen, on the other hand, was captured and occupied and by the close of Kamose's third year had been rebuilt.[41]

With the expulsion of the Hyksos Egypt's advance southward began in earnest. Aḥmose, Kamose's successor, turned on "Khent-ḥen-nafer[42] to destroy the Nubian Troglodytes" as soon as he had put an end to the Asiatic regime in the Delta.[43] A counterattack on the river by a Nubian force under one *33t³*,[44] presumably representing the riposte of Kerma, was beaten back at one of the cataracts and the commander and his troops captured.[45] A dozen years later the Egyptians returned: in the seventh and eighth years of Amenophis I, presumably when the young king came of age, an expeditionary force penetrated to a point south of the Second Cataract, where it encountered the Kushites. "Then His Majesty smote that Nubian Troglodyte in the midst of his army, and brought (them) off in a strangle-hold without any loss; those who fled were laid prostrate as though they had never been . . . !"[46] Survivors and their cattle were chased into the desert.[47] Egypt had now regained the entire Second Cataract to a point eighty miles south of Senwosret III's old frontier, and Amenophis I was able with impunity to occupy Saï Island, an erstwhile outpost of Kerma, a mere sixty-eight miles north of the Kushite capital![48]

At the close of Amenophis I's reign Kerma, though immeasurably weakened, remained intact, but the following decade witnessed its dramatic collapse and destruction. Thutmose I, Amenophis's successor, at the outset of his reign planned a major campaign,[49] which, thanks to several surviving inscriptions, may be traced in some detail. The old channel through the First Cataract was dredged,[50] and late in his first year[51] his troops crossed the frontier, heading south in a flotilla of warships. A little more than a month later the expedition reached the Second Cataract at Tangur, and here disaster was barely averted at the rapids of Dal. A captain, Aḥmose, son of Abana, saved the situation "at the 'Bad Water' in forcing through the fleet over the 'Place-of-capsizing'" and was at once promoted to marine commander.[52] Shortly afterwards they reached Saï[53] and prepared for battle. Precisely when and where the king of Kush chose to make his stand are unknown, but it was presumably north of Kerma. Apart from the platitudes of the Tombos stela (see later in this chapter), the only account of the final engagement is that of the aforementioned marine commander Aḥmose.[54] Thutmose I himself took the lead (in his flagship?), burst in among the Kushite vessels, and shot the enemy leader in the neck with his first arrow.[55] It was all over: a rout ensued. And although two of the sons of the Kushite king escaped to fight again, the regime of Kerma was at an end. The city was destroyed, its inhabitants captured.

It is from this signal victory, known afterwards as the "day of the slaughter of the Perfect God,"[56] that the Egyptian empire in Africa must be dated.[57] In order to secure the south to a point optimal for strategic purposes, Thutmose and his army marched through Dongola and reached Ḥagar el-Merwa beyond the Fourth Cataract two months later.[58] Here, where the land route from Lower Nubia regains the Nile, the king established a southern frontier. A rock-carved tableau shows Amunre facing the Horus-name of the king; a text beneath this depiction pronounced a formal curse on any Kushite who might trespass across the line.[59] Scarcely six weeks later the army had retraced its steps to the ruins of Kerma, and commands were given to build a fort[60] and to erect a formal triumphal stela at Tombos, seven miles to the north of the former capital.[61] Although the stela was finally written up several years later,[62] Thutmose's accomplishment was to remain unchallenged: the kingdom of Kush, with its capital Kerma, had ceased to exist, and everywhere in the south as far as Ḥagar el-Merwa the Egyptian empire was supreme.

THE EGYPTIAN EMPIRE IN KUSH

lthough Thutmose I's reign may be construed as a watershed in the history of the Sudan, his crushing victory did not mean that Egypt was automatically accepted by the autochthonous inhabitants. For more than a century it had to battle against increasingly isolated and weakened communities that saw no reason why they should relinquish their autonomy. On the morrow of the demise of the kingdom of Kerma, for example, two of the surviving sons of the Kushite ruler who had died in the encounter with Thutmose made common cause with "a chief on the north of Kush"[1] and attempted to set up three independent regional states.[2] Acts of harassment and rapine followed, directed at the Egyptian colonists of a fort Thutmose I had founded somewhere in Nubia.[3] Egyptian retaliation was swift and overwhelming, with the result that riverine Nubia was cowed, but the more remote Sudanese enclaves continued to "plot in their valleys."[4] Ten years later[5] the Egyptians returned, now under a young queen, "in power, in valour, in [justification]"; the army "went overland with horses over the mountains," and the recalcitrant tribesmen were slaughtered in untold numbers. So smoothly did this military exercise run that Hatshepsut felt at no risk circulating among the troops to bind captives herself.[6] Scattered graffiti around the Second Cataract between years 12 and 18[7] may betray punitive action against the last holdouts, action that will have been brought to a conclusion in year 20, when Hatshepsut's co-regent Thutmose III authorized a rock inscription at Tombos commemorating "the overthrow of him that attacked him."[8]

THE CONSOLIDATION OF THE AFRICAN PROVINCE

By the middle of the fifteenth century B.C., less than one hundred years after the annihilation of the kingdom of Kerma, a regime of "control and order" was in place in Nubia and Kush as far south as Dongola.[9] Egypt had eliminated all independent enclaves formerly acting as intermediaries in trade with the more remote parts of the Sudan. Before Thutmose I died, in fact, the mechanisms are attested whereby for more than three centuries goods and personnel would move from the Sudan to Egypt by impost or impressment. Ineny, the great factotum of Thutmose I, speaks in his tomb of viewing the Kushites (*nḥsyw*) given as a body of prisoners of war "to the endowment of Amun at the time when vile Kush was overthrown."[10] At Deir el-Bahari Dedwen the Nubian deity is presented by the propagandist as a *pro*-pharaonic numen, leading Sudanese captives to the Egyptian queen;[11] and, like Ineny, Puyemre, the deputy high priest of Amun under Hatshepsut, speaks of "witnessing the weighing of great heaps of incense . . . ivory, ebony, electrum of Amaw . . . various aromatic plants . . . and the living captives which H.M. brought from his victories."[12] By the fourth decade of Thutmose III's sole reign an enforced etiquette obliged Sudanese chiefs to present themselves at Pharaoh's court, as they had done in the past (see "The Confrontation with Egypt" in Chapter 5), bearing their benevolences of gold, ivory, ebony, giraffes, monkeys, panthers,[13] spices, incense, gems, electrum, and especially gold.[14] Although the amounts listed in Thutmose III's "annals" are modest, this is only because the impost in question is a *particular* tax, namely, the labor tax[15] levied on specific chiefs and in this case directed to the king and entered in his daybook.[16] Other surviving sources recording income for the temple of Amun, for example, contain astounding sums, 36,692 *deben* of gold alloy in one case![17] As far south as Napata Egyptian settlements began to spring up, the inhabitants of which were addressed in royal proclamations and treated to spectacles.[18]

The successful imposition of such a *pax Aegyptiaca* makes it difficult for us to take seriously the insistent and repeated claims of kings of the later Eighteenth and Nineteenth Dynasties that such-and-such a tribe had just rebelled and was about to wreak untold havoc if not checked. At times the military campaigns that were thus provided with a rationalization were closer to theatrical extravaganzas: the messenger arrives breathless with news of the uprising, the king enters the shrine to secure the god's blessing, the fleet sets sail in all its splendor, the people cheer, and so on.[19] Or: the king appears on a dais in glory in Thebes, with his troops arranged in their battle squadrons, while the entourage rejoices and 2,657 men file past bringing a vast tribute from the southland never seen before under the ancestors (see fig. 9).[20] The campaign of Amenophis III's fifth year[21] was prominently celebrated by rock tableaux at Aswan and later gave rise to a legend; but the textual record is vague and bombastic. The king

Fig. 9. Nubians bringing tribute to Pharaoh. Beit el-Wali, Nubia, thirteenth century B.C.

speaks of a tribal leader whom he captured and boasts of taking tens of thousands of prisoners,[22] but the texts employ stock phrases and fail to locate the encounter.[23]

Many of the "campaigns" in the later New Kingdom must have been thinly disguised forays in search of booty and slaves. Thutmose III's "expedition" in his year 50 may have been little more than a tour of inspection.[24] Akhenaten's action against a tribe at the junction of the Nile and Wady Allaki was prompted by a vague report that the Kushites were "seizing all the sustenance." In the event 80 Kushites were impaled—a sobering object lesson!—and 145 captives were brought back as slaves along with 361 head of cattle. The rows of docile blacks in Horemheb's tomb are specifically stated to be part of the "benevolences," literally what was brought, from the Sudan.[25] A message that "the doomed ones of the land of Irem are considering rebellion" was enough to call out the troops under Sety I to chase the tribesmen into the desert, plunder their wells, and bring back 434(?) slaves.[26] By Ramesses II's reign the lively scene of Pharaoh charging into a mass of fleeing Nubians had become a generic tableau (fig. 7), devoid of specific time or place.[27]

THE VICEROY OF KUSH AND HIS ADMINISTRATION

Buhen stelae enable us to trace a sequence of four or five generations of fortress commandants beginning under the Kerma/Kushite regime and extending into the early Eighteenth Dynasty.[28] They called themselves *sr*, "magistrate, administrator," a rather colorless title; but some added the more specific *tsw n Bhn*, "commandant of Buhen."[29] In one case a commandant used the title "king's-son,"[30] and this may well be a harbinger of things to come. For "king's-son" was commonly used in the Second Intermediate Period to designate a royal plenipotentiary not of royal blood and often with military functions.[31] Already under Kamose, presumably at the time of his southern campaign, a certain Tety was appointed as "king's-son" and shortly afterwards a Djehuty, and both left their graffiti on the rocks at Toshka.[32] These are but names to us, but shortly a new incumbent was to be appointed. Into the hands of one Aḥmose-so-taiyet, the scribe of offerings of Amun,[33] was placed the task of handling affairs on behalf of the king in the newly won Nubian territories. Like Tety and Djehuty, he received the title "king's-son" with the added designation (to make his bailiwick explicit) "superintendent of the southern countries." His son Turo, who eventually succeeded him, began as a "temple-scribe, god's father and overseer of cattle (of Amun)" and was appointed commandant of Buhen.[34] Later incumbents show a similar early training in the priesthood (or diaconate) of Amun;[35] a few came from the palace administration.[36] From the late fourteenth century a military training was sometimes deemed adequate for a "king's-son of the southern countries."[37] From the reign of Amenophis III this office, which moderns have dubbed "viceroy of Kush,"[38] was upgraded by the addition of the rank title "king's-scribe."[39] But over the five centuries of its existence the office of viceroy remained under the immediate control of the crown, its occupants being drawn from low-ranking officials completely beholden to Pharaoh for this status and favor (see fig. 10).

It is not to be imagined that a complex system of administration in the south came into being fully developed on the morrow of Aḥmose's campaigns. The process of devising a workable government for Nubia and Kush was ad hoc and occupied the better part of a century. At first, under the first three reigns of the dynasty, the "king's-son and superintendent of the southern lands" was really a bailiff without a bailiwick; and only with the final destruction of the Kerma regime under Thutmose I and II did the office begin to realize its potential. Although later in the New Kingdom the chief task of the viceroy was the dispatch of the annual tribute quota,[40] this duty seems to have been discharged by others in the early days of the Eighteenth Dynasty. Harmini, the erstwhile mayor of Hierakonpolis who must be dated as flourishing during Amenophis I's reign,[41] was at some time in his career made responsible for Nubia: "I passed many years as mayor of Hierakonpolis, and I brought its tribute to the Lord of the Two Lands. I was praised (for) no one found any mistake of mine. As a trusted one of my lord I reached old age in Nubia (Wawat). Each and every year I went north bearing its tribute to the king, and justified did I return thence (for) no one found arrears of mine."[42] There is no reason to assume that Harmini's floruit

Fig. 10. Viceroy of Kush: "King's-son of Kush, fanbearer on the king's right-hand"; thirteenth century B.C.

antedates the establishment of the office of viceroy: during the formative period spheres of authority were ill defined and probably overlapped to a considerable extent.

With the reign of Amenophis III the viceroyalty had achieved the apogee of its evolution. The viceroy had his headquarters at Aniba[43] and was responsible for the territory from Hierakonpolis to Karoy. Apart from the general oversight of this vast territory—more than a thousand miles in length—the viceroy's chief concerns were the collection and dispatch of the annual taxes (see fig. 9)[44] and gold production.[45] A support staff of scribes and a domestic establishment grew up at Aniba around the viceregal person.[46] At Kubban, where gold production was centered, there were supervisors and scribes.[47] In the tomb of the viceroy Huy a scene depicts long lives of individuals, young and old, Egyptian and Nubian, bringing gold rings and gold dust to "the chief of the stable Hatay" and the "scribe of the gold-count[48] Hornufer."[49]

The model for the administration over which the viceroy presided was supplied by Egypt itself. In imitation of the two viziers of Upper and Lower Egypt, the Sudanese administration spawned two deputies, one for Nubia and the other for Kush.[50] A "treasury of the Lord of the Two Lands in the Land of Nubia"[51] was located at Aniba, with a treasurer responsible for preparing tax lists and shipments.[52] Departments of agriculture and livestock are reflected in such titles as "overseer of the double granary,"[53] "scribe of the granary,"[54] "overseer of cattle,"[55] and the ubiquitous "bailiffs (or administrators)."[56]

THE GARRISON OF KUSH

By the joint reign of Thutmose III and Hatshepsut a permanent military presence is attested in the Sudan. To house them the former built a permanent frontier fortress at Napata, nearly one thousand miles south of Aswan; on a stela erected at the site he tells us, "Lumber comes to me from Kush, consisting of boards of *m3m3*-wood and furniture without limit, of southern acacia wood. My armed forces in Kush (namely,) those who are there, hew them by the millions."[57] Hatshepsut is the first to speak of a "standing-army" of Kush,[58] a term that would become standard for the Egyptian forces of occupation south of the First Cataract. Modeled on similar forces in both Asia and Egypt proper, the garrison had a commanding officer,[59] battalion commanders,[60] quartermasters,[61] and army scribes.[62] No garrison was ever a desirable posting for a soldier, but the hot south was particularly uninviting: service there was regarded as a disgrace and tantamount to exile.[63] Soldiers were settled in hamlets along the Nile and could be called out at a moment's notice,[64] squads being organized by village.

Although the garrison of Nubia was originally designed to hold down the Sudan and engage in policing and punitive action when needed, by the end of the Nineteenth Dynasty it had acquired increasing independence and had become a lawless and unpredictable force. The unrest in Irem and Akita[65] and the stasis that brought reprisals under Merenptah[66] may be evidence of a much deeper malaise in the fabric of Nubian society. Whether the garrison of Kush had any involvement in the civil strife that soured the end of Merenptah's reign[67] is unknown, but it certainly was expected to play a role in the conspiracy to assassinate Ramesses III[68] and later is found involved in tomb robberies.[69] Seventy years later, as we shall see,[70] the garrison once again impinged itself on the politics of the realm, this time in a bid for supreme power.

THE PROBLEM OF THE ACCULTURATION OF THE SOUTH

As is abundantly clear from the outlines of the viceroy's civil service and the arrangements for a military presence, Egypt itself was serving as the model on which everything was being patterned.[71] From Amenophis III on—in some cases before[72]—texts speak of towns,[73] villages,[74] and fortresses,[75] administered by a *ḥ3ty-ˁ*, "mayor,"[76] modeled on the time-honored Egyptian pattern; and the use of the term *township (sp3t)* indicates that the Egyptian concept of metropolis and adjacent glebe (= *territorium,* or "nome") had taken root in the south.[77] Many of the new towns, both new settlements and restored forts from the Middle Kingdom, centered upon temples that provided an economic structure and the rationale for amassing large bodies of workers in one spot. Many of these new towns were walled.[78]

The demographics of southern settlement and the relations between Egyptians and natives continue to produce debate.[79] To what extent did the native population undergo acculturation, and what percentage of the inhabitants at the height of the empire were Egyptian colonists? Archaeology makes one point quite clear: although the latest C-group burials, contemporary with the early Eighteenth Dynasty, are rich and native in inspiration,[80] from Hatshepsut's reign on a gradual "Egyptianization" is evident in burial customs.[81] Native chieftains turn up, bearing Egyptian names or intermarried with Egyptians,[82] but their progeny did not survive as power holders. The coming of the empire meant the imposition of an administration from without in which Nubians had no special place, and local autonomy was the exception rather than the rule.[83] The southland was placed under a "plantation economy"[84] in which the best land was confiscated for crown, temple, or high-ranking courtier, and Egyptian colonists were introduced as civil servants and farmers.[85] To work the land as farmhands and provide a pool of unskilled labor for the temples, prisoners of war were brought in from Canaan.[86] Agricultural produce was by and large taken to Egypt and only the bare necessities left to support the infrastructure. The Nauri decree of the outgoing fourteenth century B.C.[87] gives a comprehensive view of the personnel resident and on the move in Nubia and Kush and the population they controlled. The prime tasks for which they were responsible comprised the following: gold production, tax collection, the transfer of population, extraordinary service, and the agricultural corvée. The personnel named, apart from the viceroy and his staff, are heavily weighted toward the military: battalion commanders, charioteers, stable masters, captains, fortress commandants, and the soldiery at large. The civil arm is represented by mayors, village commanders, agents, and superintendents of Nubians. This last title betrays an indigenous population, isolated and controlled *en bloc.*

The answer, then, to the question of Nubian demography during the period of the Egyptian empire must be that a powerful and substantial minority of Egyptian military, bureaucratic, and civilian personnel exercised absolute dominion over a larger and thoroughly cowed native population. Some of the latter, in particular the families of erstwhile chiefs, were exposed to Egyptian ways and adopted them to a greater or lesser degree (see fig. 2),[88] but the native Nubians had, as a class, been reduced to a servile status and deprived of any voice in their governance (see fig. 11a,b,c).

Fig. 11a. Nubians adoring Akhenaten at the jubilee. Thebes, early fourteenth century B.C.

Fig. 11b. A Nubian in Akhenaten's bodyguard. Thebes, early fourteenth century
B.C.

Fig. 11c. A scene inscribed or painted beneath the royal balcony: Nubian and
Canaanite captives in submission to Akhenaten. Thebes, early fourteenth century
B.C.

THE TEMPLES

In its goals to extend the frontier, exploit all available resources, and reduce the aboriginals to peonage, Egyptian policy (if we can use a word denoting sober political reflection) can be seen no more clearly than in the numinous world of the cult. Herein Egypt overwhelmed the native precursors. Whatever duties and modes of worship the Sudanese had devised prior to the New Kingdom, few survived the Egyptian occupation.[89] Falcon cults, which tended to abound in Nubia, may reflect local hypostases or numina, but it seems more likely that they are avatars of Horus (i.e., the king of Egypt), "Lord of Foreign lands," transplanted to foreign parts.[90] The same may be true of Thoth and his emblems, which turn up associated with Thutmose III[91] and Amenophis III.[92] Along with the Egyptian settlers went their gods, especially those of the cataract and Upper Egypt;[93] and in keeping with Egyptian practice, a female numen gained an identity in the south as "Hathor mistress of Wawat."[94]

But most preeminent during the New Kingdom are the cult centers devoted to the formal worship of the pharaohs.[95] No sooner had Egypt reoccupied the south than shrines to the pharaonic genius began to arise, first in the repeopled settlements of the Middle Kingdom and later as nuclei of new towns. These temples not only provided places of worship in a "national" cult for colonist and native alike, but they also constituted a monumental statement in stone averring the legitimacy of the king of Egypt as "lord of Nubia." Most of the temples were constructed

Fig. 12. Granite lion from Gebel Barkal; mid–fourteenth century B.C.

Fig. 13. Facade of the great rock-cut temple of Ramesses II at Abu Simbel; thirteenth century B.C.

Fig. 14. Facade of the lesser rock-cut temple, dedicated to Nofretari, queen of Ramesses II, at Abu Simbel; thirteenth century B.C.

under the Eighteenth Dynasty, beginning with a vengeance under Thutmose III[96] and continuing under Amenophis II,[97] Amenophis III (see fig. 12),[98] Akhenaten,[99] and Tutankhamun.[100] By the Nineteenth Dynasty, though new colonists and towns were not being implanted in the south, temple building continued at an astonishing rate. Ramesses II constructed no fewer than ten south of the First Cataract (see figs. 13, 14).[101]

It is difficult to identify the precise economic role of these temples in the life of Nubia. Were they independent institutions, forming the nucleus for landed holdings? And where were such holdings located: in Nubia or Egypt, or both? Did they enjoy independent endowments? The fact that in Ramesside times the phrase "in the House of Amun/Re" is appended to the names of Nubian temples[102] suggests the role of a subsidiary shrine of some major temple in Egypt proper. But the picture is complicated by the almost complete absence of any reference to Nubian temples from administrative documents in Egypt.

THE ECONOMIC EFFECT ON EGYPT OF NUBIAN GOLD

Recent trends in interpreting the expansion phenomenon of the Eighteenth Dynasty and later,[103] many of a seductive ingenuity, are currently giving rise to assumptions and interpretations the trendsetters may never have intended. These include (1) that it is increasingly appropriate to adopt terms and concepts derived from modern economic state theory in order to elucidate the phenomenon of ancient "empire"; (2) that imperial authorities indulged in long-range planning and were aware of costs of production and the benefits of cost-effectiveness and that this is reflected in artifact distribution in the periphery; and (3) that products and resources from the African sphere were used to "finance" state activities elsewhere. None of these must go unchallenged.

It has become faddish among some Egyptologists to consider the ancient Egyptian a species of *homo economicus,* such as we imagine ourselves to be, fair game for the application of the economic theory of rational expectations. Yet superimposing modern, and often infelicitous, concepts and terminology (which themselves are already under attack by economists!)[104] upon the ancients risks ignoring what they themselves had to say. And in fact they had a great deal to say. First and foremost, ideological, not economic, considerations of preemption, revenge, and honor far outweighed what to us would be a far-sighted economic view of enlightened self-interest, especially in the formative stages of the empire. No ancient source ever betrays a prior concern for resources, trade routes, or middlemen. On the contrary, Pharaoh took military action to "smite the foreign rulers who had attacked him,"[105] "to overthrow him that had attacked him,"[106] to repel "all lands as they moved against him,"[107] "them that had intended to bring destruction upon Egypt"[108] or "who had trespassed the frontiers."[109] The safety of the community dominates the texts justifying and explaining empire.

The characteristic lawlessness of non-Egyptians itself constituted a threat to Egypt's security: Pharaoh struck Kush first "in order to extirpate uproar throughout the foreign lands and to stem invasion from foreign parts."[110] The Nubian had to be attacked "for he had planned an uprising against Egypt."[111] Such an uprising could be construed as "rebellion" (*bšt*) when Egyptian colonists had been attacked, their cattle stolen, and their land confiscated.[112]

Frequently in inscriptions of the early Eighteenth Dynasty Egypt appears in the trope of the defenseless woman, the mother who expects loyalty from her children[113] but who requires a champion (male) to defend her. Kamose's intent was "to rescue Egypt whom the Asiatics have destroyed,"[114] and Thutmose III was "the saviour of Egypt, fighting in the breach."[115] Thutmose I was already aware of the figure: "I have made powerful those who were (formerly) terror struck, I have removed the evils from her (Egypt), I have made Egypt chieftainess, with every land being her chattel."[116]

One of the best expressions of the idea of empire and the rationale behind it is contained in the stela of Thutmose III from Buto:[117]

> The southerners are in his grasp, the northerners are under his
>   authority, the Two Banks of Horus are in awe of him,
> all lands and all foreign countries lie together under his sandals;
> they come to him with heads bowed, groveling at his might;
> the foreign chiefs of each and every land say: "he is our master!"
> It is he they serve through fear of him!
> There isn't a land he has not trod to extend the boundaries of
>   Egypt in might and power! Myriads and millions are of no
>   concern to him,
> He is an active king who makes great slaughter in battle among
>   the nomads to a man, who makes the chiefs of Retenu
>   altogether bear their labor taxes,
> taxed with an annual labor-quota like serfs of his palace;
> he is more effective than a numerous army of millions behind
>   him,
> a unique fighter, a brave for whom no other of equal

(accomplishment) has come along in any land among his
troops,
the foreign rulers or the southerners or northerners;
he is a king deserving of praise commensurate with his strength.
Egypt is strong since he came (to the throne)—no country is a
concern to her;
she never has to attend on the southerners or seek out the
northerners,
knowing that her champion is like Min with uplifted arm,
the King of Upper and Lower Egypt, Menkheperre, the bowman
of Montu,
who sets his frontier on the horns of the earth, on the highland
of Miu!
Kush is with him as his serf, directing to him her labor taxes
of numerous and endless gold, ivory and ebony!
There is no king that has done what he has done, among any of
the kings that ever were!

This conveys the essentials of the imperial experience: the divine approbation of the monarch, his overwhelming power and victory, the intimidation of the world, the likening of Egypt to a defenseless woman, and
the king's role as its honorable champion. There is nothing here that can
be fitted into modern economic theory. The rough-and-ready reality was
that Egypt, in order to protect itself, was "expanding the frontiers"[118] and
that the inhabitants of foreign parts thus engulfed had been reduced to the
same footing as the Egyptian underclass: share-cropping tenants ($n\underline{d}t$)[119]
whose possessions, wealth, and even agricultural produce could be (and
were) claimed by Pharaoh.

It is difficult to square the assumption of long-range planning and
consciously conceived "policy" with the hard pharaonic evidence. At every stage one encounters a certain quixotic temperament ill suited to sustained pursuit of a goal over generations and given to ad hoc decision
making. A Kamose might tell us what his desire or aim (*ib*) was, an
Amenophis II might provide a thumbnail sketch of his behavioral mode
vis-à-vis Nubians, or an Akhenaten might give his views on Canaan, but
these scarcely merit the term *government policy* in a modern sense.[120]

That distribution of Egyptian or Egyptianizing artifacts in the periphery reflects conscious "policy" by the central administration is difficult to
maintain. Not only does such a thesis ignore the studied disinterest by the
Egyptian authorities as to where goods ended up, but it also is not pref-
aced by a study of municipal taxonomy and spatial parameters. In trying

to assess the impact of an imperial "center" upon the settlements of its "periphery,"[121] one must be aware of the hierarchy of settlement imposed by the "center," for in any imperial structure it is largely within the competence of the administration to enhance and embellish, or denigrate and impoverish, the towns within its hegemony, and this will have a direct bearing on the presence or absence of artifacts. Therefore, it is well to note (a) that imperial Egypt spoke of all the settlements within its dependencies as "towns (of Pharaoh),"[122] denying them the formal *niwt*—metropolitan states did not exist therein, (b) that only two generic terms were common, namely, "town" (*dmit*) and "hamlet" (*wḥ3t*),[123] and (c) that the Egyptians had unconsciously "graded" settlements into several ranks: headquarters, garrison towns, "name" towns,[124] depots, way stations (*hydreia*). It would be interesting to investigate how the dispersal of Egyptian(izing) artifacts follows the outline of these categories.

In Egypt during the New Kingdom the means, and possibly the right, to send Egyptian products and artifacts abroad in large quantities lay solely in the hands of one authority and six or seven of his delegates: the king, the vizier, the chief treasurer, and the heads of three or four temples.[125] The objective of caravans and expeditions mounted from Egypt was not so much trade as exaction or extortion of specifics from smaller polities—Egyptians were "target"-traders[126]—gift exchange at a higher level. The monopoly of power largely excluded entrepreneurial commerce.

To authorities who could wield such immense power expense was wholly meaningless. Expeditions went to the Sudan with hundreds of donkeys via the oasis route at great cost, eschewing the more convenient riverine transport; tens of thousands of people might be uprooted and exiled a thousand miles away at a cost prohibitive to any economizing polity; ten thousand men might be sent to quarry a few blocks of stone that mere hundreds could have extracted. One can only conclude that once again, as in the classic case of pyramid construction, the pharaonic state was indulging in a display of conspicuous waste[127] in its demonstration of the unlimited power of the god-king. It was the godlike and heroic image that was striven for, rather than the frugal, not only in outward display but also in underlying agenda.

The Egyptian acquisition by conquest of the mineral wealth of Nubia has sometimes been presented under the guise of a system of finance facilitating Egypt's international role in the world.[128] Whatever may be useful about the model, the term *finance* seems an infelicitous choice and wrongly applied *en tant que tel*. This term derives from a money economy,[129] user-friendly in eliciting services or securing commodities from independent or semi-independent sources but useless in a monopolizing pharaonic system.

That the newfound Nubian mineral wealth somehow underpinned or enhanced Egyptian influence and activities elsewhere is yet to be demonstrated. It is not consonant with the known evidence to require *ex hypothesi* a major injection of such wealth from the south into Egypt's coffers to provide the wherewithal to create and sustain Egypt's position elsewhere. Already in the halcyon days of the Old Kingdom Egypt's sphere of influence had extended as far as the Aegean,[130] and in the New Kingdom Nubia had been won long before the Nubian gold mines had reached anywhere near their peak of production. The winning of an Asiatic empire was effected by ragtag, native levies traveling on their bellies; they were recruited from the factors and menials of temple estates, for large expeditionary forces one in ten being taken.[131] Their rudimentary requirements were supplied from home—witness Anastasi I[132]—their rations grown on the banks of the Nile. And in this the New Kingdom expeditionary forces differed little from the Old Kingdom hosts who had undertaken little more than razzias and slave raids in south and north, long before Nubia had become a significant factor in the Egyptian economy. For the first century and a half of the Egyptian empire in Canaan, the cost of maintenance of an Egyptian presence was borne by the locals themselves, a burden only gradually lifted during the thirteenth century by the pursuance of the Egypto-Hittite war.[133]

Revenues in precious metals coming from the south were in the overwhelming majority destined for Pharaoh's treasury and temple treasuries, the latter, though enormous, being "within the system" and under tight pharaonic control. The overriding aim of the Egyptian administration throughout its history was *accumulation,* not export or disbursement.[134] Although some gold and silver circulated commercially at home and abroad, this was a relatively paltry amount. The mass of this wealth was held "in reserve" as it were.

One real and often overlooked use to which the Egyptian state put its increased revenues in precious metals is to be identified in the loyalty/reward system (*fq3*), not to be confused with the system of state emolument. And this system operated mainly within the Egyptian community, rather than in foreign parts. Of course Pharaoh might proffer rewards, trivial in the broad scheme of things, to foreigners "who were upon H.M.'s water"; but this had been going on since the Old Kingdom, long before substantial amounts of Nubian gold entered the picture. Nubian gold might have seemed to be a new "carrot" to be dangled before the noses of foreign potentates: it scarcely constituted the sine qua non of Egyptian activity in the world and in reality amounted to a tiny fraction of available resources.

THE COLLAPSE OF THE EMPIRE IN KUSH

The end of the Egyptian "provinces" of Kush and Nubia is not recounted in any connected record, but tantalizing clues turn up from time to time in "asides" in business and administrative documents.[135] The career in office of the last functioning viceroy that we know of, Paynehsi, occupies roughly the first two decades of Ramesses XI's reign[136] and seems in no way out of the ordinary. He prepared a tomb for himself, in keeping with the common practice, at the viceregal headquarters at Aniba,[137] and his name is found in pietistic texts at Buhen.[138] But then, in year 12 of his suzerain, his name appears in the heading of a routine document of grain receipts from farms in the Thebaid, with the impressive titulary "flabellum-bearer on the king's right hand, king's-scribe and general of the army, superintendent of the granaries [of Pharaoh; king's-son] of Kush, superintendent of the southern lands, the *dux* Paynehsi of the battalions [of Pharaoh . . .]."[139] The implication is strong that at the time of writing Paynehsi was either in Thebes or responsible for its administration. What had suddenly extended his bailiwick into Upper Egypt?

Paynehsi's floruit overlapped the end of the tenure in office of Amenophis, the high priest of Amun. This worthy was son of the high priest Ramesses-nakht, who had served under Ramesses III seventy years before and who had apparently wrested from the king the right to pass on his office to his sons.[140] Amenophis appears first in Ramesses IX's tenth year, when he is shown being rewarded "for the many fine monuments he made in the House of Amunra-sonther in the 'Great Name' of the Perfect God"[141] and "for the diligent job you have done of the harvest taxes, dues and labor taxes of the personnel of the House of Amonra-sonther."[142] These activities must have occupied a more or less extended period of time, so that Amenophis would not have come into office simply on the eve of the tenth year.[143] Whether he survived in office into subsequent reigns remains moot,[144] but there is a good likelihood that he did. In a biographical statement written in later life Amenophis,[145] in a testimony to the grace of the god he served, recounts how someone (clearly an enemy) "seized it (the Temple of Amun?), and spent eight full months in it, while I suffered grievously under him." Yet the speaker was able to triumph eventually over "the one who had violated me, and I appealed to Pharaoh, my lord." It is almost beyond dispute that this same "violation" is reflected in the court transcript of the evidence given in the trial of a gang of thieves which took place in Ramesses XI's nineteenth and twentieth years.[146] The robberies included grave robbing and stealing precious metals from portable shrines and temple doors, crimes in broad daylight which could be committed only if normal police controls were nonexistent. The thefts had been committed much earlier than the time of the trial, many of the witnesses, now adults, having been children at the time. One of the depositions runs as follows:[147] "The barbarians came and they seized the temple (Medinet Habu) while I was tending some asses of my father's; and Pahat, a certain barbarian seized me and took me to Ipip just when the violation of Amenophis who had been high-priest of Amun was about to reach six months (duration). In fact, I came (back) only after this portable shrine had been purloined and set on fire, nine full months into the violation sustained by Amenophis who had been high-priest of Amun." The "barbarians" had come in force: "It was when I was a little boy that my father was killed, and my mother told me: ' . . . when the battalion commanders of the barbarians killed your father, they took me for questioning.'"[148] That a Paynehsi was involved in the "violation" is made explicit: "I left the House of Pharaoh just when Paynehsi came and violated my master, although there was no violation on his part."[149] A "Paynehsi" is mentioned in other contexts also as having perpetrated crimes in Thebes, including wrongful appropriation[150] and murder.[151]

A strong case has long since been made for an occupation of the Thebaid at the expense of the high priest by Paynehsi (the viceroy) at the head of "barbarians" (i.e., troops from Kush). The occupation is termed a "violation," *thi,* a word that means basically to stray (over a line), to trespass, to transgress (against someone's rights), and then to damage, neglect, or disobey.[152] But once it is termed "the war of the high-priest,"[153] and it is tempting to link the incident to other references such as "when Paynehsi destroyed Hardai"[154] and "the war in the northern sector (i.e., Lower Egypt)."[155] Though in part a fanciful tale, P. Pushkin 127, set towards the close of the Twentieth Dynasty, makes mention of "the flames of war" engulfing the four cardinal points of the land.[156]

If the above-mentioned reconstruction is speculative, the motivation of the protagonists is much more difficult to ascertain. Was Paynehsi really the perpetrator and his victim Amenophis the wronged party? And what role did Pharaoh play: had he called in Paynehsi in the face of uprisings in the homeland, or had he backed Amenophis *against* Paynehsi as the biographical statement may be construed as implying? And who fomented the "war": Paynehsi? Amenophis? or some third, unnamed party?

It used to be assumed that the floruit of Amenophis represented the last effort of the high priesthood, now possessed of political power equal to that of the monarchy, to wrest the reins of state from Pharaoh. True, some passages in contemporary texts seem to portray an arrogant high priest, countermanding police orders and refusing rations to strikers,[157] but this could be dismissed as anecdotal evidence. Certainly the biographical statement published by Wente represents the speaker as a loyal subject of Pharaoh, more sinned against than sinning.

The following is an acceptable scenario based on the sparse sources at our disposal:

1. Sometime early in Ramesses XI's reign, for unknown reasons,[158] civil war erupted in Egypt and lasted nearly one year. It was attended by looting and murder.
2. Into the Thebaid came the viceroy Paynehsi with Nubian troops, and Amenophis the high priest was suppressed and temporarily relieved of power.
3. Shortly thereafter and by unknown means, Amenophis was restored to office, but he died soon after; his immediate successor remains unknown.[159]
4. Paynehsi continued to exercise control over the Thebaid until year 12 and perhaps beyond: he is still in the royal administration in year 17.[160]

At this juncture an unknown entered the picture. Herihor,[161] a man of probably military background,[162] turns up in Thebes as high priest of Amun with an impressive array of titles:[163] "heir apparent, he who is over the Two Lands, great courtier in the entire land . . . field marshall of Upper and Lower Egypt, *dux* . . . superintendent of construction on His Majesty's monuments, manager of Upper and Lower Egypt, overseer of the granaries, vizier."[164] Paynehsi is nowhere to be found: Herihor is obviously the "king's man" and has no qualms about taking the title "viceroy of Kush."[165] In year 19, probably pursuant to an oracle,[166] the great god Amun issued an edict appointing Herihor as governor in Thebes and a northerner, Smendes, as "officer" in the north.[167] Whether this catapulting of two new men into ad hoc positions of power—note that neither is a vizier—was done at the instigation of the king or in disregard of him is difficult to say at present. That Ramesses XI was considered by contemporaries a virtual nonentity is a recorded fact;[168] yet he continued to come south for the important Theban festivals,[169] and his authority was respected.[170]

Clearly, however, year 19 marks a break with the past. A new era, dubbed "Renaissance" by contemporaries, had been inaugurated, and for the remainder of Ramesses XI's reign dating by the new era alternates with the king's regnal years. In everyday affairs Herihor continued as "high-priest of Amun," his official claim to administrative power,[171] and in colloquial speech he was called "boss" and "magnate";[172] but in the privacy of the temple, where centuries of cult tradition demanded a *royal* presence as celebrant, Ḥeriḥor donned the guise of "Pharaoh" and took an official titulary.[173]

The province of Kush had come to an end. If Payneḥsi's intervention in Egypt had been a bid for power, it failed. The new regime of Ḥeriḥor could tolerate no rival. Payneḥsi is last heard of fighting against Ḥeriḥor's successor in Nubia proper, at the close of Ramesses XI's reign.[174] Then all evidence ceases.

THE SILENT YEARS
THE ABANDONMENT OF LOWER NUBIA
AND THE RISE OF NAPATA

B y the time of the first millennium B.C. the southland had entered a "dark age." Ḥeriḥor and his successors might well have displayed the old title "viceroy of Kush" as an expression of their claim to jurisdiction over the old Sudanese province,[1] but it became increasingly a hollow claim. By the close of the Twentieth Dynasty, if not before, the inscriptions cease in Nubian temples, and signs of an active administration are absent: the last texts at Kawa belong to the viceroy Nebmarenakht[2] (temp. Ramesses VI and VII), at Buhen to Ramesses XI,[3] and at Napata temple service peters out under Ramesses IX.[4] The last taxes from Kush are recorded late in Ramesses XI's reign (year 23).[5] A clear view of the south disappears with Piankhy's war against the recalcitrant viceroy Paynehsi,[6] and for centuries we must suffer an almost total absence of archaeological material, for a period of "low Niles" had set in when the Thebaid suffered hunger,[7] and communities in Lower Nubia, unable to sustain themselves, moved south to Dongola.[8] Since the prosperity of the area had depended in the imperial age in part on an exchange of goods with Egypt, the economic decline of the erstwhile motherland and the process of depopulation resulted in an interruption in trade which proved calamitous for the Sudan.[9] Egyptians and Egyptianized Nubians alike disappear,[10] and the "high life" of former times cannot be found. The great temples of the Eighteenth and Nineteenth Dynasties stand derelict and abandoned, tragic reminders of an age that will never return.

THE REVIVAL

The first signs of a revival in the fortunes of the northern Sudan are to be dated as occurring in the first and second quarter of the ninth century B.C.,[11] when the evidence points to a community taking shape in the environs of Napata. This site, lying beneath Gebel Barkal, had supported a settlement of Egyptians at least as early as the reign of Thutmose III.[12] The worship of Amun, the guarantor of the empire, had been implanted at the site, and a shrine built by the reign of Tutankhamun had been expanded into a formal temple.[13] As time went on, the cult exerted an irresistible attraction over the native Kushites, who treated it as their own and settled in Napata to create a permanent community. From about 890 B.C. the burying ground of this community at neighboring Kurru yields a series of large graves.[14] These at first are in a native tradition in which a pit and chamber are covered by a simple tumulus, and the corpse is either flexed or laid upon a bed,[15] but later development leads to the veneering of the tumulus with stone and the creation of mastabas in imitation of the Egyptian type.[16] At the same time trade revived: the Theban high priest Osorkon refers, in the twenty-fourth year of Takelot II of the Twenty-second Dynasty, to "fine gold of Khent-hen-nefer" and "dry myrrh of the best of Neḥsy-land" among the gifts given to Amun,[17] and the contents of the Kurru graves begin at the same time to display Egyptian trade goods.

Who was the family buried at Kurru and what was the ethnic makeup of the Napatan community over which it presided?[18] It was once fashionable to allow fancy free rein: priests of Amun had fled from Thebes after the end of the New Kingdom and set up a "theocracy" at Napata, or one Pashedbast, son of a Pharaoh Sheshonq, had settled there and fathered the Kushite royal house.[19] Needless to say, scarcely a particle of evidence exists to support either of these notions. The worship of Amun of Napata was of long standing, and the jar mentioning Pashedbast is clearly a trade item. To judge by their later representations and their names, the members of the ancestral Twenty-fifth Dynasty appear to have constituted an autochthonous family of Sudanese blacks exercising the headship over local tribes in the Dongola.[20] None of their birthnames can be derived from the Egyptian onomasticon, and when in a scene provided with color they are depicted, their color is chocolate brown, in contrast to the russet tone of the Egyptians.[21] Moreover, their rule of inheritance is alien to Egyptian custom and involves inheritance through the king's sisters: from elder to younger brother, then to eldest brother's son.[22]

The family of chiefs buried at Kurru—and presumably we are dealing here with a chiefdom—come into the light of history some five generations after the cemetery had begun with a certain Alara, the first to be known by name.[23] Significantly, when mimesis demanded that the evolving chiefdom adopt a script, it was Egyptian hieroglyphic that was chosen. Although retaining its own Nubian dialect as the communal vernacular, the Twenty-fifth Dynasty could only conceive of the "triumph-stela" and other public records in the Egyptian language.[24]

In fact, the entire frame of cultural reference of the incipient kingdom of Napata was Egyptian. Alara, by enclosing his name in a cartouche, perceived himself in a *pharaonic* guise. When he and his successors felt constrained to memorialize themselves in relief and statuary, they chose the artwork ready at hand, namely, the Ramesside temples of Nubia, the artistic decoration of which became models for the Kushites.[25] Later, with the Thebaid in their grasp, the scions of the Twenty-fifth Dynasty succumbed to the attraction of the traditional, blockish art of Thebes, with its high, bold relief, heavy musculature, and prognathous profiles.[26]

But it was the cult of Amun which held the Kushites in thrall and forged an unbreakable bond with the Thebans for more than two centuries. The center of Kushite power lay under the very walls of Napata,[27] within the shadow of the house of Amun "of the Holy Mountain," and the Twenty-fifth Dynasty worshiped and served this god, mainly in his local ram avatar,[28] with all the fervor and piety of converts. Amun, and he alone, creates the *true* king, and the kings from Napata are like his children and his chosen ones.[29] By their insignia the Kushite kings identified themselves closely with Amun,[30] and from the time of Alara they followed the practice of dedicating sisters and daughters to the service of the god.[31] Thus, even before a political dimension was added to their relationship with the Thebaid, the Kushite kings must have longed for Thebes as much as any crusader for Jerusalem.

The early eighth century B.C., through its dearth of textual record, imposes upon us a most regrettable silence, for it must have been then that the young Nubian kingdom was in the process of consciously borrowing and adapting the pharaonic traits later to inform Sudanese civilization of the Twenty-fifth Dynasty. Along with script and lingua franca (initially introduced and nurtured by "literati" imported from Egypt?) went a body of technical know-how that was to prove all-important in the south's bid for power. It must have been before 750 B.C., in fact, that knowledge of advanced methods of warfare and the hardware to utilize them reached the kingdom of Napata. Chariotry, personal armor and weaponry, and especially siege techniques involving towers, siege mounds, and battering rams all bespeak an awareness of the improvements in warfare at home in the Tigris-Euphrates Valley.[32] How they arrived in Napata is open for discussion, but the Levant and Egypt itself undoubtedly acted as intermediaries.[33] One way or another, when the Twenty-fifth Dynasty appeared on the world stage, it was well equipped to take on the most successful superpower of the day.

Alara was succeeded before the middle of the eighth century B.C. by his younger brother Kashta. His name occurs in inscriptions at Elephantine, so that presumably at least the region of the First Cataract acknowledged his overlordship.[34] With him the history of Kush becomes united with that of Thebes.

EGYPT UNDER THE LIBYANS

If the Kushites had expected a warm reception by a united Egypt, bent on a chaste and reverend service of a national deity mutually adored, they must have been rudely shocked. The Egypt they burst upon was a far cry from that of the New Kingdom six centuries earlier. A foreign ethnic element had not only insinuated itself into the Nilotic landscape but had also assumed the rule of the country.

Egyptian resistance in the twelfth century B.C. to an eastward and southward pressure of population from Libya and the Aegean had proved only partly successful. Three major battles in the fifth, eighth, and eleventh years of Ramesses III (first quarter of the twelfth century B.C.) admittedly stopped the uncontrolled movement of these aliens into Lower Egypt, but from all accounts the effort had been Herculean and had left the state exhausted. The onset of the period of reduced inundations and the intestine feuding of the ruling family of the Twentieth Dynasty contributed to the weakening of Egypt's economy and its ability to control its frontiers. Throughout the course of the late twelfth and early eleventh centuries, its Asiatic and African empires withered away, and it was forced to countenance the settlement of the very Aegean groups that had tried to break into the country by force on the very threshold of the eastern Delta in southern Palestine.[35] On the western Delta the Libyan enclaves found no effective check to their peaceful incursions, and groups of the Meshwesh and (to a lesser extent) Labu drifted into Lower Egypt and made themselves a nuisance to the settled inhabitants (see fig. 15).[36] As soldiers, the Libyan tribesmen impressed the Egyptians, who accepted their services on a mercenary basis. The chief of the Meshwesh took up residence in Herakleopolis, which had been a military base from Ramesside times,[37] and functioned as the commander in chief of the armed forces. Although his action was not exactly a coup, Sheshonq's role as chief of the Meshwesh and generalissimo of the army cannot have hindered his assumption of regal power on the death of Psusennes II about 931 B.C. Thus was inaugurated the (Libyan) Twenty-second Dynasty, with its seat in Tanis in the northeastern Delta.

Despite their reputation for bellicosity on the battlefield, the rule of

Fig. 15. Libyan tribesmen. Thebes, tomb of Ramesses III, twelfth century B.C.

the Libyans was seldom strong or efficient.[38] They seem to have kept apart, living on the fringes of Egyptian settlements, and to have retained their own onomasticon and probably their own language, as well. Libyan soldiers were provided with plots of land for their upkeep and probably owed a sort of feudal loyalty to their chiefs. Libyans worshiped Egyptian gods, and some intermarriage with Egyptians is attested at the upper levels of society, but nothing could rid them of the stigma of being foreign and rather barbaric.

This unsavory reputation was enhanced by Libyan treatment of Thebes. Although the Thebaid did not have to suffer Libyan occupation—the Mahaswen tribe that made incursions in the south in the Twentieth Dynasty shortly disappeared—it nonetheless was obliged to watch helplessly while its power was drained away and the office of high priest of Amun was taken over by Libyans. Moreover, the high priest, usually a prince of the reigning Twenty-second Dynasty, often did not deign to shoulder his duties in Thebes but resided in the fort at Tehneh in Middle Egypt, appearing only for major festivals. Royal inspectors and taxmen from the north were free to interfere in Theban affairs with impunity,[39] and after the reign of the founder of the house almost no royal building activity was authorized in the southern city. One or two Thebans who attained high rank in the priesthood dared to enclose their names in cartouches, mimicking perhaps the example set by Ḥeriḥor,[40] but no independent dynastic succession resulted from the act. The Libyan kings had a reputation for "rages," and one was lucky to avoid harsh treatment.[41]

One hundred years after the assumption of power by the Libyans, Theban grievances had become so severe that further tolerance was impossible. Possibly Pharaoh Osorkon II had felt a premonition of doom, for at his *sed*-festival in his twenty-second year (c. 845 B.C.) he had issued a proclamation in Thebes's favor: "I have exempted Thebes in its length and breadth; it is purified and given back to its lord (i.e., Amun). There shall be no interference with it by the inspectors of the king's-house, (for) its people are exempted for an aeon."[42] But in the event it may be seen as too little too late.

Barely seventeen years after the promulgation of this edict, the city of Thebes rose in open revolt against the hated foreigner in the north.[43] For the third time in Egyptian history the Thebaid was taking the lead in a nationalistic insurrection to oust a perceived usurper. In the Eleventh (twenty-first century B.C.) and Seventeenth (sixteenth century B.C.) Dynasties the uprisings had proven successful and had produced a prosperous, unified country: doubtless the Theban patriots of 832 B.C. looked for a similar outcome to their actions. The insurrection broke out with such suddenness and severity that contemporaries remarked on the lack of portents preceding the event which might have forewarned them.[44] Soon the rebellion spread, and a good portion of Upper Egypt had taken up arms against the king in Tanis. Vandalism seems to have attended the uprising, as temples and monuments to Libyan rule suffered desecration. Theban scribes, moreover, willfully destroyed documents and records in an effort to frustrate the Libyan administration. The reaction of the contemporary Takelot II, though swift, lacked sureness or skill. He placed responsibility for quelling the disturbance in the hands of his brother Osorkon, the high priest of Amun, who maintained his residence at Tehneh in Middle Egypt. With armed forces at his disposal Osorkon defeated the rebels and restored his southward march; he entered the city unopposed and set about to settle the issue once and for all. Despite the fact that he issued six decrees increasing offerings and granted charters of immunity to local institutions, he could not resist meting out punishment that was draconian, if not barbaric. The scribes and administrators who were deemed mainly responsible were rounded up and burned alive.[45]

In no way did these measures solve the problem. Barely four years later the revolt of the south broke out afresh and raged for nearly a decade, this time engulfing most of Egypt in the uproar. Although the end of the affair is not clear to us—Osorkon's apologia is clearly distorted and fuzzy in order to place him in the best light—it would seem that stalemate dictated some kind of accommodation. The Libyan dynasty was not unseated, but neither was Thebes defeated.

The aftermath brought on the sure decline and fragmentation of Libyan authority. The long reign (fifty-two years) of the weak Sheshonq III, whose floruit encompasses the first third of the eighth century B.C., witnessed the growing independence of a number of Delta principalities ruled over by "great chiefs of the Me(shwesh)"[46] and the arrogation of regal status by the rulers of four cities[47] in the Delta and Middle Egypt.[48] Libyan "foreignness" to Egyptian ways coupled with the exigencies of politics and hallowed form resulted in a modification in the notion of head of state which could accommodate more than a single *nsw* (king) in the land.[49] The jumped-up "kings" did not fight among themselves or against the Twenty-second Dynasty king in Tanis but lived in a sort of equilibrium dating events each by his own reign. Nonetheless, a certain parochialism is now discernible in town culture, manifesting itself in the local cult and the close relationship of the local ruler to the nome deity.

THE SUDAN INVADES EGYPT

In the eyes of the youthful Nubian kingdom the vista that now opened to view in the old mother country to the north was anything but comforting. Frankly it was appalling. Gone were the piety and reverence and fear of god that had characterized the traditional Egypt of the New Kingdom. Egyptians were now a bastard race, shot through with the barbarity of godless foreigners. They cared nothing for true kingship and the election of god; their ignorance of the proper way to serve god bothered them not at all. They flouted god's law even in their daily lives: why, some of them even wore wool and ate fish!

About 737 B.C. Kashta was succeeded on the throne at Napata by his son, whose name was Piankhy or (perhaps) Piya.[1] If Alara and Kashta are but faceless names to us, Piankhy suddenly confronts us with a fully developed personality, at least for the purposes of rhetorical propaganda, thanks to the lengthy and most important records he has left behind.[2]

THE TWENTY-THIRD DYNASTY AND THE DIVINE WORSHIPER

Despite its rebellion, Thebes and the cult of Amun remained a force to be reckoned with in the body politic of the eighth century. Unable to throw off the Libyan yoke, Thebes had nonetheless, by its supreme efforts, crippled the Twenty-second Dynasty and indirectly contributed to the breakup of Middle Egypt and the Delta. It had to be courted, and the chiefs and kinglets of the north did not fail to do so. It became customary, in imitation of an earlier practice of the Twenty-second Dynasty, for northern dynasts to dedicate a daughter to the priesthood of Amun, as a songstress or hierodule.[3] Along with the little girl—for the daughters who were dedicated were undoubtedly of young age—went monetary considerations and concessions of other sorts, designed to win favor with a southland that had brought itself to everyone's attention. Ironically, the staff of the Temple of Amun, especially the upper echelons of the priest-hood, had suffered a serious diminution of power, yet it was these indi-viduals who now found themselves privileged to choose which northern nonentity they would memorialize. So now it was the contemporary Twenty-second Dynasty monarch, or now an ephemeral king of Letopolis, who graced the records of the height of the inundation with his regnal years[4] or king Thotemhat of Hermopolis or a Harsiese (of no fixed address) whom a local notable chose to mention on his statue.[5]

As the eighth century wore on, there was one northern dynasty, no less worthy of oblivion than the rest, which Thebes took to its heart more than the others—that of King Pedibast and his descendants. Pedibast was probably of Bubastite origin,[6] as the name implies, but the territorial ju-risdiction of his regime and even his principal seat of residence remain problematical, at least on the basis of present evidence. Manetho, the priest-historian of the third century B.C., claims Tanis to have been the seat of origin of the dynasty (which he labels Twenty-third),[7] but the exca-vations at the site have revealed few traces of a Pedibast[8] and none of his successors.[9] On the basis of a passage in the Piankhy stela, the residence of the dynasty has been postulated as Bubastis, with a bailiwick extending north-northeast to Ranofer west of Tanis; but even if that be the case around 717 B.C., we cannot say for certain that the same situation ob-tained three generations earlier. The burial of a queen mother alleged to be of Twenty-third Dynasty date at Tel Moqdam[10] has diverted attention to that site (ancient Leontopolis), and it is very tempting to view Bubastis and Tel Moqdam as constituting a political axis in the eighth century. Pedibast is in fact attested at Bubastis, but so is the late Twenty-second Dynasty in the persons of Pemiu and Sheshonq IV,[11] and the stela on which Pedibast is mentioned might be construed as an equivocal accep-tance of his authority.[12]

Pedibast and his descendants are slightly better attested at Thebes.[13] Shortly after his accession Pedibast was recognized by the Amun priests, and his regnal years were used in lieu of those of the Twenty-second Dy-nasty to date events.[14] Pedibast restored the tenth pylon on the south, "making for him (Amun) a great gate of sandstone, after he found it fallen to ruin."[15] Somewhere on the approach to the Khonsu Temple Osorkon III constructed a building of unknown purport (a porch?), with reliefs showing himself and his son Takelot as high priest.[16] Later in his reign Osorkon associated Takelot with him as joint king, a co-regency memori-alized in the charming little shrine of Osiris, northeast of the main Amun Temple,[17] which Osorkon erected shortly after.

Pedibast appears to have employed Theban notables in his administration, which from their description sounds far-reaching and effective.
The "hereditary prince, count, sole friend, fan-bearer on the king's right
hand" Ḥory, who held priesthoods in the service of Amun, Montu, and
Ptaḥ, functioned as Pedibast's secretary of correspondence and in this capacity was assigned the task of an inspection of the economy of the entire
land.

> I was indeed chief of the palace and administrator for the plebs.
> Myrrh it was to the heart of my lord (for) he lived (only) to hear
> my tongue. I directed the king for the good of the Two Banks
> (=Egypt), to fare in loyalty to the god; and he grounded the Two
> Lands in the concept of my heart . . .[18] foremost magistrate in the
> land . . . who provides Egypt with his laws as far as the sandy
> beaches. . . . I was a confidant of the unique one, one who filled the
> palace with his teaching and established procedure for the magis-
> trates, one whose pen brought together the Two Lands. I was sent
> on a mission of the lord of the Two Lands to restore Egypt for its
> lord, for he knew my excellence over the Two Lands and my status
> among the grandees. I was chief commander of the entire land, be-
> loved of his lord's heart, who gives orders to the plebs while the
> courtiers are silent; who reports to the king on the labor of the land
> and administers the country for its maker; skilled in the laws of the
> palace and the instructions of the ancestors. . . .[19] My Lord assigned
> me to register the Two Lands and to put the country back into its
> state of purity with every man at his task. The grandees indeed
> consulted me, so great was my teaching.[20]

Despite the self-serving verbiage, the circumstances and importance
of the chief underlying event of Ḥory's life show through clearly. Early in
the eighth century, as the weak scion of the Twenty-second Dynasty,
Sheshonq III, lost power and influence, and as the country in the wake of
the Theban rebellion went to ruin, Pedibast sought to extend his jurisdiction by ordering a nationwide census and inventory. And in order to carry
this out he enlisted the services of a prominent Theban.

Osorkon III continued his predecessor's close association with
Thebes. Djedkhonsefankh, fourth prophet of Amun and overseer of the
treasury of Amun, describes himself as "trusted by Horus in his house,
who restores the boundaries, who restores what had fallen into ruin; who
raised the levies in the Temples."[21] His special relationship with the king is
described as follows: "When I was in the palace, I got rich in it. . . . I would

enter at the front and come out at the last, conferring over all policy that I might direct him (the king) aright. I was knowledgeable about the temples, and I established their boundaries and fixed(?) their incomes. I used to talk with His Majesty through the days; and while his magistrates would say what he wanted (to hear), I had no fear. It was I that calmed him when his mood worsened into his rages. He was content with my statements, and I brought him the tribute of every land."[22] The statements of Djedkhonsefankh sound as though he had direct access to the king on a daily basis; and since there is no reason to believe he functioned anywhere else but in Thebes, the prima facie probability is that Osorkon III resided there. He seems to have had a tomb on the west bank at Thebes,[23] and his epithets and accoutrements in art point to Upper Egypt.[24]

Despite this circumstantial evidence of an active political role, the Twenty-third Dynasty would have sunk into oblivion in the collective memory of posterity were it not for Osorkon III's elevation of his daughter Shepenwepet (I) to the office of Divine Worshiper of Amun (see fig. 16).[25] This post, a function of some member of the distaff side of the royal house (usually the queen), amounted to a sort of high priestess's office responsible for the female personnel of the cult of Amun.[26] Although an ancient institution going back to before the beginning of the New Kingdom, the Divine Worshiper was never a prominent wielder of power in the sacerdotal hierarchy, being completely overshadowed by the upper ranks of the (male) priesthood. Under the Libyan dynasty evidence is largely lacking on the fate of the office,[27] although a certain Karome (with name in cartouche) is known from the ninth century under the high priest, "king"

Fig. 16. Osorkon III (right) and his daughter Shepenwepet (center) worship Amun, Reharakhte, and Ptaḥ. Thebes, Temple of Osiris-Ruler-of-Eternity, eighth century B.C.

Harsiese.[28] Under Osorkon III Shepenwepet I was a virtual regent, with double cartouche and epithets resembling those of a sovereign: "the God's-Wife of Amun, She-that-cleaves-unto-the-heart-of-Amun, Beloved-of-Mut Shepenwepet, living on *ma⁽at*, being rejuvenated like Re daily!"[29] She takes precedence over her father in the first and second room of the Temple of Osiris, in offering to Amun, Reharakhty, and Ptaḥ and to her ancestors; she is suckled by Hathor and enjoys the distinction of wearing two double crowns.[30]

THE ASSYRIAN EXPANSION AND THE RISE OF SAÏS

Osorkon's appointment of his daughter probably came shortly after his twenty-third year and was part of a broader settlement in which his son Takelot (III) was associated with him on the throne. In the Temple of Osiris the iconography and texts associated with Takelot suggest Lower Egypt,[31] and it is a fair guess that the son was designated as a co-regent in the north at Bubastis. The south was to be left to Shepenwepet as a sort of titular "queen" and to the shadowy Amun-rud, possibly her brother.[32]

In retrospect it seems ludicrous that Osorkon's settlement had any chance of drawing the country together. The last king of the Twenty-second Dynasty, Sheshonq IV, although acknowledged at Memphis,[33] had little real jurisdiction outside the environs of Tanis, his capital. Thebes completely ignored him. His regnal years were honored in the Delta and occasionally upriver, but he himself suffered insult through the passing over of his name on formal stelae. The great chiefs of the Me in their Delta principalities remained strong within their bailiwicks, and few showed anything but a parochial interest in politics. Takelot III may well have been a noble ancestor, to whom the nobles of the seventh century B.C. might trace their ancestry,[34] but he left scarcely a mark on Egypt's political life.

Unfortunately for Egypt, the creation of this political vacuum coincided with the meteoric resurgence of Assyria under the energetic leadership of Tiglath-pileser III.[35] In the west Assyrian expansion meant the defeat and annexation of such major buffer states as Arpad (741 B.C.) and Damascus (732) and the drastic attenuation of the territories of the surviving states of southern Palestine such as Israel, Ashkelon, and Gaza (732). For the next century history would call upon these weakened principalities to play the role of buffer and intermediary between Egypt and Assyria, a role that more often than not they were unable to fulfill. For Assyria wished to come to terms with Egypt directly: after the reduction of Gaza about 732 B.C. the Assyrian forces marched on to the "Brook of Egypt," planting victory stelae in the area.[36] A local sheikh was empowered to keep watch on the Egyptian frontier on Assyria's behalf, and Phoenician lumber merchants were strictly forbidden to trade with either the Philistines or the Egyptians.[37]

All this could be construed as a slap in the face to a weakened Egyptian state, incapable of reaction; but in fact a reaction was produced which was to affect the history of Egypt profoundly for four centuries. Sometime shortly after 730 B.C.[38] a Libyan chieftain by the name of Tefnakht appeared on the western side of the Delta, in the district known as the "West." In an obscure move he ejected the rightful chief of the Labu, Ankhhor, from his post in the city of Saïs and took it over himself.[39] He then proceeded to extend his authority to Buto on the north and Yamu on the south, molding the three townships into a homogeneous "Kingdom of the West."[40] By the thirty-sixth year of Sheshonq IV (728) he appears with the titles "Great chief and *dux*, great chief of the Labu, prophet of Neith, Edjo and the Mistress of Yamu."[41] Four years later Sheshonq IV died, apparently without surviving issue, and two centuries of rule by the Twenty-second Dynasty came to an end. A stela in process of inscription by Tefnakhte was abruptly halted—the cartouches were not filled in, and the text breaks off in midsentence—for in that year Tefnakhte asserted the primacy of his own career as the regime by which the community dated its years: in short, he adopted the kingship.[42]

Precisely how Tefnakhte effected his rapid rise to a position of authority in Lower Egypt is not completely known, but already in the year Sheshonq died he appears to have been well known. The west side of the Delta, from Memphis to the Mediterranean, was his bailiwick, and the principal fiefs of the great chiefs of the Me and the assorted "royal" townships acknowledged his rule.[43] These included the Sebennytic region on the lower central Nile under Akenosh[44] (who in retrospect came over somewhat reluctantly); Busiris under Chief Sheshonq, apparently a distant relative of the late Twenty-second Dynasty king;[45] Mendes under Chief Dedamunefankh, a scion of the long-lived family of Hornakht,[46] and Athribis under Prince Bakenefi, great-grandson of Sheshonq III.[47] King Yewepet in Leontopolis[48] and King Osorkon IV of the Twenty-third Dynasty in Bubastis and Ra-noufe[49] are surprising additions to the list in view of their kingly pretensions, but this may be more an index of the character of Tefnakhte and the forcefulness of his aggrandizement. Certainly none of these petty dynasts of Lower Egypt broke from their parochial interest to declare themselves candidates to save Egypt on the demise of the Twenty-second Dynasty.

Tefnakhte's growing reputation and success proved a seeming confirmation of Egypt's potential strength, despite three centuries of lassi-

tude. The impression Egypt had made on the world during the New Kingdom remained very strong in western Asia, where the legends and exploits
of the mighty Egyptian conquerors lived on in garbled legend. Those "political observers" who were more astute and who sensed the inherent
weakness of post–New Kingdom Egypt gained little following among
contemporary governments, and few heeded the words of a Hosea or an
Isaiah.[50]

With the threat of Assyria a present reality and a perceived savior in
the person of Tefnakhte close at hand, there should be little wonder that
the surviving city-states of the southern Levant appealed to Egypt for military assistance. In 724 Israel, the erstwhile northern kingdom of the He-
brews reduced since 732 to little more than the city of Samaria, sent envoys to Saïs[51] and in the hope of help rebelled against Assyria.
Shalmaneser V, successor to Tiglath-pileser III, and the Assyrian forces
marched immediately to the west and invested Samaria.[52] Before
Tefnakhte could act, the Israelite king Hoshea was captured (early 722
B.C.), and the city fell in September of the same year, suffering the deportation of 27,280 of its inhabitants.[53] Shalmaneser, however, died before
the end of the year, and Tefnakhte seized the opportunity of the change of
regime to take the initiative. He championed the cause of the refugee
Hanno, former king of Gaza, who had fled to Egypt ten years before to es-
cape the advancing forces of Tiglath-pileser III.[54] Together they con-
cluded an agreement, and Hanno raised a revolt in Gaza. At the same time
rebellion broke out against the Assyrians in central Syria.[55] For two years
the rebellion raged, until Sargon II, the new Assyrian king, turned his attention to the west in 720 and marched upon Syria. Opposition collapsed,
and Sargon moved towards Gaza.

This time the Egyptians acted. Assembling an army under the direction of a general named Re'a,[56] Tefnakhte[57] dispatched it to Rapihu
(modern Raphia, ten miles south of Gaza), where Hanno had mustered
his Philistine forces. Let Sargon himself describe the sequel: "Hanno, king
of Gaza and also Sib'e, the *turtan* of Egypt (*Mu-ṣu-ri*), set out from
Rapihu against me to deliver a decisive battle. I defeated them; Sib'e ran
away, afraid when he (only) heard the noise of my (approaching) army,
and has not been seen again. Hanno, I captured personally. I received the
tribute from Pir'u of Musuru, from Samsi, queen of Arabia (and) It'amar
the Sabaean, gold in dust-form, horses (and) camels."[58]

THE INVASION OF PIANKHY

I t must be remembered, when attempting to write a history of Egypt's foreign involvement from about 900 to 525 B.C., that for most of our textual material we are reliant on non-Egyptian sources. The battle of Raphia points up the difficulties for the historian inherent in such a situation. If Sargon's victory had been so complete, why had he not pursued—it could easily have been at a relaxed gait—the terrified Re'a and mopped up the Delta townships one by one? The sequel suggests that Sargon was putting the best face on a military engagement that, although a decided repulse to the relieving forces of Hanno and Re'a, was certainly not the overwhelming victory his construction of events placed upon it.

In fact, in Egypt Tefnakhte's reputation suffered hardly at all. In the years 719–718 B.C. he began to build on the continuing strength of his Delta base. His detractors might well have derided his supporters by calling them "dogs at his (Tefnakhte's) heels," but the opponents of the Eleventh and Eighteenth Dynasties might well have used the same terms in a losing cause. Tefnakhte was not weakened at all by recent events and began to cast his eyes on those Egyptian principalities not yet within his ambit. He already had Memphis: now he needed Middle Egypt.

Tefnakhte's march south was a demonstration in force (see map 3). Of the two petty kingships whose jurisdiction extended over Middle Egypt from Asyut to Memphis, Namlot of Hermopolis declared for Tefnakhte, but Peftjawabast of Herakleopolis[1] refused. Despite this recalcitrance, all of Peftjawabast's fortresses except his capital opened their gates to Tefnakhte on both sides of the Nile.[2] Tefnakhte's circuit, up the Bahr Yussef and back down the Nile, confirmed his new acquisitions, and he then proceeded to place Herakleopolis under siege. Peftjawabast's desperate appeal for help, relayed southwards by the few who dared resist the rising power in the Delta, precipitated the momentous events of the next few years.

72

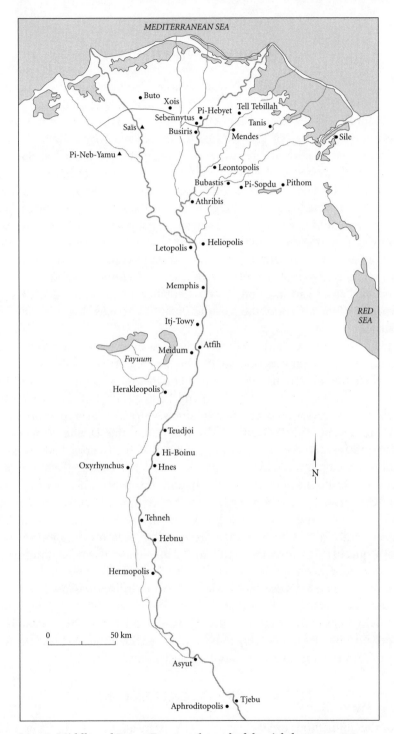

MEDITERRANEAN SEA

• Buto
Xois •
Sebennytus •
• Pi-Hebyet
• Tell Tebillah
Saïs •
• Busiris
• Tanis
Mendes •
• Sile
Pi-Neb-Yamu ▲

• Leontopolis
Bubastis • • Pi-Sopdu
Pithom
• Athribis

Letopolis • • Heliopolis

Memphis •

Itj-Towy •
Meidum • • Atfih
Fayuum

Herakleopolis •

• Teudjoi
• Hi-Boinu
Oxyrhynchus •
• Hnes

• Tehneh
• Hebnu

Hermopolis •

RED
SEA

N

0   50 km

Asyut •

• Tjebu
Aphroditopolis •

Map 3. Middle and Lower Egypt at the end of the eighth century B.C.

PIANKHY AND THEBES

The exact date of Osorkon III's death is at present impossible to compute, but it probably occurred before Tefnakhte had appeared on the scene and therefore about 730 B.C., if not before. When the old king went to rest in his tomb on the west of Thebes,[3] he left a threatened Thebaid in the hands of progeny too weak to offer their subjects much protection. Takelot III, presumably posted in the north (see Chapter 8), cannot have survived him long. In Thebes itself another son, Amunrud, appears in minor inscriptions[4] and lived long enough to produce at least two daughters, one who married king Peftawabast of Herakleopolis[5] and a second who became a singer of Amun and was buried at Medinet Habu.[6] Amunrud himself did not last long, although his ultimate fate is unknown. With his disappearance all semblance of rule by those of Libyan descent over the Thebaid came to an end, and shortly thereafter[7] in an unrecorded but apparently bloodless coup, the Kushite Piankhy extended his control over Thebes.[8]

Far from opposing the move, Thebes saw every reason to welcome a southern, black-skinned monarch who revered Amun and his city as much as the indigenous inhabitants. Piankhy imposed a garrison on the town under two generals, Pawerem and Lemersekny, but their yoke was light, and there was no purge of individuals who owed their appointments to the Twenty-third Dynasty.[9] In fact, even the Divine Worshiper Shepenwepet (I) (see fig. 16), though a scion of the late royal family, was not removed but was allowed to continue in office with all the honor accorded a titular head of state. Piankhy did, however, oblige her to make one concession that set a precedent for two centuries to come: she had to adopt as her "child" and Divine Worshiper in training Piankhy's younger sister Amunirdis.[10] Both women are duly honored on the monuments with queenly accoutrements and titles, the senior partner taking only slight precedence over her apprentice. But there could be no doubt about the mechanism the Kushites had devised: Amunirdis represented *their* interests in Thebes, and through her emissary[11] as well as his generals Piankhy kept close control of the Thebaid. And it was thus through a Thebaid willingly shouldering the Nubian yoke that the desperate cries for help from the north were transmitted to Piankhy.

THE KUSHITE COUNTERATTACK

For the momentous events that followed we are almost wholly dependent on a large granite stela found in 1862 in the ruins of the Amun Temple at

Napata and now in the Cairo Museum.[12] The stela is carefully inscribed with 159 lines on faces and sides. The vignette at the top illustrates graphically the obeisance of some of the notables mentioned in the text. The latter represents a valiant and surprisingly successful attempt to compose in the classical language, with only slight contamination by the contemporary vernacular. It also illustrates how far the Sudanese authorities had come since Alara in their ability to commandeer literate Egyptian scribes, for despite the fact that few, if any, Nubians of the day could read the account, the composer of the text has produced a coherent, rhetorical narrative in which his own erudition is on display in his choice of the occasional archaic idiom.[13] Having sung the praises of the composing scribe, one must not assume that he had free rein, even though the king he labored for spoke a different language. In its every aspect the stela serves Piankhy's interest in carefully creating, then developing, a royal persona, and virtually every turn of the "plot" is used either directly or as a foil to point up some trait of the king's character. And *plot* is an apt term in this regard, for the text is far removed from chronicle, annals, or daybook: it is, in fact, pure narrative.[14]

Clearly the personality profile of the king which shows through the account of the inscription is precisely what Piankhy wished to have promulgated. From a Drake-like insouciance in the face of impending invasion, to a supreme confidence in his own ability, to a puritanism easily outraged (justifiably so, it seems), Piankhy appears to us as a bluff agent of the wrath of god (in this case Amun) against the apostate and perverted generation of contemporary Egypt. His rule of behavior points up that apostasy, as Nubian shames Egyptian. His advice to his soldiers as to how to deport themselves as guests in Thebes is a model of pious admonition! Only before Amun does everyone bow, only in his shrine is everyone to be pure: before him no one bears weapons, only he can grant victory; Piankhy is fastidious in his observing of dietary laws and prudish in his eschewing of women.

That self-serving motive having been made plain, one must admit that there is no compelling reason to disbelieve the broad outline of the story. Although motivation may be suspect, the events by and large are not. Clearly Piankhy's eventual decision to intervene was occasioned by Tefnakhte's military expansion into Middle Egypt, but his tardy response may have been due to his underestimating his opponent, rather than the calculated restraint borne of confidence in himself and Amun as the stela maintains.[15] Significantly it was the declaration of Hermopolis in favor of Tefnakhte which spurred Piankhy to action. Only then did he instruct his garrison commanders resident in Egypt immediately to proceed to

Hermopolis and place it under siege, simultaneously dispatching a force from Napata. At some unspecified point on the Nile between Thebes and Asyut,[16] the Nubian expeditionary force met and defeated a flying column dispatched south by Tefnakhte to intercept them and on the following day virtually annihilated the survivors who had fled across the river. Pursuant to what was perceived by the forces of the north to be a signal defeat, Namlot interrupted his participation in Tefnakhte's siege of Herakleopolis and fled south to Hermopolis, entering his city just before the Nubians surrounded it entirely. The Kushite commanders, Pawerem and his colleagues, at this point displayed a flash of genius. Keeping Hermopolis under siege, they made a lightning attack down the Bahr Yussef and seized Oxyrrhynchos by surprise.[17] The rest of the rebel forts belonging to Herakleopolis now closed their gates and prepared to withstand investment, but the southern forces were not lacking in military hardware. Battering rams were employed against Tehneh,[18] and the city fell with great loss of life, including that of one of Tefnakhte's sons, who had presumably been placed there as commander. The example was salutary for southern success, and neighboring Ḥi-boinu (modern Sharuna) surrendered without a fight.

These victories and strategic moves effectually sealed Tefnakhte's fate, even though (for the rhetorical purpose of building up Piankhy's profile) the stela continues for 130 lines more! The text pictures the king as dissatisfied with his generals' work and coming north at a leisurely pace, being careful to pay his respects to Amun, to finish the job properly. He was on hand to receive the surrender of Hermopolis and to fulminate over the starvation of Namlot's horses like an outraged SPCA official.[19] He even deigned to allow Peftawabast, the very victim on whose behalf he had ostensibly come north, to bring tribute, prostrate himself before him, and submit to yearly taxation! What magnanimity!

THE SIEGE OF MEMPHIS

Few forces were left to block Piankhy's triumphal advance northwards, but the text makes the most of the rhetorical opportunity. Persekhemkheperra, the old fort built by Osorkon I two hundred years before, was found ready to withstand a siege, but Piankhy's words alone proved sufficient to unnerve the defenders: "O ye who live in death, ye poor wretches who live in death! If a moment passes without (the fort) being opened to me, look, you are as good as dead!"[20] And the gates opened, the garrison surrendered, and another son of Tefnakhte fell into Nubian hands. Piankhy repeated his blunt speech under the walls of

Meidum, about sixteen miles to the north: "'Look! You have options, and choose how you like! Open and you live, keep (the fort) closed and you die! . . . ' Thereupon they opened the gates immediately and His Majesty entered into this town."[21] The next fortified strong point Tefnakhte had prepared, Itj-towy (modern Lisht), twelve miles north of Meidum, did not even wait to suffer Piankhy's homily but opened up at once upon the approach of the southern army.

Although the three forts just named, which had provided a buffer on the latitude of the Fayum, constituted rich prizes for Piankhy, they were "small fry" when compared with Memphis. (They might well have held out against the Kushite forces much longer, in the hope of succor from the apex of the Delta, but one can only speculate on the effect of the tactic of surprise and the unexpected military prowess of the southerners on the defenders.) Piankhy tried his rhetoric on the Memphites: "Let not the primordial capital of Shu[22] shut its gates and fight! Let him that would enter, enter; and him that would go out, go out—there won't be any interference with traffic! I (only wish to) offer a hecatomb to Ptaḥ and the gods who are in Memphis."

But the Memphites were made of sterner stuff than Piankhy supposed, and they had no use for disingenuous palaver. Their immediate response anticipated in a curious way the Mendesian levies against Nektanebo II[23] or the sallies of the gentlemen apprentices, artisans, and shopkeepers of Londonderry during the siege of 1690: "Thereupon they shut their gates and sent forth an army against some of His Majesty's troops, consisting of artisans, builders and sailors."[24] The pompous rage of Rosen at Londonderry and Piankhy at Memphis at such an insult displays the comical purblindness of both: neither could appreciate that they faced a *popular* and *spontaneous* opposition at the grassroots level! (But at the time, of course, popular will counted for nothing over against god's will.) This failure to comprehend the enemy fully may have been endemic in the dynasty; certainly fifty years later it was to prove the undoing of Nubia's hold on the northland.

Now, however, in the summer of 717 B.C., victory went quickly and predictably to the Sudanese warlord. Tefnakhte had heightened the walls of the city and allowed the river to come right up to the fortifications on the eastern side and had installed a garrison of eight thousand men to defend it. He himself was not present in the city, and Piankhy's amanuensis wastes no time imputing cowardice. By night, he says, Tefnakhte stole into the city to encourage his troops and then before dawn fled "mounted upon a horse—never giving thought to his chariot!—and went north in fear of His Majesty."[25] The following day Piankhy completed the investment of the city and pitched his camp on the north near the harbor.[26] Suggestions by officers at a council of war that Memphis be formally blockaded were rejected probably because of the strength of the garrison, and the king's plan for a direct assault on the harbor carried the day. The merchant fleet of Memphis, lying within the harbor, was confiscated and pressed into service for transporting the troops. Piankhy ordered an immediate attack in force: "Forward against it (the city)! Scale the walls and penetrate the houses along the river! As for any of you that makes penetration over the wall, there is to be no lingering in the vicinity! [Push on] before you are counter-attacked! He who holds back is a coward!"[27] A single day was all that was required: the city "was taken like a cloud-burst and many people were killed in it."[28] The inhabitants of the surrounding townships "opened their keeps and fled headlong, and no one knows where they went."[29]

PIANKHY AND THE DELTA

Whether he knew it or not, Piankhy had experienced his last major engagement in the war. His final moves as recorded in the stela were curiously subdued: the usual offerings to the god of the conquered (better, "liberated" in Nubian perception) city, in this case Ptaḥ, the confiscation of the city treasure, and a desultory visit to Heliopolis to worship Re. Then the fleet and army embarked for Athribis, thirty-five kilometers north on the "Great River," the central branch of the Nile in the Delta, and Piankhy and his forces encamped east of the city.

This last leg of Piankhy's northern excursion was probably made at the invitation of Pediese, the hereditary prince resident in Athribis; Pediese, Akenosh of Sebennytos, and Awelot, king of Leontopolis, had been the first to present themselves before Piankhy after the capture of Memphis. Pediese was probably promoting himself as a go-between to forestall further hostilities, and to such a role he brought not inconsiderable credentials. Pediese had married the great-great-granddaughter of Sheshonq III, who had established Athribis as a sort of appanage for a cadet branch of the Twenty-second Dynasty;[30] by now he shared the governance of the region with his brother-in-law Nesnaw. It was probably Pediese who was instrumental in persuading the kinglets, chieftains, and mayors of the central and eastern Delta to renounce their allegiance to Tefnakhte and use the opportunity of Piankhy's presence at Athribis to make overtures to the new potentate from the south. In the event, fifteen of them showed up at the Nubian camp. But what Piankhy, through an enforced statement of subjection, required of each of them was negligible: in contrast to confiscating for Amun the treasures of all the forts of the south, Piankhy demanded essentially only a gift of horses and the handing over of the royal accoutrements of each of these Delta princes![31]

The settlement with Tefnakhte is even more puzzling. The stela represents Tefnakhte wilting at news of the defection of his Lower Egyptian colleagues and dispatching (presumably, from the fastness of Saïs, his home) a messenger to Piankhy's camp. Tefnakhte's abject plea for mercy is well written but overdrawn, and I wonder if he ever said it. Piankhy's emissary, the chief lector Pedi-amun-nebnesuttawy, who was sent to Saïs to secure a surrender—why did Piankhy and his army fail to go?—returned with but a perfunctory gift and the tersest of oaths: essentially in four brief denials and a single statement of compliance Tefnakhte promised not to transgress Piankhy's directives and not to interfere with his neighbors! The oath of loyalty conforms not at all, in either length or substance, to contemporary treaty oaths.[32]

There is something suspicious in all this. The advance of the Nubians had been impossible to counter: every fortified city had fallen to them with ease including the royal city of Memphis. Thereafter the best Piankhy could do was to meet the enemy at a powwow on neutral ground, as it were. Yet more than eighteen Delta cities of major proportions, presumably fortified, remained to be reduced, and the chief villain, Tefnakhte, refused even to meet with the conqueror. One is strongly tempted to conclude that the incessant sieges, assaults, and battles over many months had exhausted the Nubians; by the time Memphis was won, the north had, it is true, been reduced to the expedient of uncoordinated and half-hearted resistance, but Piankhy, too, had reached the point of loss of both strength and élan. All that was left were the niceties of a formal agreement to terminate hostilities, the offering of lip service to the winner, and the handing over of a symbolic gift.[33]

It is unlikely that Piankhy retained, after he retired south, much influence at all north of Herakleopolis. Since he is known to have controlled the oases in his twenty-fourth year (713 B.C.),[34] he must have been acknowledged in Middle Egypt, and certainly the Thebaid remained firmly and willingly in Nubian hands.[35] But Memphis defied him by refusing to have anything to do with him and by continuing to acknowledge the political primacy of Saïs, and since approbation by the Memphite priesthood was tantamount to official approval,[36] Piankhy had lost the final contest with his enemy Tefnakhte.

THE TWENTY-FOURTH DYNASTY

Tefnakhte died very shortly after Piankhy retired, but not before dedicating a parcel of land within his domains to Neit of Saïs.[1] Apart from legends surrounding his name in later times,[2] this is the last we hear of this interesting renegade-founder. He was already middle-aged. Two of his grown sons had been lost in the war against Piankhy; a third lived to succeed him.

BOCCHORIS "THE CONTEMPTIBLE"

As far as we know, Piankhy did not contest the accession of Tefnakhte's son Bakenrenef, who is better known to us under the Hellenized form of his prenomen, Bocchoris (Waḥkare).[3] Tefnakhte's son has cut a remarkable figure in later legend. Why this should be is not altogether clear. It is true that certain legendary figures of heroic stature in Egyptian history tended to attract unto themselves "floating" motifs of folkloric composition. But Bocchoris was no heroic figure. Nor, with one exception, is he the focus of "floating" folklore. We are left wondering whether there was, in fact, some truth in what classical sources say of the man.

First, it was asserted that he was physically ugly and temperamentally mean. "After the kings mentioned above (Cheops, Chephren and Mycerinus) Bocchoris succeeded to the throne, a man who was altogether contemptible in appearance but in sagacity far surpassed all former kings. . . . He was very weak in body and . . . by disposition the most avaricious of all their kings."[4] The oxymoronic effect of this description is not unknown elsewhere in Egyptian literature and conjures up the Egyptian appreciation of the "grotesque."[5] Wise men often sustained physical infirmity.[6] A type of royal likeness in vogue in the second half of the eighth century B.C. and the first half of the seventh presents a stocky and prognathous individual who, across the generations of fickle and vacillating public taste, might be deemed ugly,[7] but admittedly we have no evidence that Bocchoris's sculptors portrayed him in this fashion.

Second, and bruited more widely, was Bocchoris's reputation for wisdom.[8] Diodorus reflects a Hellenic classification of seven lawgivers of ancient Egypt, of whom Bocchoris was the fourth:

> A fourth lawgiver, they say, was the king Bocchoris, a wise sort of man and conspicuous for his craftiness. He drew up all the regulations which governed the kings and gave precision to the laws on contracts; and so wise was he in his judicial decisions that many of his judgements are remembered for their excellence even to our day.[9] . . . Their laws governing contracts they attribute to Bocchoris. These prescribe that men who had borrowed money without signing a bond, if they denied the indebtedness might take an oath to that effect and be cleared of the obligation . . . and whoever lent money along with a written bond was forbidden to do more than double the principal from the interest. In the case of debtors the lawgiver ruled that the repayment of loans could be exacted only from a man's estate, and under no condition did he allow the debtor's person to be subject to seizure.[10]

The alleged innovations thus break down into four:

1. A law regulating kingship
2. Discharge of obligation on oath alone
3. Limitation on interest rates
4. Prevention of borrowing on debtor's person[11]

Opinions have varied as to whether we should accept this tradition,[12] and it is true that in Egypto-Hellenic historiography tragic heroes who (are perceived to) end a line tend to be remembered for their wisdom.[13] The economic woes that must have attended the weakening and dissolution of the regime of the Twenty-second Dynasty in the earlier eighth century must have given rise to speculation and created fertile ground for the loan shark.[14] And it may well be that laws regulating lending in favor of the borrower were required more than ever in the final quarter of that century. A similar case can be made for the historicity of a "law on kingship." As we have seen, the declining Libyan power had created a vacuum in which several parochial kingships of "human creation"[15] had thrived, and these, along with the ranking system of township rulers in the Piankhy stela, betoken a complex protocol that must have fostered a hamstringing decentralization of political power. It is altogether reasonable that Bocchoris would have moved against the supporters and components of such a system, and this, in fact, may have cost him his life.[16]

A third, and most elusive, expansion of the Bocchoris legend presents us with a seer, or at least one in whose reign momentous visions of the future were vouchsafed to posterity. The plot motifs appear in a variety of individual tales. Bocchoris appears transmogrified into "Necho the Saïte" (Nechepso) adept in interpreting the heavens;[17] or, in his reign, a sacred ram reveals the misfortunes Egypt will suffer in the future. In the latter type of prediction the misfortunes are usually brought on by an invasion of foreigners from the north, and in the Judaeo-pagan polemic of Ptolemaic times the story type is used as an aetiology on the Hebrew sojourn and Exodus.[18]

This is exceedingly difficult to untangle. Foretelling the future enters into the religion and folklore of ancient Egypt to a significant extent, but the question centers upon why Bocchoris's reign should have been singled out as the period appropriate for a prophecy. Elsewhere folklore selects kings of renown—Snofru, Khufu, Menkaure, Amenophis III—but Bocchoris is assuredly not of that class. Admittedly Bocchoris is the king under whom an event of some finality occurred, namely, an invasion that resulted in a change of regime; but the invaders came from the south, not the north, and their complete acculturation rendered them wholly acceptable to historical tradition. The prophecy of the ram assumes the presence of plague in some form, which prompts the desire to expel the foreigners, but we have no direct evidence of any historical plague in Egypt from 717 to 711 B.C.

EGYPT AND SARGON

The "historical" Bocchoris, as indicated in the preceding paragraphs, has left behind little trace in contemporary records. This is hardly surprising in that Saïs, his hometown, has never, until now, been excavated to modern standards.[19] Some allusions to him, however, might be expected from the comparatively rich records of western Asia and Memphis.

Bocchoris fell heir to a restricted jurisdiction. There was no question that his edict enjoyed no acceptance in Middle Egypt or the oases, and even in the Delta his authority was curtailed. The chiefdoms remained strong and in possession of their individual "fiefs," while Osorkon IV continued to hold Bubastis.[20] And even though the Memphite priesthood acknowledged Bocchoris to be rightful Pharaoh, his neighbors in the Delta clearly reserved for themselves freedom of action at least at the outset.

But Bocchoris could engage in relations, both peaceful and bellicose, with lands to the north and east. Scarabs of *W3ḥ-k3-r* found in late-eighth-century tombs on the island of Ischia may indicate trade,[21] and one is reminded that later Greek tradition places the founding of the Greek colonies of Cyrene and Naukratis in Bocchoris's reign.[22] And even though this dating of the founding of Naukratis is certainly incorrect, no one can doubt that the last quarter of the eighth century witnessed the arrival of Greek merchants on the coasts of the eastern Mediterranean. On the northeastern frontier of the Delta the Assyrians were active during Bocchoris's floruit, establishing a presence that could not be dislodged. Recalcitrant inhabitants were deported, a local sheikh empowered as a sort of warden of the march, and the region of Wady el-Arish secured.[23] At the same time groups of captives from the Zagros Mountains, Babylonia, and the Arabian desert were transferred by the Assyrian authorities to Philistia and Samaria.[24] Perhaps in order to tap the riches of Africa and at one and the same time to keep Egypt under surveillance, Sargon, king of Assyria, established a trading post between Gaza and Raphia, where Egyptians were invited to trade their wares (see fig. 17).[25] Sargon's move provoked a favorable response. "Shilkanni, king of Egypt, a remote place, was overwhelmed by the fear of the splendour of Ashur my lord, and he brought to me (Sargon) as his present 12 large horses of Egypt, the like of which is not to be found in Assyria."[26] The personal name in question is to be identified as the contemporary vocalization of Osorkon[27] and the individual in question with Osorkon IV of the Twenty-third Dynasty at Bubastis.[28]

In 713 B.C. a certain "Pir'u, king of Egypt" became involved in a riskier enterprise involving Assyria. Early in that year a worthy of that name was approached by a certain Yamani, a usurper at the Philistine city of Ashdod,[29] for aid in his insurrection against Sargon. In fact, the incipient revolt showed signs of involving the surviving states in the south Levant, for "[the kings] of Philistia, Judah, Edom and Mo'ab who dwell by the sea, payers of tribute and gifts to Asshur my lord, sent evil words and improper speeches (with) their presents to 'Pir'u' king of Egypt."[30] Ashdod's role in the revolt came to nought, and Yamani was forced to flee to Nubia.[31] But "Pir'u" had, willy-nilly, been tarnished in the abortive attempt, and Egypt compromised.[32]

The identity of Pir'u is not readily apparent, for the "name" conceals merely the title that was to become famous via Greek transcription as "Pharaoh" and which ultimately derives from Egyptian *Pr-'3*, "Great House."[33] But it seems unlikely to have been Osorkon IV, as the Assyrian scribes knew him by name. Only twelve years before the Ashdod affair Is-

Fig. 17. The Levantine coast, south of Ashkelon.

rael had sought aid from "the king of Egypt" in Saïs, that is, Tefnakhte, and it is most likely that "Pir⟨u king of Egypt" sat in the same seat and was, in fact, Bocchoris.

BOCCHORIS'S END

Contemporary texts do not even hint at how Bocchoris met his fate, but late folklore and the king-list tradition promoted colorful accounts. A story circulating in the fifth century B.C. and told to the visiting Herodotus[34] conjured up a blind king "Anusis" from a city of the same name,[35] who fled at the onset of the Kushite invasion and holed up in the marshes of the Delta. There he lived on an island of ashes and returned only when Sabaco, the Kushite king, withdrew from Egypt. The king list, in the version Manetho preserved, states that Sabaco captured Bocchoris and burned him alive.[36] If the *Aegyptiaca* was originally a king list fleshed out at intervals by narrative, signaled in the epitome by single laconic statements and qualifiers,[37] then behind the relative clause appended in Africanus to Sabaco must lie a more extended narrative. Execution by burning is well known in the ancient world, mainly for crimes of a political nature and treason,[38] although other offenses are attested.[39] Although flight to the inaccessible marshes, a well-known place of refuge, could easily be derived simply from the geographical setting of Saïs, Bocchoris's homestead, death by fire fits the historical situation rather well. In the light of the intolerance, endemic in the Saïte house, of multiple monarchic regimes in the Egyptian homeland, and bearing in mind the reminiscence of a "law of kingship" ascribed to Bocchoris, it is tempting to interpret his reign as a continuance of his father's attempt to reestablish a pharaonic "federalism." The ad hoc kingships of parochial creation, such as had flourished under Sheshonq III and IV in the eighth century, were inimical to both the theoretical and practical integrity of the pharaonic state, and for Bocchoris to act pursuant to this conviction meant moving against Osorkon ("Shilkanni") of the Twenty-third Dynasty, or Peftjawabast of Herakleopolis or Namlot of Hermopolis (if they were still living), to terminate this rule. But these were all friends of the Kushite royal house of Napata, and Piankhy had specifically forbidden Tefnakhte to interfere with his neighbors. Of course, Bocchoris could stand on legalities and claim he was not bound by his father's oath, and an aging Piankhy may have been unable (or unwilling) to counter this casuistry. But his younger brother Sabaco, perhaps in the flush of sibling rivalry, showed more enthusiasm and could act upon his "brotherhood" with at least one of the kings aforesaid.[40]

Within twelve months of Piankhy's death in 712 B.C.,[41] events proceeded in precipitate haste. The Ashdod revolt ended in disaster for Egypt, and the rebel fled up the Nile Valley; Sabaco, newly arrived on the throne, found himself providing (unwillingly?) asylum to the fugitive; Osorkon died, leaving Bocchoris sole claimant to power in the Delta. The die was cast: Bocchoris was, in the eyes of Kush, without any legitimate claim to kingship, having failed in the pattern set by his father to take the oath in the new Kushite king's name. In the autumn of 712 the Sudanese army moved north into Egypt and, as Piankhy's forces had done five years before, overwhelmed native resistance. The last pathetic defiance is reflected in the unofficial texts, scratched or painted on objects secreted in the burial of an Apis bull at Saqqara, which happened to die about this time. Here we gain a glimpse of a populace connecting the event to the reign of Bocchoris and still loyal to him.[42] We hear no more: the end is a lost page of history.

THE RESISTANCE TO ASSYRIAN
EXPANSION

nlike his deceased older brother, Sabaco did not retire to
Napata after his victory over the north.[1] Thebes became a fo-
cal point for the new regime, enhanced by the presence of
Amenirdis I, Sabaco's sister, as Divine Adoratress of Amun,
but whether Sabaco himself established the city as his residence is uncertain. Though they wore upon occasion the expected crowns of the pharaohs, Sabaco and his successors had a distinct preference for the
tight-fitting Nubian cap (see figs. 18, 19) with streamers and double
uraeus, almost symbolic of the union of Egypt and Kush.[2] Drawing upon
the remote past for inspiration, but with present intent, Sabaco chose the
prenomen of Pepy II, the longest-lived pharaoh of all time (twenty-third
century B.C.), Neferkare, and pointed to the dawn of a new day with the
choice of "He-who-makes-the-Two-Lands-Glisten" as principal epithet.[3]
For the first and only time before the nineteenth century of our era the
Nile Valley, for a stretch encompassing the last fifteen hundred miles to
the Mediterranean Sea, was united under a single government.[4]

SABACO AND SARGON

The sudden onslaught of Sabaco's forces and the easy absorption of Lower
Egypt into their domain preempted any move the Assyrians may have
been contemplating with regard to their southern frontier. For fifty years
beginning in 711 B.C. Egypt presented a strong, if not united,[5] front
against any threat from the north, and this perceived strength effectually
deterred any test of its reality. Egypt, Moab, and Edom remained the accepted southern limes of the "Sargonic" empire.

But there is evidence that, although Sabaco initially reserved the right
of action, he had within seven years of his conquest effectually relin-

Fig. 18. Shabaka (Sabaco).

quished some of his power in favor of his brother and eventual successor
Shebitku (co-regent by 705 B.C.).[6] Shebitku had no desire at first to
adopt anything but a conciliatory mood toward Sargon II. He refused to
extend the right of asylum to Yamani, who had fled to Kush for protection; and returned him to Assyria.[7] Seals and sealings of Sabaco, clearly
the indication of the presence of papyrus documents long since decayed,
have been found in Nimrud in Sennacherib's palace.[8] At the very least

Fig. 19. Taharqa, enthroned. Recycled blocks from the temple of Edfu, seventh century B.C.

this evidence signals a correspondence between the two superpowers of the day and perhaps justifies us in postulating a grudging but erstwhile acceptance of each other.

Who or what set of circumstances brought about the dramatic change in relations is not known with any certainty at present. Ever since the resurgence of the Assyrian state in 911 B.C. under Ashurnasirpal II, the success of the westward advance had been predicated upon the knocking out of the Syrian power centers and the control (or at least the neutralizing) of the Levantine ports. The reduction of the inland cities of Syria scarcely elicited any response from the Nile,[9] but any attack on the Phoenician cities of the coast impinged on a sphere of influence Egypt had claimed for two thousand years.[10] Both Tiglath-pileser III and Sargon II had attempted to neutralize Judah, the last surviving inland state of any power, by directing their attention to reducing the coast and rewarding the communities of the steppe,[11] but this strategy ran directly counter to clearly perceived Egyptian interests. And it was the maelstrom that was created through the excitement of conflicting loyalties in Philistia which finally brought a hostile Kush into the fray.

THE COALITION AGAINST ASSYRIA

It is arguable that good relations between Kush and Assyria continued until the death of Sargon II in 705 B.C.; thereafter both major powers seemed for the moment to have lost control of the situation.[12]

Viewed from the vantage point of Judah in the hinterland of the southern Levant, now was the time to assert independence. Sargon had died, unable to defeat Egypt or otherwise to reduce its strength; the new Assyrian king was an unknown quantity; the new regime in Egypt had twice proven itself able to overwhelm all military opponents on the battlefield; the Levantine coast remained free and powerful commercially and its communities for the most part inimical towards Assyria. Small wonder, then, that in the ensuing confrontation with the power beyond the Tigris it was Hezekiah of Judah who took the lead.[13]

Both textual evidence and archaeological evidence converge in providing a vivid picture of Judah's preparations for insurrection. Hezekiah renewed the fortifications of his border cities, especially on the north and west, whence the Assyrian counterattack was to be expected, and the ubiquitous jars stamped with the winged scarab[14] which turn up in excavations at this time reflect the attempt of the royal commissariat to make the collection of food and redistribution more efficient.[15] At the same time embassies were busy going to and fro, and Jerusalem became a hotbed of intrigue. The Chaldaean Marduk-apla-iddin, also a rebel against Assyria, dispatched a legation to Palestine to bolster Hezekiah's resolve,[16] and Hezekiah himself pressured the Philistine and Phoenician cities to join a coalition against Sennacherib.[17] Almost certainly the Judaean king made contact with Egypt and persuaded the new Kushite regime to guarantee military support.[18]

In almost all quarters Hezekiah's overtures bore fruit as city after city rallied to the call, but in Ekron of the Philistines the local king, to the dismay of the populace, refused to renounce his oath to Sennacherib. For this courageous stand he was swept off the throne in a popular uprising,[19] placed under arrest and sent to Jerusalem in chains. Hezekiah used the incident as justification for annexing Ekron to Judah and thus won a foothold in the coastal plain.[20]

The incarceration of a loyal Assyrian vassal was sufficient cause for punitive action, and in 701 B.C. Sennacherib mustered his army and moved west rapidly. Despite a disinclination to involve himself in the Levantine coast,[21] Sennacherib was able to settle affairs with Tyre and Sidon (whose king had fled)[22] and then received homage from the cities of the Levant.

But none of the kings of the southern coastlands, with the exception of Mitinti of Ashdod, presented themselves at this "durbar," a clear affront to the imperial dignity. Consequently Sennacherib continued his march down the Mediterranean coast, capturing Joppa and environs, a reversal of fortunes which prompted many of the Philistines to capitulate at once. Sidḳiya of Ashkelon, however, did not move quickly enough,[23] and he and his entire family were deported to Ashur.[24] Sharru-lu-dari, son of the former king, was reinstated and burdened with an annual tribute.[25] Then Sennacherib moved up into the foothills of Judah, reducing Azekah and Gath and finally coming to rest beneath the walls of the fortress Lachish, which he promptly invested.[26]

One can imagine the gloom that must have descended upon Hezekiah. The careful planning of four years had come to naught, and the coalition had virtually collapsed. Hezekiah was ready to capitulate. He sent to the Assyrian camp promising complete submission and accompanying his offer with tribute.[27] By the time Lachish fell and neighboring Libnah was besieged, Hezekiah must have been panic-stricken, but it was at this juncture that events took an unexpected turn and forever enshrined Isaiah as the archetypal prophet.

THE BATTLE OF ELTEKEH AND ITS AFTERMATH

As the Assyrians had begun their march down the coast, the call had gone out for the Egyptian army,[28] and their arrival found Sennacherib's forces already committed to the reduction of Hezekiah's hill forts. In fact, the Egyptian expeditionary force's sudden appearance in Philistia came as something of a surprise to the Assyrians, who certainly would not have become entangled in a siege in the Shephelah had they known that "an army beyond counting" (Sennacherib's words) was advancing against them! But now it was Shebitku who was in command. In the event, the Egypto-Kushite forces were able to penetrate beyond Ashdod and were making a bid to outflank the Assyrians by recovering Joppa when Sennacherib hastily quit the hill country to intercept them. This he did on the flats of Eltekeh about sixteen kilometers south of Joppa.[29]

The longest account of the subsequent battle is that of Sennacherib himself: "The officials, patricians and common people of Ekron . . . had become afraid and had called for help upon the kings of Egypt and the archers, chariotry and cavalry of the king of Kush—an army beyond counting—and they had actually come to their aid. In the plain of Eltekeh their battle lines were drawn up against me and they sharpened their weapons. Upon a trust-inspiring oracle delivered by Ashur my lord, I fought with them and delivered a defeat upon them. In the mêlée of the battle I personally captured alive the Egyptian charioteers and their princes and also the charioteers of the king of Kush."[30] It is clear from the use of the terms "kings of Egypt" and "king of Kush" that the Egyptian expeditionary force comprised both Nubian troops and the parochial militias of the Delta "Great Chiefs of the Me," whom the Assyrians persisted in mistaking for "kings" (šarru).[31] This is an important point, as it indicates that Shebitku had been successful in subverting and co-opting the local dynasts of Lower Egypt. Less clear is the veracity of Sennacherib's claim to complete victory. In particular, the motif of engaging personally the chariots of high-ranking officers derives from the much publicized episode at the Battle of Kadesh, which through art and recitation passed into oral tradition and exerted an exceptional influence throughout the Near East.[32] Moreover, the Assyrian moves that are reported to have taken place *after* Eltekeh only confuse the general picture: the reinstatement of Padi, the punishment of *some* Ekronites, the reduction of the Judaean forts, the investment of Jerusalem, and Hezekiah's tribute. But neither Ekron nor Jerusalem is said to have been captured, and on Sennacherib's own admission the tribute followed his withdrawal to Nineveh. Since the capture of the hill forts clearly preceded Eltekeh, it is tempting to construe the information as out of place chronologically in the sequence of Sennacherib's account.

References to the battle in Egyptian sources are difficult to identify. The head-smiting scene on the pylon at Medinet Habu which shows Sabaco executing his enemies, including northerners, belongs to a genre too vague and too easily appropriated to be used as historical evidence.[33] Less easily dismissed is the "Toronto scarab," which describes Sabaco in the following terms: "(3) whom Amun loves more than any king that ever was since the earth (4) was established—he has slain those that rebelled against him in Upper and Lower Egypt (5) and in every foreign land. 'Those-that-are-across-the-sand'[34] who had rebelled (*sic*) (6) against him fall to his slaughter; they (7) come of their own accord as living captives, (8) each one of them having seized his companion!—because he did (9) good for his father (*sic*), so greatly did he love him!" This is all high-flown jargon, familiar to those conversant with the rhetoric of Egyptian inscriptions, but within the lexical parameters acceptable to the ancients, "Those-that-are-across-the-sand" could serve as an oblique reference to anyone beyond the Sinai!

The Tang-i Var stela has introduced the interesting possibility that not only Sabaco but Shebitku also was present at Eltekeh. If Shebitku's co-regency had begun in 705, his triumphal entry into Thebes[35] would be dated as taking place in 703. He could very well, therefore, have been present in the north at the very time action in Asia was being contemplated.

The incident that, from the convergence of three sources, must have immediately followed the battle of Eltekeh constitutes the crux of the entire event. We quote first the biblical author: "And on that night the messenger of Yahweh went out and slaughtered 185,000 in the camp of the Assyrians, and when reveille sounded next morning, these were (found to be) all corpses. Then Sennacherib the king of Assyria departed and went home."[36] A tale told to Herodotus when he was in Egypt, 250 years later, recounts a similar incident: "Next on the throne after Anysis was Sethos, the high priest of Hephaestos . . . they abandoned their position and suffered several losses during their retreat."[37] Berossos also, apparently, recounted an unsuccessful siege of Pelusium (paraphrased by Josephus) and then stated: "Now when Sennacherib was returning from his Egyptian war to Jerusalem, he found his army . . . in danger, for god had sent a grievous plague upon his army; and on the very first night of the siege (of Jerusalem?), 185,000 were destroyed with their captains and generals."[38]

Although the alleged quotation from Berossos sounds too reminiscent of the biblical text and may have been embellished by Josephus, the three sources quoted in the aggregate support the contention that some unexpected "act of god" prevented the Assyrians from realizing a victory. The localization of the disaster either at Pelusium or after the retreat from that city was introduced by false analogy with a number of important battles fought near the site between Egyptians and Asiatic invaders.[39] Curiously the environs of Ashdod and Ashkelon, near which the event must, in fact, have taken place, retain traditions of disease and associations with mice. I Sam. 4–6 contains the picaresque tale of how the Philistines, flushed with success after defeating the Israelites and capturing the ark, came down with an embarrassing complaint and felt constrained to make propitiatory offerings of images of mice, "which are destroying the land."[40] (R. A. S. MacAlister claims to have witnessed the depredations of mice in the area in 1904.)[41] Herodotus records the legend that the Scythians, retreating north after Psammetichus I bought them off, plundered the temple of Aphrodite Ourania at Ashkelon and were struck with "women's disease."[42]

Whatever the truth about the ending of Sennacherib's campaign in 701, it was followed by an embarrassing retreat from the southern Levant which lasted more than twenty years.[43] A hard-fought encounter and the lucky onset of an epidemic had caused the Kushites' stock to soar, and for the next generation the stage belonged to them.

"TAHARQA THE CONQUEROR"

The date of Sabaco's death is unknown at present. His latest dated inscription records a fifteenth year with a calendric of the eleventh day of the month Payni (= the tenth month),[1] so that, if this text is accepted as genuine, he must have survived into the summer of 698 B.C. In accordance with Kushite custom, the throne passed to the eldest brother's eldest son, in this case Shebitku, son of Piankhy (see fig. 20). If the Karnak quay graffito number 33 actually refers to Shebitku's coronation in his third year,[2] we might be justified in postulating a co-regency, and since it is now clear that in 705 Shebitku held executive power,[3] his association with his brother could scarcely have occurred later than that date. If we treat the year 15 of Sabaco seriously, then only at the turn of the century would Shebitku have enjoyed sole rule. Certainly, however, by the close of 698 B.C. Shebitku was sole ruler, the first Kushite, in fact, to accede to the throne on Egyptian soil. Certainly in his third year Shebitku was in residence in Thebes, possibly the first Kushite monarch to reside there.[4]

"FROM THE LAND OF NUBIA, A FINE LAD!"

There may have been some uncertainty, as Shebitku's reign progressed, as to who had the right to succeed him.[5] At some unspecified date, but certainly between 697 and 692 B.C., Shebitku summoned his brothers (and probably also his cousins), who were still in Napata, northwards to Thebes. The purpose may have been to gather together under the king's watchful gaze a batch of royal siblings tending towards unruliness and to let Amun decide the successor (though scarcely the co-regent).[6] Taharqa describes the event as follows from a vantage point several years after he himself became king: "Now His Majesty (i.e., Taharqa) was from the land of Nubia, a fine lad, the king's brother a beloved darling. Then

Fig. 20. Shebitku (left) worships Amun with his daughter (right). Thebes, Temple of Osiris-Ruler-of-Eternity, early seventh century B.C.

north he came to Thebes among the fine lads whom His Majesty king Shebitku had sent for to the land of Nubia; and with him there did he remain."[7] Taharqa was around twenty years old at the time, the age at which the ancient Egyptian state usually called up the new generation for entry into the draft lists.[8]

If we are to believe Taharqa, he evoked spontaneous love and affection from both court and populace: "Now I came from Nubia among the king's brothers whom he had called up thence and I remained with him, for he loved me more than all his brothers and all his children, and I was singled out from them by His Majesty. The hearts of the patricians came over to me, and everybody had (only) love for me."[9] Yet the process of selection still had to be undergone, and the rhetoric meets the demands of the description of the ideal king. He is Amun's son, Amun predicted great things of him, Amun chose him within (the sanctuary?), and so forth.[10] Only in the cryptic reference to "that which had not been known of me"[11] is there any hint that his accession might be argued from Taharqa's plea to the god: "Save me from the mouth [. . . unknown . . .] of their utterances, and turn them back on their own heads!"[12] Is he merely acting the part of a loving husband and father when he beseeches Amun "[preserve m]y wives and let my children live, and keep death away from them for me"?[13] Or is he apprehensive lest (as turned out to be the case) one of his own sons be bypassed for the kingship, as he had supplanted Shebitku's?

In any event, the Kushite practice of favoring surviving brothers at the expense of sons lent justification to Taharqa's claims to power, and when Shebitku passed away, sometime in 690 B.C.,[14] Taharqa came to the throne amid general rejoicing (see fig. 21; see also fig. 19). He enjoyed a coronation in Memphis, once again a "first" in the annals of the Kushites in Egypt,[15] and as was the custom of the times, he backdated his accession to the calendric New Year's Day.[16]

THE REIGN'S FIRST DECADE: AN AUSPICIOUS START

A thumbnail description of the new king contained in the stela of year 6 encapsulates the traditional expectations of any "Horus" newly ensconced upon the throne.

> Now His Majesty is one who loves god, one who spends the day and stays awake at night seeking out useful things for the gods, building [their] temples [which had fallen into] ruin, fashioning their images as (they had been) on the First Occasion, building their storechambers, provisioning their altars, making them divine

Fig. 21. Taharqa. Thebes, reused block beside the sacred lake, seventh century B.C.

offerings of every sort, and making their libation tables of electrum, gold, silver, and copper. So the heart of His Majesty was at peace doing useful things for them every day, and this land had abundance in his time, as it had in the days of the Eternal Lord; everyone reclined in the sun and no one said: "Oh would that . . . !" about anything. *Ma\(at* pervaded the land, and wrongdoing was driven into the ground![17]

The sleepless monarch mulling over what is best for the land, the renewal of temples, *implementa* and endowments, the prosperity of the people, the triumph of *ma\(at*—none of these topoi are new, and in fact the very jargon recalls standard rhetoric as old as the Middle Kingdom.

But Taharqa's scribal editor did not mouth platitudes: his lord very much lived up to the mark that the mythology of kingship had prescribed. The rebuilding of temenos walls and the refurbishing of Medinet Habu was under way by year 3[18] and the additions to the Edfu Temple by year 5.[19] We cannot doubt that projects designed to benefit the cults of Amun and the Theban triad, whether at Napata or Thebes, were also begun at the very outset of the reign.

Amun's recompense added a personal element to a stereotypical program. The end of the eighth century B.C. had witnessed in northeastern Africa increased rainfall and heightened inundations,[20] and Taharqa's sixth year (685 B.C.) was marked by an exceptional flooding of the Nile. No more opportune event could have impressed on Egyptians the divine selection and continued favor the southern potentate enjoyed, and Taharqa made the most of it.

There occurred in His Majesty's time, in the sixth year of his reign, miracles the like of which had not been witnessed since the time of the ancestors; for his father Amunre loved him. His Majesty had been beseeching his father Amunre lord of Karnak for an inundation so as to prevent want in his time. . . . When it came time for the rise of the inundation (the river) rose greatly day by day, and through many days it rose at (the rate of) one cubit a day. It reached the cliffs of Upper Egypt and overtopped the mounds of Lower Egypt: the land lay languid in the Primeval Sea, nor did the new earth emerge from the river.[21] Its (maximum) height was 21 cubits, one palm, two and one-half fingers at the town of Thebes. His Majesty had the annals of the ancestors brought to him[22] to see (what) inundations had occurred in their time; (but) the like of this was not found therein. For lo! rain fell in Nubia and made all the mountains glisten.

Following this "editorial" adumbration of the event, the excited voice of the king himself is heard:

[Never had] the like been seen since (the time of) the ancestors! The Inundation came like a cattle thief and flooded the entire land. The like was not to be found in the writings from the time of the forefathers, nor could it be said "I heard (that) from my father"! It made all the arable land fertile . . . it killed off the mice(?) that were in it and the snakes inside it, and it curbed the ravages of the locusts. It did not allow the south winds to steal it. I heaped up the harvest into granaries: incalculable was the amount of Upper and Lower Egyptian grain, and the various (other) cereals native to the land.[23]

In the same year the queen mother Abala was summoned from Kush, and she came north to Memphis to see her son for the first time since he had departed from her in Shebitku's reign. Taharqa was very proud of the event and was quick to liken it to Isis's viewing of her son Horus, risen upon the seat of his father, Osiris. All the happenings of this eventful year were given wide publicity in writing all over Egypt.[24]

"HIS MAJESTY LOVED THE ART OF WAR"

With the repulse of the Assyrians in 701 B.C. the southern coast of the Levant became a power vacuum into which it is tempting to imagine that, given the Kushite élan, Shebitku would have quickly moved. The evidence for the 690s, however, is extremely sparse. Shebitku copied some of the bellicose titulary of Thutmosis III, but this can scarcely be accepted as indicative of anything.[25] Slightly more arresting, perhaps, is the scene on the northern face (eastern side) of the outer wall of the Temple of Osiris-Ruler-of-Eternity at Karnak.[26] Here Amun proffers the ḫpš-sword to Shebitku, with banal phrases regarding fighting foreigners: "(Amunre) I grant thee thy power like Montu! . . . I give thee the southerners to thy Great Crown, the northerners to the red crown . . . King of Egypt, ruler of foreign lands,[27] sovereign who seizes all lands." It is difficult to ascertain whether this scene reflects the events of 701 or later activity in the Levant.

For Taharqa's reign the evidence is now more extensive, thanks to excavations and the publication of new texts over the past twenty years. The texts that establish a tentative chronology are the Kawa inventories,[28] which cover donations to the temple of Kawa in Nubia over the first decade of the reign (i.e., 690-681 B.C.). Until Taharqa's eighth year (683 B.C.) the entries are innocuous enough, covering cult paraphernalia and supplies, all of which could have had an origin in the Nile Valley. In the eighth year, however, the entries suggest much more: "one bronze statue of the king smiting foreign countries" and "the children of the chiefs of the Tjeḥenu." In Taharqa's tenth year (681 B.C.) the list includes "cedar . . . Asiatic bronze . . . good gardeners from the Mntiw of Asia." The personnel and the wood mentioned are booty; the statue's symbolism is clear. One can only conclude that between 684 and 681 B.C. Taharqa had been militarily engaged in both Libya (cf. "Tjeḥenu") and Asia. Other scattered allusions to the activity may now fall into place. The renovations at Thebes which Montou-em-het mentions made use of "true cedar from the best of the terraces (namely, of Lebanon)" and "Asiatic copper," perhaps tribute from these same foreign campaigns.[29] The Libyan campaign may be commemorated by the inclusion of "oasis" and "Tjeḥenu" in lists of conquered places.[30] The precise range and objective of the warfare described in a fragmentary stela from Karnak are not definitely identifiable, but it probably falls during the same decade. The fragmentary phrases make clear the nature of the operation: the enemy "did all this in marching against me," but I (Taharqa) set forth "hastening to the place where they were . . . they were destined for a severe and grievous blow. . . . I had no compassion on the least of them [. . .]"; and soon they were "fleeing before me with fear pulsating through their limbs." After the victory Taharqa "[placed the captives(?)] in quarters, I settled them in villages, and [their] cattle [in . . . , the . . . came, their benevolences] in their hands." Finally comes the appeal to Amun: "O thou lord of the gods! May years be granted me! [. . . thou(?) hast] been in my heart since I was a youth. It was thy 'Great Name' [that was upon my lips . . . I have given] thee the valuables of every land, and borne (the contents of) their treasuries to thee to Karnak!"[31]

The results of this military activity are clear from western Asian sources, and although the Libyan action may have been punitive, the push to the north gained territory. Esarhaddon implies that southern Philistia as far north as Ashkelon, at least, was in Egyptian hands when he attacked in 671 B.C.,[32] and Tyre and Sidon on the Phoenician coast had become enthusiastic supporters of Taharqa.[33] If after 722 B.C. Assyrian policy, insofar as it was clearly thought out, had been directed towards securing the Levantine coast[34] and Transjordan, thus isolating the Palestinian highland, it had proven only partly successful. Only in Transjordan had the Assyrians extended influence unhindered,[35] and this was the least profitable arena for victory. On the coast Egypt continued, at least potentially, to enjoy a slight advantage.[36]

"TAHARQA THE CONQUEROR"

The Kushites had conquered Egypt, repulsed the Assyrians, and even gone over to the attack. The confidence in ability born of success without setback imbued the victors with an exhilaration that invited original modes of celebration. In the following unique stela one glimpses the triumphant pharaoh on public view in all his regalia, glorying in the physical fitness of his crack troops and participating in their training:

> His Majesty commanded that his army which he had mustered run every day [in] their five [battalions(?)]. Said His Majesty to them: "How good is what my father Amun has done for me! [The like] has not happened [to] any other king! He has granted me to decapitate the Nine Bows which are (now) strewn beneath my sandals. What the sun-disk encircles labors for me, without (any) resisting me throughout that which heaven encompasses! There is no coward among my troops, no weak-armed among my recruits!" The

king himself journeyed to the highland to view the excellence of his army [and] ⌈they⌉ [came on] as comes the wind, like kites flying with their wings, the household troops[37] included,[38] (so) sure-footed there was no distinguishing between them. The king for his part was like Montu, unequaled among his troops. His majesty was intelligent and strong in every activity, a second Thoth! The king himself was mounted on a chariot to view the running [of] his army; and (in fact) he ran with them over the desert of Memphis at the hours of sunset, and they reached the Fayum at dawn. They were back at the Residence (= Memphis) at the hour of [____]. He singled out the best among them, and had them eat and drink with the household troops.[39]

This stela conveys a different impression than the conventional view of Taharqa, destined from the outset to be a tragic loser. Obviously in the outgoing first quarter of the seventh century B.C., he was supremely self-confident as a commander[40] and believed he had brought his troops to such a peak of training that no foreign power could threaten Egypt on the battlefield.[41] We have to pose two questions: why, in view of the caliber of his armed forces, should he have lost so suddenly and ignominiously; and why, despite his defeat, he should have survived in historical tradition as a conqueror. But before we take up the threat these questions carry forward, the Kushite success must be chronicled on the "home front."

EGYPT OF THE "BLACK PHARAOHS"

The kings of the Twenty-fifth Dynasty had thus reinvigorated Egypt. Success had been enjoyed on the battlefield, and at home the extensive building program had signaled a revived economy. In the administration and state ideology, also, the Kushite regime had awakened Egypt and brought an end to the disastrous decline of the previous four centuries.

THE ADMINISTRATIVE DECLINE OF THE THIRD INTERMEDIATE PERIOD

The decades following 1150 B.C. witnessed the growing importance of two factors that profoundly affected Egypt. The redrawing of the ethnic map of the Near East resulted from the arrival of new Indo-European-speaking peoples, hostile to Egypt, in the very regions of the Levant to which, through empire or treaty, Pharaoh had had free access heretofore. It was no longer an easy matter to obtain silver, iron, boxwood, oil, aromatics, and luxury manufactures, and trading for them became increasingly difficult through the reduction of Egypt's economic base.

If Egypt had little control over what was happening in foreign parts, it had none over its own climate. The second factor, more insidious and far-reaching, was the change in weather patterns in northeastern Africa, which resulted in a progression of low Nile inundations. A decrease in food production entailing a decline in population left a growing number of farms untended,[1] with the result that marginal arable land tended to be ceded to desert or fen. Government documents from the close of the Twentieth Dynasty (early eleventh century) suggest that grain production was down significantly from what it had been a century and a half earlier.[2] The loss of agriculture was more serious in Upper Egypt than the Delta, where animal husbandry provided a somewhat more reliable livelihood[3] and where foreign ports were closer. Throughout the twelfth and eleventh centuries one senses a gradual withdrawal of the organs of administration from the valley (Upper Egypt) to the north, a move that accelerated dramatically with the collapse of the Ramesside house. Even in the Delta the center of the country's administration over the same period gravitated along a northeastern axis, from Memphis to Pi-Ramesses, and eventually to Tanis: here trade with Levantine cities might be expected to offset the decline in Egypt's internal economy.

Not only did the bureaucracy seek more northerly centers of operation; it also shrunk in size and began to disintegrate altogether, with catastrophic effects on the body social. When under the Nineteenth Dynasty Egypt had been rich and its population increasing,[4] the civil service had been made to function with practical success on the basis of three principles. First, at the head of the organization there had to be a CEO (= Pharaoh) of an able, hardworking, and charismatic caste who could judge character well. He had perforce to effect his decisions through a cadre of executive officers (*srw*, "magistrates," in modern vernacular "take-charge guys") who were chosen countrywide on the basis of ability and family and who operated nationally, not locally. Finally, at the bottom of the pyramid there had to be a support staff (*smdt*) chosen on a parochial basis, who functioned locally and were not shifted about.[5] As the population declined and the ranks of the executive officers, the *srw*, thinned, the government found itself unable to affect its will on a *national* basis, and parochial tendencies began to dominate. The prosperity of the state had depended on the competence of the members of the *srw* to maintain agriculture and industrial production, collect taxes, and recruit and organize labor on a grand scale, but now it became increasingly difficult to ensure their competence or their numbers. Disquieting geopolitical tensions were also beginning to split the unity of the country: from the First Cataract to Asyut a "House of Amun," tied more to Nubia than to the north, was beginning to take shape, and lower Middle Egypt and part of the Delta came to be dominated by settlements of Libyans. Such incipient divisions tended to rob the central authority of power and to contribute to the difficulty of tax collection and redistribution on a national scale.

The decline of the overarching umbrella organization of the *srw*, set up on a national basis, cast to the fore other power structures of purely local creation and purview. The local temple and its community enjoyed an increase in prominence in the Tanite period. Its priestly functionaries perforce adopted a quasi-political role in administering the local bailiwick, now more and more identified with the temple and its god, and the practice they favored of garnering as many hereditary prebends as they could from widely scattered temples made this "old-boy" network of priests into a substitute (albeit a poor one) for the erstwhile cadre of *srw*. The foreign enclave was another structure that fell heir to power at this time. The settlements of the Libyan tribesmen owed their allegiance primarily to their chiefs and displayed an ill-advised tendency to deny loyalty to any broader, national ideal. Increasingly the local township found itself having to carry on without the direct support of the crown in terms of temple subsidies and state-run building projects. This situation thrust the municipal administration into a slightly more independent role and eventually was to promote the local "mayor" to the status of the "nomarch" of old.

What Egypt was losing through the concatenation of these disparate and debilitating factors had become painfully evident by the beginning of the first millennium. There was little money for construction, and the pool of foreign labor, the prisoners of war of imperial times, had dried up. Pharaoh rarely went through the land on progress, as his New Kingdom predecessors had done annually; and his dwindling roster of officials scarcely budged from the capital. In fact, when a magnate did make a tour of inspection, it was deemed a singular event and worthy of inclusion in a biography! Shipping and communication along the Nile declined, and even maritime trade gravitated into the hands of the Phoenicians. As towns found themselves largely responsible for their own defense, the fortified keep or "donjon" became a characteristic feature of the Nilotic landscape.

THE MONARCHY

The chief office in the Egyptian state, that of "King of Upper and Lower Egypt," suffered a decline commensurate with that of other organs of state and aspects of culture; in fact, the progressive weakening of Pharaoh was the bellwether for all Egypt. The outward trappings might well have remained, but the contrast with the ephemeral nature of the officeholder created almost a caricature. Officially one could be a "mighty bull: beloved of Re, . . . with a powerful sword, defeating hundreds of thousands . . . with great strength, giver of the life of the Two Lands"[6] and still elicit the contemptuous comment: "As for Pharaoh how can he ever reach this land? Of whom, indeed, is Pharaoh the master? . . . Do not be concerned about what he might do!"[7]

The monarchy suffered from blows that it was beyond its control to ward off—low Niles, inimical neighbors, changing trade patterns—but it also adopted measures deleterious to its own welfare by trying to maintain impossible standards. In particular, the great Ramesses II had cast a long shadow down the centuries following his death, and by the beginning of the first millennium his sixty-seven-year reign, filled with stunning feats of military prowess, statecraft, and construction, had begun to form the major ingredient in the folkloric mix that produced the legendary "Sesostris."[8] Ramesses II had set a mark that kings for six centuries felt constrained to strive for, but it soon became nothing more than donning a "Ramesside costume." Royal epithets and titulary simply parroted those of the great Ramesses, his pretensions to foreign conquest were repeated, even his aquiline profile in art can be found on a figure labeled "Osorkon" or "Takelot" (see fig. 22)! To judge from his letters and those verbatim transcripts that can be deemed to be his own words, Ramesses II was a

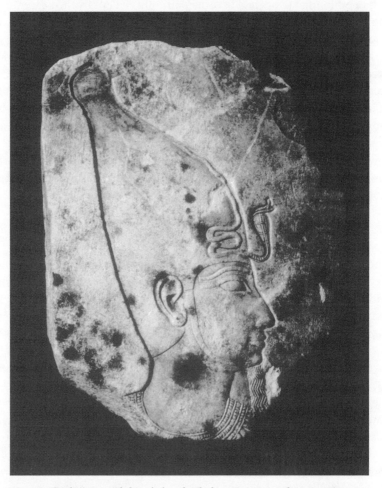

Fig. 22. Trial piece with king's head. Thebes, East Karnak excavations.

rather pedestrian individual, but one endowed with the physical and psy-chological drive of a Frederick the Great. In the 700s, however, no one re-membered this: Ramesses had become a model similar to Franklin D. Roosevelt. He had to be copied and, when that proved impossible, at least imitated. But the cost was measured in loss of imagination and intuitive reaction never put to the test.

The Ramesside experience had produced an "Amun-theology" that effectually, though not formally, replaced the ideology of the Perfect God on earth by shifting the focus to a new hypostasis of power. This theology tied Amun at a political level to the terrestrial event of Egypt's triumph, in part to fill the void created by the failure of god on earth. Amun became identified with a national theocracy as "the first to become king, god of the first occasion."[9] This was a theology of otherworldly, rather than im-minent, sovereignty, spiritualized power wielded ineffably and manifest through the nation. "Indeed! Thou (Amun) hast let every country and ev-ery land know that thou art the 'Power' of Pharaoh l.p.h., thy child, against every country and every land! Thou it is that hast made powerful the land of Egypt—thy land alone!—not through the agency of any army, but only through thy great might!"[10] In all this humans have no inde-pendent role: their function as ruler stems solely from Amun's empower-ment.

The titularies of the kings of the Twentieth through the Twenty-third Dynasties bear out this assertion.[11] Eight of the ten members of the Twen-tieth Dynasty bear prenomina of the type ADJ.+$m3't$-r', and four imitate Ramesses II with Wsr-$m3't$-r'.[12] Seven of the eleven kings following Siptaḥ imitate Ramesses II by using the added epithet stp-n-DN, "he whom god X has chosen";[13] of eight kings from Smendes to Osorkon I whose titularies are known, *all* employ the same epithet. Of the nine kings from Osorkon II to the close of the Twenty-third Dynasty who achieved an en-try in the official king list,[14] seven mimicked the great Ramesses by adopt-ing the prenomen Wsr-$m3't$-r' stp-n-DN.

If mimicry suggests lack of self-assertiveness and imagination, it also betrays an uncertainty regarding legitimacy. Of the six kings from Smendes to Osorkon II whose Horus-names are known, *all* invoke the god (usually in a causative construction) to affirm divine agency in legiti-mizing the claim to kingship (Amun for the Twenty-first Dynasty; Re or Atum for the Twenty-second).[15] By the time of Sheshonq III and Pamay the epithet stp-n-Imn, "he whom Amun has chosen," has become almost obligatory, and the Twenty-third Dynasty uses it to the exclusion of any other.

A king uncertain of himself and his legitimacy, lacking in financial resources and manpower and hemmed in by the "fiefs" of his congeners, the Great Chiefs of the Me, would command little authority or even respect beyond the immediate township in which he resided. The loss of his persona as true "Lord of the Two Lands" and "Master of the Cult" (*nb irt ḫt*) would be felt in two areas, one secular, the other sacerdotal: municipal authority and the priesthood. There was a strong tendency, therefore, to view the headship of a town and the high priesthood of a god as essentially *kingly offices*. The cult demanded in theory a royal celebrant, and sure enough the Tanite period throws up several high priests of Amun who adopted the full royal panoply. Hermopolis, Herakleopolis, and Bubastis are preeminent cities of royal association, and in the eighth century each of them is found to be ruled by a headman claiming to be king, with full titulary, crown-cum-uraeus,[16] and hereditary rights. It is these sacerdotal and popular "kingships" that Piankhy contemptuously refers to in the statement "Gods make a king, men make a king."[17] His characterization of himself (or possibly Amun?) as "the one whom no dukes created"[18] shows clearly the origin of the "popular" brand of king as a *primus inter pares* among the local aristocracy.

But no matter to what extent a sacerdotal kingship might promote itself during the Third Intermediate Period, the fact remains that such a rulership had irrevocably forfeited any true capacity to function in priestly celebration. Kings and high priests lacked liturgical competence, and in consequence their thus derived political stock plummeted during the eighth century B.C. The extent to which their sacerdotal role ostensibly predominated is the measure of their political weakness. The temple functions in question now increasingly gravitated into the competence of "parish clergy," leaving the high-flown priestly prebends to be garnered by kings and "soldier-bishops."

The Twenty-fifth Dynasty concept of kingship[19] takes the form of a vibrant and imaginative restatement of what can only be called "Amun-theology," but it now has the added element of the ideology of an "Amun" of provincial origins, namely, Amun of Napata. "Amun of Napata," says Piankhy, "granted me to function as ruler of every foreign land."[20] In many respects one can hear clear echoes of the birth-and-selection rhetoric made famous in the self-serving mythology surrounding the figures of Hatshepsut and Thutmosis III, whose origins are probably to be sought in the Middle Kingdom approach to kingship. The monarch was selected and prophesied before birth. Of Piankhy Amun says: "I said about you in your mother's womb (that) you would be ruler of Egypt; I knew you as sperm when you were in the egg (that) you would be the lord that I had made!"[21] Piankhy was indeed "one who emerged from the womb already marked as ruler . . . whom his father knew and his mother recognized was destined to be ruler (even) in the egg!"[22] Taharqa refers to Amun as having "prophesied these things of me before thou didst allow me to accede to the throne."[23] Sonship and divine likeness are lightly stressed: Piankhy is "a divine likeness, living image of Atum,"[24] and Taharqa declares to Amun, "I am thy son, it being thou that hast m[ade me in(?)] thy ⌈being⌉."[25] The father in time-honored perception is viewed as acceding to the son's every request: "Now as for everything that issues from His Majesty's mouth, his father Amun makes it happen immediately!"[26] More stressed are Amun's perspicacity in selection and the freedom of his choice: the god "had chosen him in the womb before he was born";[27] "thou didst choose me within the⌈sanctuary(?)⌉and didst make them say of(?)[28] me: 'Look! Amun makes a Pharaoh out of whom he likes!' and thou hast made me realize that the one whom thou installest [is(?) . . .]." Amun's sovereignty and his status as font of *all* political and cosmic authority are basic to the Kushite concept of pharaonic monarchy; and we are probably correct in viewing this unabashed promotion of the national god of the African south as a counterblast to the north. Amun alone could grant legitimacy: "I am the one (Amun speaking) that gave you authorization: who can share that with you? I am lord of heaven: what I grant to Re, he grants to his children, whether gods or men. I am the one that grants you the title deed: who will share that with you? No other king has been (so) authorized (for) I am the one that grants it to whomever I will!"[29] Amun stands at the summit of hierarchical authority: "O Amun! There is none that lays down the law to thee! Thou art the one that lays down [the law to others(?)]."[30]

Pharaoh shows two faces. He may "have done what no (other) Pharaoh has done," yet he is "with thee (Amun) as (but) a servant";[31] and like a servant, his approach to his master is tentative, if not obsequious. "Let me not enter upon any matter which thou dost disapprove of . . . let me not do anything which thou dost disapprove of."[32] "As for what thou wilt say to me, viz. 'Go, go!' I will go [. . .]!"[33] To the world, however, the king is god's plenipotentiary, fully empowered with a mandate that can never be questioned. "The one to whom I say—'You are king!' he functions as king; the one to whom I say—'you are not king!'—he never functions as king! . . . the one to whom I say—'Accede (to the throne)!'—he accedes (to the throne); the one to whom I say—'Do not accede (to the throne)!'—he never accedes (to the throne)!"[34] Says Piankhy to Namlot, that abject sinner: "Don't you know god's shadow is over me? He never frustrates what I do . . . I have done nothing without him! He it is that ordered me to act!"[35]

THE TWENTY-FIFTH DYNASTY VERSUS
THE DELTA DYNASTS

The theory of kingship just described, derived from a Theban past but stressing potentiality in a novel fashion, had transformed Pharaoh into more than a mere son of the god. He was now a divine protégé, god's CEO and heaven's hatchet man rolled into one. He would need all the powers deriving from these roles, as he articulated Theban Amun's bid for supremacy over the north.

For the principal dynasts of the Delta we possess two lists, fifty-five years apart—that of Piankhy in his famous stela (c. 717 B.C.),[36] and that of Ashurbanipal (in the 660s).[37] The former is more carefully composed, and therefore more useful than the latter, in that it carefully observes hierarchy of power and primacy of bailiwick (see map 3). The "monarchies" are listed first, that of Bubastis, stretching north over the land between the Tanitic and Pelusiac branches as far as the sea,[38] and that of Leontopolis (Ta-remu and Ta'an), occupying the central Delta on the central branch (in the reach of modern Tanta-Mit-Ghamir) and extending along the right bank of the Mendesian branch of the Rekhty-water.[39] By the reign of Sabaco these "kingships" had been terminated. Then follow four of the great chiefdoms of the Delta, which, with the exception of the third, Pi-sopdu, occupy the lower extent of the central branch of the Nile: the principality of Mendes-Hermopolis Parva,[40] from modern Mansura-Simbelawein to the Dakahlieh plain and north to Dikirnis;[41] the principality of Sebennytos, stretching from modern Samanūd north to the coast; and Busiris, from modern Mit Ghamr to Samanūd, on the left bank of the central branch, coextensive with old L.E. 9.[42] The chiefdom of Mendes, the family of Hor-nakht, can be traced through five generations beginning in the early eighth century B.C.[43] and has left numerous remains at the site of Tel er-Rub'a.[44] In the last quarter of the eighth century it was ruled by Chief Djed-amun-efankh and half a century later by a Puyam;[45] whether these were later scions of the Ḥornakht family is debatable,[46] but the principality nonetheless remained strong. The family in Sebennytos can be traced no earlier than the time of Piankhy, when one Akenosh functioned as chief, but his descendants can be traced for at least three generations into the mid–seventh century.[47] Like the Mendesian house, the family of chiefs of Busiris can be traced from the early eighth century B.C.[48] During Piankhy's campaign the incumbent Sheshonq[49] died, and his successor, Pemu, was left to offer allegiance to the Kushites.[50] Two further generations of a Sheshonq (II) and a Pemy (II) carried the chiefdom into the early Twenty-sixth Dynasty.[51]

Impinging on Piankhy's list of the great bailiwicks of the lower central Delta is the sequence of fiefs strung out along the eastern, desert access through the Wady Tumilat. These comprise Athribis (L.E. 10), Pi-sopdu (L.E. 20), and Parbaethos (L.E. 11), which form an arc flanking Bubastis on the east, and Pigruru in the Wady Tumilat proper.[52] Of these Athribis was most powerful and, as we have seen, played an intercessory role vis-à-vis Piankhy. The city had enjoyed its position of preeminence since around 800 B.C., when Sheshonq III had established his erstwhile eldest son, Bakennefi, as ruler of the locality,[53] and from that point this cadet branch of the Twenty-second Dynasty had united Heliopolis and Athribis in a sort of princedom.[54] Just before Piankhy's invasion the then heir Bakennefi (II?)[55] had placed a son, Nesna'y, in the great chiefdom of the eleventh township and married his daughter to Pediese, who replaced him in Athribis. A generation later a Bakennefi III, son of Padiese, still retained the princedom of Athribis under Taharqa and Ashurbanipal.[56] Under Piankhy Pi-sopdu was ruled by a Patjenfy, and from about 710 to 690 a man with the same name ruled the tenth township in Parbaethos.[57] If they are the same individual, as seems likely, it would mean an aggrandizement of the sphere of Pi-sopdu's authority at the expense of Athribis, a political move for which Sabaco might be responsible. Whether the Padikhonsu who is found in Parbaethos in Psamtek I's eighth year[58] is a descendant of Patjenfy is unknown. A similar enhancement of parochial power may be attested for the Wady Tumilat. Under Piankhy a Nakht-ḥornasheny is found as great chief of the Me in Pigruru, and half a century later a like-named individual[59] rules a place named Pi-sapti-'a. The latter has been variously identified, but no suggestion is convincing.[60] It seems to me that in Assyrian ʾa what we have is a vocalization of ww, "district," and that the designation "Pi-sopdu-the-district" means the territory of the nome-bailiwick of which Pi-sopdu was the principal town, that is, the western debouchment of the Wady Tumilat.

The Piankhy list ends with two unlocated great chiefs of the Me, the high priest of Letopolis, and the local mayors of the region of Memphis, but the logical arrangement of a Piankhy is not mirrored in the list of an Ashurbanipal. The latter places Saïs (by now the principal center of vice-royalty in the Delta) in first position, a primacy it had enjoyed since Tefnakhte asserted his power. The family had not been unseated by the Kushites: in fact, Tefnakhte's grandson Necho I now occupied the fiefdom.[61] The rest of the list is organized by the preoccupation of a foreigner approaching Egypt by land from the northeast, and the imagined route is in a sense reduplicated. Si'nu, Pelusium,[62] follows Saïs in second position and is followed in turn by Natho; Ṣa'anu, Tanis, occupies seventh position and is again followed by Natho! Whether there were two sites with this name seems very doubtful to me—certainly Herodotus II, 165, does not suggest it—and one should not be surprised at confusion on the part of the Assyrian scribe.[63] The fact that Natho in both positions, three and eight, in the list of Ashurbanipal is associated with sites in the central and northeastern Delta eliminates Tell el-Yehudiya as a candidate and would militate in favor of Tel Muqdam.[64] Thus two of the "royal" cities of the eighth century, Tanis and Leontopolis, had survived as parochial centers of power while a third, Bubastis, had been absorbed. The incumbent of Tanis, to judge by his name, may well have been a scion of the old Libyan house;[65] the names Pishanhor and Wenamun at Natho, on the other hand, are not in themselves suggestive of family identity.

The remainder of the Delta names represent the proliferation of political subdivisions after the Kushites took over. Punubu is presumably the *Pr-inbw* on the western Delta,[66] perhaps a fragment of the original "Kingdom of the West," now under a Tefnakhte. Uḫni has been identified with either Tel el-Muqdam or a faubourg of that site,[67] but an identification of Natho with Muqdam might eliminate the first. If the Bakennefi of Uḫni is the same as the Bakennefi of Athribis, we might construe this as evidence of Athribis's expansion at the expense of Leontopolis. Pi-hathor-*unpiki* seems to contain an allusion to Hathor (mistress) of *Mfk3t*,[68] but whether this is Kom abu-Billo[69] or an eastern Delta site is difficult to say.[70]

In sifting the evidence just reviewed, several facts about the Kushite policy toward the Delta become clear.

1. The Twenty-fifth Dynasty, whether through choice or inability, found itself disinclined to terminate the chiefdoms of Libyan descent which they found ensconced in the north.
2. With the subversion of the old "royal" cities of Tanis, Leontopolis, and Bubastis, a fragmentation of their large bailiwicks ensued, resulting in the increase in parochial power centers.
3. Despite its defeat, Saïs continued to be felt to be a sort of *primus inter pares* among the cities of the north and, along with Athribis and Pi-sopdu, was considered by the Assyrians responsible for the Delta.
4. If the dynasts sought a theoretical basis for their continued control of their towns, they found it in their hereditary claims on a local priestly function.[71]
5. The Kushite kings refrained from construction projects in the Delta, which would have betokened and actually entailed the redistribution of wealth to support the dynasts' local cults.[72]

The Kushites' response to the dynasts was shrewd, if not revolution-ary. The old mechanism of marriage was found useful. The "hereditary princess, much-charming and much favoured, possessed of charm and of sweet affection, the king's-daughter Amunirdis," who had formerly been Divine Worshiper of Amun, was married off to a hereditary prince Mentuhotpe of the eastern Delta, lately raised to the vizierate.[73] The chronic failure of the dynasts to cultivate loyalty to any authority higher than their own family prompted a Kushite response that recalled time-honored hostage taking. In an ironic reversal of the old policy of Egyptian conquerors towards the blacks of the Sudan, Taharqa trans-planted Delta people, including sisters and wives of the chiefs, to the tem-ple estates of Nubia as servants and priestesses.[74] This deportation resem-bled the practice the Assyrians had carried out over three centuries, and had Taharqa retained control of the north, it might have been followed by the exile of the dynasts themselves.

THE KUSHITE ADMINISTRATION OF UPPER EGYPT

In contrast to the Delta, the Sudanese rulers of Egypt were "at home" in the valley of the Nile. Hermopolis, Asyut, and Thinis might have been al-lowed to retain their own ruling families, but to a greater degree than their compatriots farther north they were compromised by their proximity to the center of power. Namlot in Hermopolis, who survived into Ashurbanipal's time,[75] is a pious dedicant to the regime of the Divine Worshiper,[76] and Nespamedu of Thinis[77] is related by marriage to Theban magnates.[78]

Thebes was sufficiently enamored of its pious co-religionists from Napata to allow the Twenty-fifth Dynasty a free hand. Possibly as a result of the denigration of the office through its callous absorption into a mili-taristic governorship by the scions of the Libyan royal house, the high priesthood of Amun had long since suffered a political eclipse that was to prove permanent.[79] Power in the Thebaid now resided with the royal house, which exercised it through the person of a female member (usually a daughter of the reigning king).[80] Assuming the role of "Divine Wor-shiper" of Amun, the princess enjoyed all the outward trappings of roy-alty: the cartouches, regal epithets, and graphic symbolism (see figs. 23, 24; see also fig. 16).[81]

Such paraphernalia, however, was but the heraldry of an institution of deep roots and broad control, for the Divine Worshiper disposed of a court and a political establishment that, in a sense, reendowed Thebes with a "royal" presence.[82] The dignitaries who surrounded her, and the

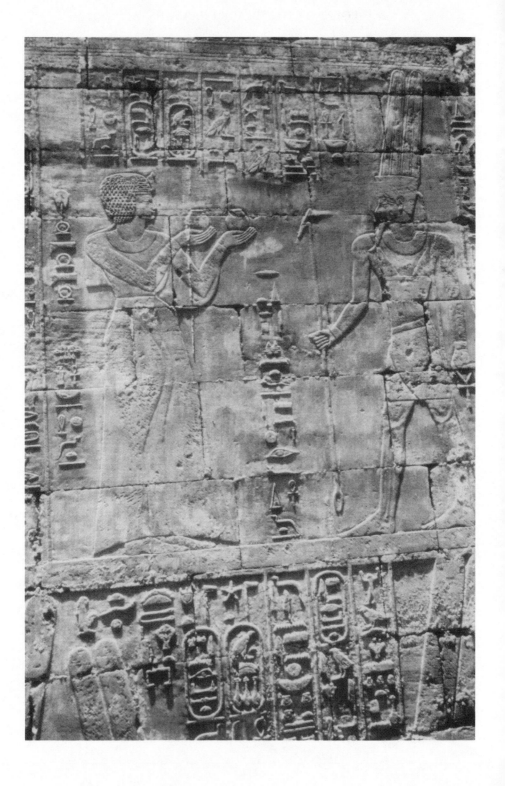

Fig. 24. Shepenwepet I before Montu (upper) and Harendotes (middle). Thebes, facade of the Temple of Osiris-Ruler-of-Eternity, early seventh century B.C.

Fig. 23. *(opposite)* Amunirdis I worships Amun. Thebes, Temple of Osiris-Ruler-of-Eternity, early seventh century B.C.

descending hierarchy of servants under her, have left impressive memorials in the form of sculpture and tombs, all bespeaking an infusion of real wealth in the Thebaid. The Divine Worshiper presided over a royal "salon" in which chamberlains and palace managers were prominent; she was entertained by singers, sistrum players, and perhaps even eunuchs. Her ceremonial partakes of "mysteries," and she was watched over by a security staff. Like a king she disposed of servants who were responsible for the regal accoutrements and crowns, and a cadre of officers concerned with provisions saw to the alimentary needs of this crowd. The Divine Worshiper had scribes (male and female!) of every skill—accountancy, epistolography, draftsmanship—and a host of "followers" and "servants" attended to her every need. She possessed artisans in their ateliers, goldsmiths in their smithies, unskilled labor in workhouses—even miners trekked through the mountains avid for precious minerals. Her wealth was deposited in a treasury and used to support construction, and on her death, part of it would sustain an elaborate mortuary cult, as though she were a king.

It is difficult to determine whether this "princess court" was more theme park than city hall. Did the Divine Worshiper really exercise political power? There is good reason to believe that she was appointed while yet a little girl, so that it is unlikely she could have exercised her own will freely. It is true that we possess next to no historical texts of any genre from Dynasties 25 and 26; nonetheless, even in private memorials no Divine Worshiper ever figures in any of the major events of the time, whether in decision or implementation.[83]

In fact, the Divine Worshiper appears more as a figurehead than as a "queen" in her own right: administrative control rested in the hands of her majordomo and her close relatives who occupied priestly functions. The majordomo was at first chosen from the ranks of the local populace: Harwa under Shepenwepet II and Akhamenru later in Taharqa's reign.[84] Later a respectable pedigree attached itself to holders of the office. The upper ranks of the Amun priesthood were filled by Kushite princes: the office of high priest by Harmachis, son of Sabaco, that of second prophet by Nes-shutefnut, son of Taharqa.[85] Before the end of Kushite domination Harmakhis was to hand on the high priesthood to his son, Harkheby.[86]

Despite their high birth and membership in the ruling house, none of these was to rival the rank and power attained by a most unlikely candidate, a commoner named Montou-em-het. Son of the mayor of Thebes and priest of Amun, Nesptaḥ, and a simple "housewife," Montou-em-het had, by the early years of the seventh century, worked his way through the ascending ranks of temple scribe, inspector of priests, chief of the temple,[87] fourth prophet of Amun, and finally mayor of Thebes. In the last capacity he could boast that he had "all Upper Egypt under my charge, (from) the southern boundary at Elephantine (to) the northern at Hermopolis. I showed my ability to Upper Egypt and my affection to Lower Egypt, and the townsfolk prayed to see me, like Re when he manifests himself, so great were my accomplishments and of so high degree my competence!"[88] Montou-em-het appears in his inscriptions as a throwback to a type of traditional patrician well known from as early as the late Old Kingdom but noticeably absent under the Libyan hegemony. Such a one was proud of his city and concerned for its welfare and renewal: "a useful refuge for (his) city.[89] Passing the night vigilant over those he is responsible for."[90] He is proud of his family, especially of "my son who is upon my seat, my able heir who has grasped my institution."[91] Piety informs his every act: he was one who "followed his god without ceasing, who opens the temple to see what is in it, each chapel being under (his) seal."[92] In a time of renewal after neglect, piety also meant restoration of god's house and his property. Montou-em-het prides himself on "reconstituting what was in fragments, filling in the lacunae throughout the townships of the entire southland,"[93] and this inevitably required an ability to read what the ancestors had written and, more to the point, access to authoritative texts.[94] Time and again Montou-em-het refers to his careful following of the ancient archetype by employing the phrase "in accordance with (the prescription) which is in book so-and-so."[95] He viewed his role as "[calling] to remembrance what has passed . . . restoring ritual which had fallen into neglect."[96]

THE BUILDING PROGRAM

Montou-em-het was particularly proud of his program of restoration, which focused primarily upon Thebes but extended north as far as Hermopolis, as well. His jargon favors such expressions as "I restored his temple as it was in former times. . . . I built it as I found it, but improved over what the ancestors had made . . . I built his temple better than it had been formerly."[97] If one takes him seriously, one would have to conclude that the erstwhile Libyan regime had left the country in dilapidation, and as an excavator of Karnak over eighteen years, I should have to agree that Montou-em-het is indeed telling the truth. Thebes, at least at the end of the eighth century B.C., was a small, undistinguished town with temples sadly in need of repair, but on the eve of the Assyrian conquest it had again achieved a "world-class" status under the guidance of

Montou-em-het. Well might he boast "I am the one that made Thebes festive [and exceeded] what was done by ancient kings."[98]

Montou-em-het's program centered chiefly upon the restoration of the cult, its paraphernalia, and support structure, rather than the wholesale rebuilding of temples. Mostly he speaks of constructing the gem-encrusted portable barques of the gods and the statuettes (the "Protected Images")[99] they contained. (In the period of economic decline such portable conveyances were the first to be stripped of their gold, silver, electrum, gems, and cedar poles, thus rendering them unusable.)[100] He also polished up old offering tables and created new ones and redug sacred lakes. Regularization of the calendar of feasts and the reestablishment of temple income both figured on his agenda. Outside Thebes the gods thus favored included the Bull of Medamud, Min of Koptos, Horus of Khemkhem,[101] Isis and Osiris at Abydos and an avatar of Thoth near Hermopolis.

In the long stretch of the valley beginning at Thebes and extending south into the Sudan, there is understandably evidence of greater building activity than farther north. At Edfu Taharqa contributed to the existing temple of Horus; blocks of his, reused by Psammetichus II a century later, were unearthed at this site a decade ago beneath the Ptolemaic peristyle court (see fig. 19). The same king made dedications to Hemen at Asfun, north of Esna.[102]

THEBES UNDER THE TWENTY-FIFTH DYNASTY

T he city that benefited most from the Sudanese occupation of the lower Nile was understandably the city of Amun himself, Thebes.[1] The "southern city," as it was known in a jargon fashioned in the Memphite-dominated north, had suffered a dramatic and damaging drop in population and diminution in spacial extent at the close of the Twentieth Dynasty, when the royal administration severed all ties with the city. Magnates and bureaucrats whose presence and lifestyle in Thebes were underwritten by the court had no further purpose in remaining in the city and therefore no per diem allowance, and their villas were suddenly abandoned. The new regime, centered upon the person of Ḥeriḥor, a military adventurer who had conned his way to the position of sole responsibility in the Thebaid, chose to construe local administration as identical to the running of his own large, private estate. Pharaoh took no further interest in Thebes as the place to deposit booty, honor Amun, and glorify his own exploits and stopped underwriting the cost of new additions, reliefs, and statuary in the temples, and most certainly Ḥeriḥor and his kin were not interested in doing it for him! The result for the modern historian is the prospect of a 360-year period (c. 1070–710 B.C.) when the timid, single-column texts in the Theban temples attest to nothing more than the repair of a gate or wall for which, we are safe in assuming, monies had to be scrounged from the bottom of the company coffers. Commoners' hovels began to encroach on the sacred courts, and sturdy walls were required to keep them out.

Thebes's status changed dramatically with the coming of the Nubians. Protégés of Amun, they transformed the southern city into a royal city once again. Though he was buried in his native Napata, Piankhy introduced his own commemorative cult in Thebes, where his portable barque shrine was still carried in procession fifty years after his death. Sabaco and Shebitku did much more. The former added a treasury on the northern

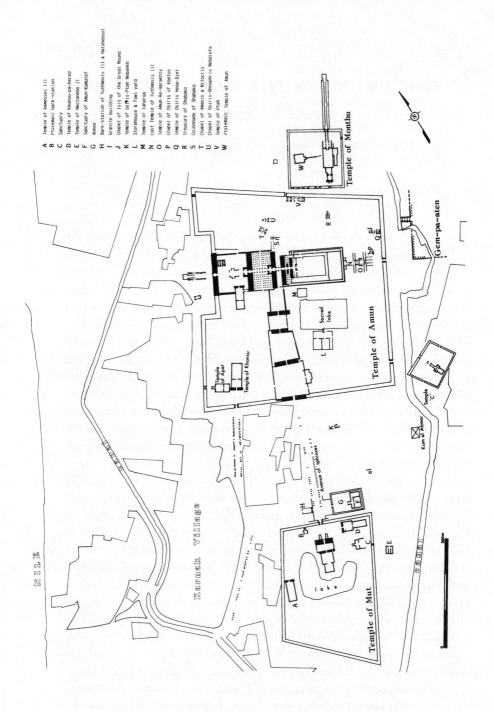

A Temple of Ramesses III
B Ptolemaic bark-station
C Sanctuary
D Temple of Khonsu-pa-khered
E Temple of Nectanebo II
F Sanctuary of Amun-Kamutef
G Annex
H Bark-station of Tuthmosis III & Hatshepsut
I Granite building
J Chapel of Isis of the Great Mound
K Temple of Osiris-Ptah Neberekh
L Storehouse & fowl yard
M Temple of Taharqa
N East Temple of Tuthmosis III
O Temple of Amun-Re-Harakhty
P Chapel of Osiris of Koptos
Q Temple of Osiris Heqa-Djet
R Treasury of Shabako
S Colonnade of Shabako
T Chapel of Amasis & Nitocris
U Chapel of Osiris-Onnophris Nebdjefa
V Temple of Ptah
W Ptolemaic Temple of Amun

NILE

Karnak Village

Temple of Monthu

Gem-pa-aten

Temple of Amun

Temple of Khonsu

Temple of Apet

Sacred lake

Avenue of sphinxes

Kom el Ahmer

Temple "C"

Temple of Mut

lake

CANAL

side of Karnak's Temple of Amun, a sure sign of an increase in the divine income. He also constructed a "Mansion of Gold" in the same area for the manufacture of cult images and temple paraphernalia.[2] The same king began the refurbishing of structures fallen into dilapidation: Thutmosis IV's golden porch before the fourth pylon,[3] the margins of the Karnak sacred lake,[4] the pylons at Luxor[5] and Medinet Habu.[6] Shebitku renovated and added a forecourt to the small temple of Osiris-Lord-of-Eternity, in the "Great Mound of Wēse" northeast of the main Temple of Amun.[7]

Already under Sabaco the policy had been set of reconstructing gates and temenos walls, rather than demolishing existing structures and building anew. If any new shrines were to be constructed, they were confined to the periphery of and the approaches to standing temples.[8] Sabaco had established the precedent: after the conquest he had given commands to the "superintendent of construction in Upper and Lower Egypt . . . Padinḥor . . . to build enclosure-walls around the temples of Upper and Lower Egypt in order that priests and servants might perform service for them and that the gods might come into their shrines."[9] Taharqa followed suit: "He made it as his monument for his fathers the gods, the lords of the Mound of Djēme,[10] renewing the enclosure wall which his fathers, the ancestors, had made for the gods, the lords of the Mound of Djēme, and surrounding their temple with a brick wall of good and enduring workmanship. For His Majesty had found (it) fallen to ruin, crisscrossed with paths in the holy place on its north side. He sanctified the holy cella for her master."[11]

The "Mound of Djēme" was the sacred area of the community of Djēme, which had grown up around Medinet Habu, the mortuary temple of Ramesses III (twelfth century b.c.). This essentially was the center of population on the west bank in the Late Period. Here the Twenty-fifth Dynasty enlarged the original temple of Hatshepsut and Thutmosis III, and here the Divine Worshipers built their mortuary chapels.

What was to be the final glorious restoration of Karnak dates from Taharqa's reign (see fig. 25). As the established pattern demanded, the approaches received the main attention. A magnificent and towering baldachin of stone with lofty lotiform columns nearly one hundred feet high was erected between the quay (already adorned with records of the heights of the inundations) and the second pylon,[12] then the facade of the temple. The porch of the latter was partly decorated with reliefs,[13] as was the door of the tenth pylon marking the southern egress towards the Mut complex.[14] Before the Khonsu temple a colonnaded porch was built[15] and

Fig. 25. (*opposite*) Karnak and environs.

possibly a precursor to the temple of Apet in the same vicinity.[16] Southwards in the Mut enclosure additions were made. On the north the Montu enclosure received equal attention: a colonnade before the temple,[17] the subsidiary temple of Harpre,[18] and refurbished apartments represented today by only reused blocks.[19] Within the temple proper Taharqa's additions were discreet and unobtrusive. On the northern side of the sacred lake near the northwestern corner a low stone "podium" was constructed with chambers and a hypogeum designed for rituals associated with the "Litany of Re."[20] Within the innermost shrine Taharqa contented himself with decorating the wall of a room north of the barque shrine with a figure of himself as a suppliant before Amun with the text of his prayer.[21] Whereas the younger son of Piankhy may have been content with the old Ramesside walls on the south, north, and west of the Temple of Amun, the situation was different on the east. Here the city was expanding, and new structures were in order. A new wall was built to separate the Mound of Wēse,[22] although a postern of some sort must have permitted access from the Amun temple.[23] In front of the old eastern "high gate" of Ramesses II, set in the old temenos wall, a porch (*ḥ3yt*) was built consisting of rows of columns with intercolumnar screens and intended as a center of civic activity, part law court, part marketplace.

For the vast expanse of land lying to the east of the high gate (see fig. 26) great things were planned. This had been the site of Akhenaten's enormous jubilee temple in the fourteenth century B.C., but after its destruction the area had enjoyed only a brief period of domestic occupation in the Twentieth Dynasty (twelfth century B.C.). When Taharqa acceded to the throne, all East Karnak had lain unoccupied, an undulating expanse of mud-brick ruins, for more than four centuries. Following the central axis of the Karnak Temple the Nubian pharaoh extended a thoroughfare from the old high gate 210 meters eastward, at which point he intended to erect a new eastern enclosure wall with a gate to enclose the new faubourg, which was rapidly growing up over the vacant land. The foundation of the gate shows that it was 3.50 meters in width and was provided with cedar door leaves that swung inwards. The enclosure wall in which it was set was approximately 4 meters wide, but no trace of this wall now exists. In order to provide fitting adornment for the gate Taharqa removed several colossi of Ramesses II along with sphinxes that had perhaps once stood outside the original high gate, and he set them up outside the new aperture. (They were found by our expedition in 1991, fallen over and reused as paving in a fourth century B.C. street a short distance away.)[24] At approximately 50 meters due east of the "Great Mound of Wēse," wherein the Temple-of-Osiris-Ruler-of-Eternity stood, a major building of sandstone was

Fig. 26. View along the axis of Karnak from the east. In the foreground was discovered the gate of Taharqa.

laid out. Only one interior wall with flanking column bases has been recovered,[25] its eastern part having been destroyed by Chevrier's digging, but the alignment suggests that it was to have been oriented towards the existing Nineteenth Dynasty high gate of the Karnak Temple.

Neither the new eastern wall and gate nor the sandstone building ever came to much. The building was probably never finished, and domestic occupation soon spread east of the new wall. In fact, East Karnak proved to be the new and vibrant faubourg of the revitalized city.

Houses rapidly spread north of the extended axis and east of the new gate. Mud bricks were the preferred material for building, the addition of doors and roof beams qualifying a domicile as "built and roofed" as deeds declare. The law code of Hermopolis specifies a situation in which the brick is made from "alluvium brought up from the canal" (i.e., pristine building material), by which, in contradistinction, we are probably to imagine another type of house built of reused components. And in fact East Karnak provides just such an example. Almost every house contained, especially in parts exposed to the wear of frequent passage, *fired bricks* reused from some ancient structure. Many of them were stamped with the names of

Menkheperre, high priest of Amun, and his wife, Iset-em-kheby, who had flourished about 1020–1000 B.C.[26] In one of his inscriptions Menkheperre tells us that, in order to protect the Temple of Amun from squatters, he constructed a stout wall on the northern side of the sacred compound. If, as seems likely, the bricks unearthed in the houses of Taharqa's time and later come from this structure,[27] then we can only conclude that three centuries after its construction Menkheperre's wall had fallen into disuse and had been dismantled in the Kushite renovations of the temenos.

At first, during Taharqa's reign, the houses were modest affairs (see fig. 27), belonging probably to the lower middle class, but shortly a more

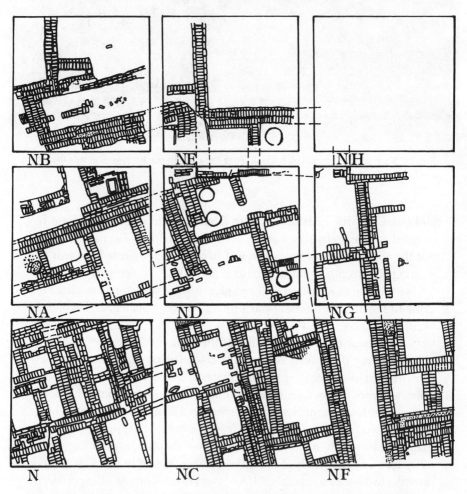

Fig. 27. Domestic structures of Twenty-fifth Dynasty date. East Karnak, early seventh century B.C.

Fig. 28. Domestic architecture—note the fired brick well in foreground. East Karnak, c. sixth century B.C.

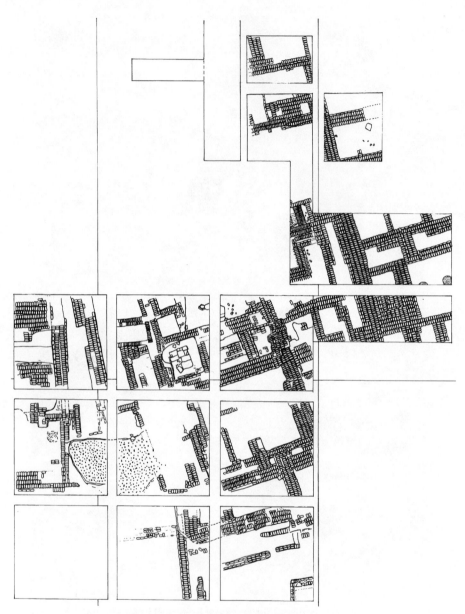

Fig. 29. Domestic structures. East Karnak, Late Period.

affluent group was to begin buying land there and erecting villas (see figs. 28, 29).[28] These villas basically belonged to the same type that is described repeatedly in business documents from the fourth through first centuries B.C., and the layout must have been common throughout Egypt from at least as early as the seventh century (see fig. 30). A small gate led into a columned antechamber of small dimensions or into a courtyard. The latter, which enjoyed no fixed position in the planning—it could be beside the main entry or in the rear of the building—varied greatly in size, from twenty to more than sixty square feet. Beyond the rooms of entry lay perhaps the most important part of the house: a block of rooms of two or three stories approached by a staircase and capped by a roof patio-cum-awning. House models from pharaonic times show us what these structures looked like,[29] but none have survived to be uncovered intact by archaeologists. Their position, however, in any excavated villa is clearly marked by a rectilinear foundation consisting of rubble-filled casemate chambers and providing a firm base for the weight of the superimposed structure (see fig. 31).

The rooms in the rear of the house were of a private nature. The kitchen area in each house is clearly marked by three or four large ovens (*tabuns* in modern Arabic), sometimes with a scatter of broken vessels and bones roundabout or within a packing of no longer used pots. In one

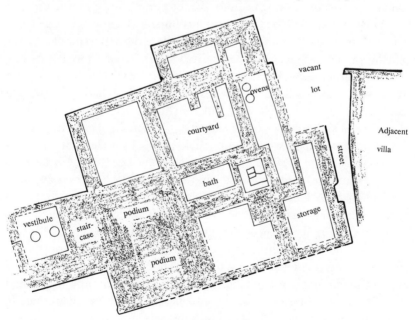

Fig. 30. Plan of a typical villa. East Karnak, sixth century B.C.

Fig. 31. Casemate foundations to support multistoried tower in villa of #30. East Karnak, sixth century B.C.

instance a macabre find cast doubt on the consistent domestic use of a kitchen: a human skull had been laid just outside the flue of a large oven. It had belonged to a woman between thirty and forty years old. Occasionally the kitchen would be associated with circular storage pits dug deep into earlier levels, but flotation failed to reveal what had been stored. In one villa a room was laid bare with an elaborate installation for bathing (see fig. 32). The mud-brick walls had been lined with plastered orthostats of sandstone and the floor provided with a shallow "trough" and socle of the same stone. Impure water was carried away by a short drain into a subfloor receptacle of stone, hewn out of a single sandstone block. In an adjacent room was found a menat counterpoise of the kind of heavy neck pendant worn by ladies of the upper class. The whole complex of apartments undoubtedly comprised what documents of house sales call the ḫrr, the women's quarters where monthly ablutions were performed.[30]

During the seventh through fourth centuries B.C. East and northeastern Karnak was densely packed with villas. Though large and often subject to partition among heirs, such houses did not always occupy all the land in the owner's possession, and "vacant lots" are sometimes mentioned in house documents. Nevertheless, house owners usually employed every conceivable means of using to full advantage the space available.

Fig. 32. Soclelike shower stall with drain. East Karnak, Late Period.

One can imagine the domestic quarrels and lawsuits that must have arisen over such crowding, but happily we are not left to speculate. A "law code" has survived in part on a fragmentary papyrus found at Hermopolis in the Demotic script,[31] and although the extant copy dates from Ptolemaic times, it is clearly a copy of a much older text of many centuries earlier.[32] Fortunately for our present purposes that part of the document we would call "the building code" is completely preserved. As one might expect, numerous laws address disputes that could have arisen only through the kind of overcrowded and congested conditions reflected by the excavations in East Karnak. Making additions to existing houses often led to conflict of ownership,[33] and litigants may have gone to court over ownership of a party wall[34] or a lane between two houses.[35]

Although a suitable space, apparently the length of a brick (32–40 centimeters), was to be left between houses,[36] it is not uncommon to find foundations sunk too close to a neighbor's house, causing that house to collapse.[37] Common complaints were that "my neighbour's drain discharges water into my house" or that his door opens onto my lot so that access to his house is across my property,[38] or that dirt from one house is cast into another.[39]

The urge to expand must have made it tempting to encroach upon the public thoroughfare, but the law was clear on this point. It was not permitted to build either on the public road ("the street of Pharaoh") or on a neighbor's lane. Failure to obey the law brought the dismantling of the offending structure and fifty lashes into the bargain![40] Now our excavations illuminate rather clearly the social milieu in which such draconian measures were enacted. Between the largest villa excavated and the property immediately to the east ran a narrow street that, in the mid–seventh century B.C., was approximately two meters wide (see fig. 29). After four successive resurfaces the villa owner relocated his eastern wall half a meter into the street, and in the next surfacing he or his heir gobbled up one whole meter of the original width, while his neighbor rebuilt his western wall forty-five centimeters to the west! Thus, two centuries after it was laid out, the "street" had been reduced to a width of barely fifty centimeters! If the laws of the Hermopolis code were harsh, it clearly reflected the simple fact that the situation was out of control.

The occupants of the East Karnak villas are, with one possible exception,[41] unknown to us, for no family archive has been recovered in the excavations; but their social status and occupation remain beyond doubt. The owners of the East Karnak dwellings clearly belonged to the upper middle class and were connected by occupation with the great Temple of Amun (see fig. 33a,b,c). We should undoubtedly be justified in extrapolating from the lists of house owners known to us from the house documents of Ptolemaic times in North Karnak, a few meters west of our area of excavation. On this basis we might identify the residents of East Karnak as midranking priests (shrine bearers and libation priests), an occasional "prophet" or superior priest, temple singers, one or two lector priests and a king's scribe, an eye doctor, soldiers, artisans, a chief carpenter, a cop-

Fig. 33a. Gold ring. East Karnak,
Late Period.

Fig. 33b. Feline goddess holding lotus. East
Karnak, Late Period.

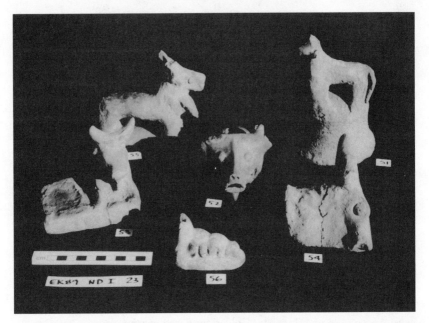

Fig. 33c. Terracotta animal images found beneath the floor of a villa. East Karnak, seventh or sixth century B.C.

persmith, and so forth.[42] None occupy the pinnacle of Theban society, but none are of the lower middle class or working class, either. That they all earn their living by service to the Temple of Amun is graphically illustrated by the evidence we possess of their *diet*. The faunal material recovered in our excavation of the villas reveals, in contrast to the record of other Egyptian sites, a surprisingly high percentage of bovine bones. Moreover, the majority of the animals in question, when aged by the osteologist, proved to have been no more than three years old when slaughtered. The luxury thus attested of being able to select and reject, argues the management of substantial herds, and points unmistakably to the temple, whose wealth in livestock was proverbial. These bulls and oxen thus had all ended their lives as sacrificial victims on the offering tables and altars of Amun and the other gods of Thebes, whose offering menus demanded the best of the herd and the choicest cuts. As was customary in every temple in ancient Egypt, the offerings constituted the income out of which came the rations or "salaries" for the entire staff of the temple, priests and laymen alike. The latter thus took their salaries "in kind" and enjoyed all their groceries at the expense of their temple employer. The cow and ox bones we have found on their kitchen floors provide concrete evidence of this system at work!

130

The residential sector described earlier was confined to the terrain stretching north of Taharqa's eastern thoroughfare extending the east-west axis of Karnak: south of that axial street the land was "zoned" for a different type of civic use. A swath of land between ten and fifteen meters in depth (north-south), lining the street on the south side, was given over to what we would call light industry. Here were located potters' kilns, complete with ash pits providing temper and holding circles for vessels yet to be fired or pots cooling down from their time in the ovens. The best preserved kiln (see fig. 34) had a flue facing northeast; many sherds were extracted from its contents and from the surrounding surface. The ovens were clearly sited so as to take advantage of the prevailing north winds yet not blow their smoke into the residential quarter. It is a good guess that these kilns provided the house owners of East Karnak with their kitchenware.

Apart from the industrial ovens just described, on the terrain south of Taharqa's axial street lay an unoccupied and undulating mound of mud-brick ruins. These dated from the Middle Kingdom, more than a thousand years earlier, when the houses of the city of Thebes had spread far to the east, but these had been abandoned and demolished even before

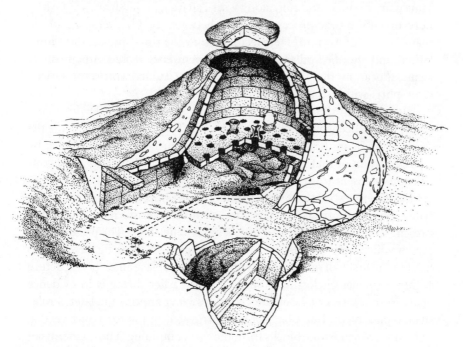

Fig. 34. Reconstruction of a kiln from remains found due east of the eastern Nektanebo gate. East Karnak, Saïte period.

the expulsion of the Hyksos and the founding of the New Kingdom in the sixteenth century B.C. From that time on the area was never to be resettled, and the Thebans of Taharqa's day were content to ignore it.

One feature of the Kushites' building program which forever commemorated their regime at Karnak was the series of small chapels (usually serviced by the Divine Worshiper) that ringed the great complex.[43] Most but not all of them provided cultic venues for the burgeoning Osirian cult and were dedicated to different avatars of the god. The earliest appears to have been the addition to the existing shrine of Osiris-Ruler-of-Eternity in the "Great-Mound-of-Wēse," which seems to have replaced an earlier mud-brick antechamber. Here scenes depict Amenirdis I, during the reign of Shebitku, engaged in foundation ceremonies and making an offering to Amun (see figs. 20, 23).[44] In the southwestern angle of the Montu enclosure Shebitku erected a shrine to "Osiris-Lord-of-Life," and again Amenirdis I officiates.[45] Early in Taharqa's reign two more chapels were erected within the environs of the temple of Montu and dedicated to Osiris-Giver-of-Life and Osiris-Lord-of-Eternity. In the latter Amenirdis I officiates, in the former her protégé Shepenwepet II and the young Amenirdis II, daughter of Taharqa.[46] The same pair celebrates the cult, along with Taharqa, in the shrine of "Osiris-Lord-of-Life" on the processional way between the Ptaḥ temple and the main Temple of Amun.[47] Here lectors intone the ritual and perform jubilation, and the *djed*-pillar is raised. Shepenwepet II and Amenirdis II again appear in the "Great Mound" in the ruined shrine of Osiris-Onnophris-within-the-*išd*-tree.[48]

Elsewhere on the periphery of the Karnak complex the Divine Worshipers have been more difficult to locate. They do not appear on the tenth pylon or in the little shrine of Osiris-Ptaḥ-Lord-of-Life erected by Taharqa south of that gateway.[49] Until recently they have also been conspicuously absent from East Karnak.[50]

In 1986-87 excavations were conducted in Temple C, a large enclosure lying about seventy-five meters east of the southeastern corner of the present temenos of Amun (see fig. 35; see also fig. 25).[51] The present temple, of which only foundation blocks remain in situ (see fig. 36a,b), was built in the first half of the third century B.C. to replace an earlier structure within a smaller enclosure. Nothing of the earlier shrine is in evidence apart from a series of casemate chambers lying around the later, Ptolemaic replacement; but a large *favissa* excavated in the forecourt yielded one hundred sandstone blocks from the earlier building. The fragments of relief brought to light depicted induction scenes, the god Amun, and Shepenwepet II and Amenirdis II (see fig. 36d–f). It seems likely, then,

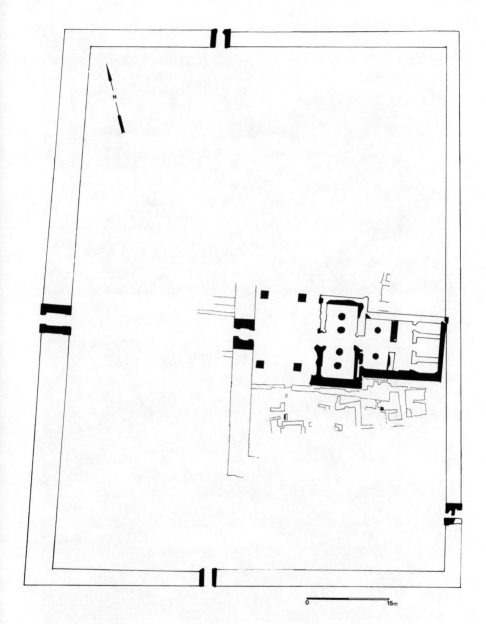

Fig. 35. Plan of Temple C. East Karnak, seventh through second century B.C.

Fig. 36a. Excavations of Temple C, 1987.

Fig. 36b. Remains of crypt, Temple C, Ptolemaic period.

Fig. 36c. Head of Divine Worshiper, Temple C, Twenty-fifth Dynasty.

Fig. 36d. Recumbent lion from the dromos, Temple C, Late Period.

Fig. 36e. Feathers of Amun-re, Temple C, Twenty-fifth Dynasty.

Fig. 36f. Fragment of scene of induction ceremony, Temple C, Twenty-fifth Dynasty.

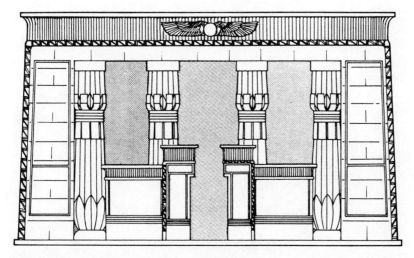

Fig. 37. Reconstruction of the putative facade of Temple C, Late Period (Lyla Brock).

that the earlier temple should be added to the list of edicules built by Taharqa and graced by his sister and daughter (see fig. 37).

Abutting on Temple C on its southern side was a small mud-brick complex that serviced the local community as a sanatorium. Increasingly common in the Late Period of Egypt's history, the temple sanatorium usually centered upon a statue, stela, or block covered with magical incantations and images inscribed on the surface (see fig. 38). The institution catered to "any man who makes the journey for deliverance of the poison of any male or female snake or any insect . . . because they were unable to obtain deliverance (elsewhere) from the bite of any venomous snake."[52] Often a particular god or illustrious ancestor was singled out and honored because of his reputed powers of therapy.[53] In the case of Temple C it was the god Khonsu, probably in his avatar as "Khonsu-the-child."[54] The mud-brick sanatorium of Temple C comprised half a dozen small cubicles built along the side of a small court, with a "kitchen" with an oven in the rear. The sacred object in this case was a beautiful quartzite stela of which we found several fragments and upon which was carved a standard magical text (see fig. 38). Possibly in the same building once stood the large stela of "Bentresh" now in the Louvre. This text, in the form of a "Novella" set in the reign of Ramesses II, six hundred years in the past, celebrated the therapeutic powers of the god Khonsu, who traveled to distant lands to heal a foreign princess.[55]

Prosperous, wealthy, and populous, Thebes during the fifty years of Sudanese rule enjoyed its last period as most favored city of the contem-

Fig. 38. Fragment of a cippos from the sanatorium, Temple C, Late Period.

porary dynasty. Though its subsequent decline was gradual, never again would it thrive as the principal power center of the realm. The unexpected events of 671 to 663 were not only to begin the drain on its treasury but also to label it (with some justification) as the center of dissent and resistance in a reactionary south.

THE END OF THE TWENTY-FIFTH DYNASTY IN EGYPT

From Dynasties 22 through 26 Egypt's desert frontiers, both east and west, remained reasonably secure. On the east the Wady Hammamat quarries were extensively worked, at least under the Twenty-sixth Dynasty, and the Red Sea offered, as it always had, an easily negotiated transit corridor to the south.[1] If bedu continued to filter into the valley through the Wady ʿArabeh or one of the wadies farther south which debouched into Middle Egypt, the government could easily co-opt them and confine them in settlements as impressed paramilitary.[2]

The problems of the Western Desert gave the impression of being intractable but in the event did not cause the Egyptians undue hardship. The Nubian invaders of the late eighth century appreciated what the oasis chain meant as a transit corridor: at least as early as Piankhy's twenty-fourth year (716 B.C.) Kushite control had been extended as far north as Dakhleh.[3] Before 700 B.C. a Kushite presence is attested at Baḥriyeh.[4] Despite the temporary setback to Egyptian interests in the west brought about by the defeat of Apries's forces in 571 B.C. at the hands of the Cyrenians,[5] Egypt's occupation of the western oases remained unchallenged[6] and from about 600 B.C. was institutionalized in the form of a regular nomarchate.[7] The Libyan enclaves of the North African coast which had dominated the Egyptian military and even the Tanite kingship were effectively reduced by Psammetichus I in his eleventh year (654 B.C.),[8] and whatever remnant remained suffered a death blow in the civil war that erupted between Apries and Amasis.

THE EASTERN FRONTIER IN THE LATE PERIOD

In such inclusive phrases as "from x to y" in which the extremities of the state are specified, the southern boundary is always stated to be Elephantine and the cataract, but the northern varies. In the earliest times it is "the East," that is, the long desert tract bordering the Pelusiac branch, by the end of the third millennium "the Ways of Horus," the beginning of the transit corridor through the North Sinai. Under the Hyksos it suffered a southwestern withdrawal to Pi-Hathor on the *Rḥ.ty*-water, but the New Kingdom firmly established the extremity of Egypt proper at the fortress of Sile (Tell Hebwa). And even though Sile's role as border fort and entry point had long since been taken over by other towns by 700 B.C., the Pelusiac branch near which it was located continued to offer the most easily defended line on the east.[9]

The five centuries that elapsed between the end of Dynasty 20 and the accession of Psamtek I constitute a virtual "dark age" in the history of the eastern frontier. As far as we know, no special effort was expended during this time to fortify the Sinai frontier, and yet the principalities along the eastern side of the Delta—Tanis, Ranofer, Pi-sopdu—suffered no ill effects from bedu infiltration. During the tenth and ninth centuries no major hostile power lay in hither Asia, waiting to pounce on the Nile Valley: until the accession of Sargon the Tanite kings used the small states of Palestine and the coast as effective buffers against Assyria. Indeed, as late as the Twenty-fourth Dynasty it was still considered possible "to extend the frontier," and both Sabaco and Taharqa proved that Egyptian forces could meet invaders in the Philistine plain and hold the line there.

The creation of the Suez Canal with its north-south alignment completely distorts one's directional sense in the eastern Delta, and one must block it from consciousness if the ancient lay of the land is to be appreciated, for the now defunct Pelusiac River, the easternmost branch of the Nile, ran in a northeasterly direction. Since the silting-up of this watercourse, desert conditions have prevailed along its lower reaches, and it is only in the twentieth century that the tract of land between Ṣalḥiyeh and the canal has been placed under cultivation. In antiquity, however, lagoons and lakes proliferated as one descended the Pelusiac branch towards Pelusium at its mouth,[10] and these posed hazards to those attempting an entry into Egypt from the north (see map 4). Travelers proceeding from Gaza would have been obliged to hug the coast, if only for the water holes, and at the Delta terminus of the route[11] would have had no other option than to pass by Pelusium. At this point they would have had either to cross the river—a daunting task, as there was neither bridge nor ferry—or continue their journey down the east bank,[12] negotiating the treacherous terrain between the lagoons. An even less inviting corridor of approach from Asia lay through the Wady Tumilat. To gain access to this route, which debouched at Lake Timsah, the traveler would

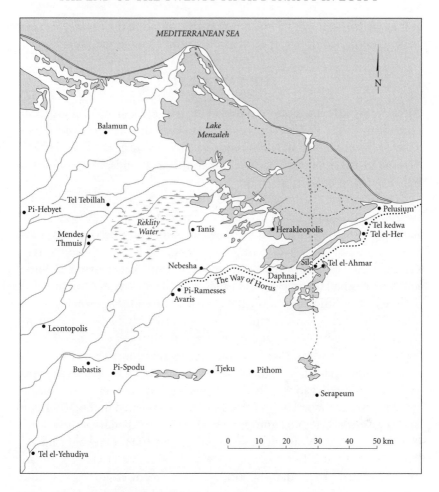

Map 4. The northeastern Nile Delta in antiquity.

have to strike south from Pelusium to the Bitter Lakes or leave the coastal route at Wady el-Arish and proceed inland across North Sinai.[13] This second itinerary had, in fact, been used by bedu from time immemorial[14] as well as Egyptians (in reverse direction) seeking access to the Sinai mines, and to this end the Ramessides had fortified the southern approaches to the Wady.[15]

It is a measure of the supreme confidence of the Kushites, or perhaps their lack of foresight, that there is no evidence that they took any steps to fortify the eastern Delta. With the exception of Sile, all the major frontier tells along the line of the Pelusiac branch are no earlier than Saïte in date.[16] (The date of the founding of Pelusium may be considered moot.)[17]

It may well be that, with a fine army and a toehold in the Levant, Taharqa never entertained the prospect that war could come to the Delta.

THE CASUS BELLI

After the rebuff meted out to Assyrian arms at Eltekeh and Taharqa's incursions into the Philistine plain in the 680s,[18] the die was cast with respect to Egypto-Assyrian relations for seventy-five years to come. Taharqa became in Assyrian eyes "accursed of all the great gods,"[19] and no casus belli needed to be sought.

The tracts of southern Palestine became the contested territory between Assyria and the Twenty-fifth Dynasty. As early as about 715–712 B.C. Sargon had established a short-lived trading post between Gaza and Raphia, possibly at Tel-Ruqeish,[20] but presumably this did not survive Hezekiah's revolt and the Battle of Eltekeh. From 701 to 680 B.C. Shebitku and Taharqa had the upper hand in the coastal cities from Gaza to Sidon, although it is difficult to know the precise nature of the formal relationship.[21] The increase in Egyptian influence probably benefited from the stasis in Assyria preceding and pursuant to the murder of Sennacherib,[22] but the Assyrian administration immediately responded. Sometime early in the seventh century B.C. the western Negev was fortified and provided with men and provisions.[23] In 679, as Esarhaddon's interest in this distant march revived, a squad of his troops suddenly appeared in the sheikhdom of Arṣia south of Raphia and packed off the local sheikh and his son in chains to Assyria.[24] It is tempting to postulate a friendly relationship between this tribe and Taharqa which Esarhaddon refused to tolerate; at any rate the sequel proves that the local Arabs were cowed into cooperation thanks to Assyria's overwhelming presence in the area. Esarhaddon was preparing the way for full-scale invasion.

In 677 B.C. Esarhaddon descended in force upon Egypt's allies situated on his western flank. Sidon, the most powerful,[25] was attacked and defeated; its king fled ignominiously over the sea but was captured and beheaded.[26] The king of Tyre capitulated and was forced to sign a treaty with Assyria,[27] and lesser rulers as far away as the Taurus followed suit.[28] The subsequent conscription of "all the kings from the Hatti-land and from the sea-coast" to contribute to Assyrian construction work underscored the complete and unrivaled domination Esarhaddon enjoyed in the Levant.

The events of the next six years were momentous in the history of Egypt.[29] The initial Assyrian attack along the northern Sinai coast was repulsed by Taharqa in 674 B.C.,[30] but whether through overconfidence or inferior intelligence, he failed to detect the Assyrian advance three years later. It may also be put down, in large part, to the cunning of Esarhaddon. The local Sinai Arabs, for whatever reason—had they been dismayed at Taharqa's inability to aid Arṣia?—offered assistance to the Assyrians and supplied them with water in their passage over the Sinai.[31] This in itself argues in favor of a route that diverged from the coastal route. Even though the latter presented a much less daunting avenue of access to the Delta than it would a century later, the fortifications at Sile (Tel Hebwa) were presumably still standing and would constitute an "early warning" post for the defenders. But Esarhaddon in his inscriptions does not mention this route, and his (albeit overblown) description of the hazards of snakes, reptiles, and waterless tracts argues in favor of an in-land desert track.

The Assyrians arrived in the Delta at a place called Migdol, which, in view of the plethora of fortified enclosures of that designation, is impossi-ble to locate.[32] Here apparently some of the "wicked enemy" attempted to block the way, an act of desperation by defenders caught off guard. But Esarhaddon easily brushed them aside and marched down the eastern margin of the Delta, the "Tract of Pre," to Ishhupri. This place too is difficult to locate, but its position clearly must be southwest of Migdol.[33] Here at last Taharqa appeared with his main forces.

Although he had obviously been outmaneuvered, it is not apparent in what respect. Had he expected the Assyrians to use the much traveled coastal route and in anticipation posted the mass of his troops at Sile? In this case he now found himself outflanked. Or had he not reckoned on a summer attack and so had not mustered his army? Assyrian sources indi-cate that Esarhaddon's plans for a second attempt at invasion were fraught with concern, and oracles and reassurances were required to steel the nerves of the invasion forces. In particular Taharqa was expected to try to block the Assyrian march in the Shephelah around Ashkelon.[34] In the event, he took advantage neither of his strategic position in the south-ern Levant nor of the tactical advantage the eastern Delta bestowed on his defenses. It may well be that both the direction and timing of Esarhaddon's advance came as a complete surprise. Taharqa had, in fact, been "outgeneraled."

But Taharqa was not lacking in personal bravery, and his elev-enth-hour resistance proved stiff. For two weeks he retreated down the eastern side of the Delta, contesting every kilometer of ground and sus-taining arrow-shot wounds on five occasions. But fifteen days were insufficient to repair old fortifications or rear new ones where none had existed. Memphis fell within a single day and was given over to demolition and conflagration. Taharqa had no time to collect his family or his treasury (both of which fell into Assyrian hands) but retreated hastily to Thebes. Resistance instantly collapsed: Lower Egypt and Memphis were in Assyrian hands. The speed of the campaign, seventeen days from the breach of the frontier to victory, was matched in degree of achievement only by the singularity of the event: it had been just one thousand years since a foreign (non-African) power had established itself by force on Egyptian soil!

The triumph, to the Assyrians, was final. The capital destroyed, the major district capitals subverted, the enemy decimated, and their leader in flight—what more need be said? The entire treasury and armory of the Egyptians now lay in Esarhaddon's hands: Egypt had lost the very wherewithal to make war! Fittingly the last word must be that of Esarhaddon himself: "I had a stela made with my name-inscription and had written thereon the praise of the valor of my lord Asshur, my own mighty deeds (when I was marching upon the trustworthy oracles of my lord Asshur), as well as my triumphant personal achievements, and I erected it for all days to come (so that) it be seen by the entire enemy country!"[35] Within ten years no Assyrian remained in Egypt. The stela has not been found.

EPILOGUE

lthough no one realized it at the time, the disaster of 671 effectually terminated Kushite aspirations to control the entire Nile Valley to the Mediterranean. Two further Assyrian invasions in 666 and 663 B.C. drove home the point that Kushite arms could not sustain the claim to hegemony over Egypt which the kings of Napata asserted. And even in the face of the Assyrians' brutality and ineptitude (which brought about their own retreat from Africa before 660 B.C.), Assyria's geopolitical stance towards Kush was shared by most Egyptians. The regents Assyria designated in Egypt, Necho of Saïs and his son and successor Psamtek, both embraced Assyrian hostility towards the Napatan regime and perpetuated it long after Assyrian troops had been withdrawn.

Taharqa and his successor, Tanwetamani, were to return, to be sure; but the sudden appearance of Assyrian forces had sent them scurrying southwards without risking battle. Thebes, where they temporarily holed up, was far more sympathetic to Kush than Middle and Lower Egypt, and perhaps here they thought a stand might be made. The swiftness of the Assyrian advance, however, terrified the southerners, and by the time Ashurbanipal's advanced guard entered the southern city, the army of Napata had retreated to its homeland. Despite pretentious claims echoing in the royal titulary and ideology for centuries in the future, the Kushites were never again to occupy Egypt.

The new regime in Egypt centered upon Saïs in the Delta. Because it derived its dubious authority through appointment by the king of Assyria, Saïs had to establish its legitimacy by force. As Assyria grew weaker thanks to civil war and a prolonged conflict in Elam, Psamtek I (664–610 B.C.) declared independence and sought to bolster his claim through the recruitment of mercenaries from Lydia, Ionia, and the Levant. Now he could face the south with a marginal superiority in personnel and equipment.

By the close of the seventh century the Egyptians were taking active steps once and for all to neutralize the surviving Twenty-fifth Dynasty. A garrison of Greek mercenaries was ensconced at Aswan before 600 B.C., and a fleet of warships assembled. Necho II led a flotilla of two dozen vessels southward about 598 B.C., ostensibly against the Kushites, and in 593 Psamtek II dispatched an even larger force comprising Egyptian, Greek, Judaean, and Aramaean contingents. While the frail king remained in the comparative safety of Aswan, his troops proceeded southwards led by Generals Potasimto and Ahmose, the latter of whom had enjoyed some limited military success in Asia. The battle was joined somewhere north of Dongola, and the Egyptians emerged victorious. The Kushites sustained thousands of casualties and could only watch as Napata and surrounding towns went up in flames. Anlamani, the Kushite king, disappeared, and for more than a century our sources virtually cease.

The events of 593 made Egypt secure and forever drove a geographical wedge between it and the Sudan: any hope the Twenty-fifth Dynasty may have enjoyed of once again returning to the Lower Nile and Delta perished. Although Kushite kings continued to be buried in pyramids according to Egyptian custom up to the early Christian era and to employ Egyptian art and architectural forms even longer, these cultural manifestations became increasingly bastardized and degenerate. Probably before the middle of the sixth century B.C. the royal family had abandoned Napata as a residence, although royal burials continued at Nuri until about 300 B.C. By the fifth century the descendants of the Twenty-fifth Dynasty had turned Meroe, two hundred kilometers north of modern Khartum, into their capital, and there they survived largely cut off from the north, a culture gone to seed in terms of its Egyptian roots. As a hybrid exponent, however, of African themes in Egyptian forms it thrived for eight centuries. Finally, about A.D. 320, the sixty-first successor of Tanwetamani disappeared, and the state was overwhelmed by the rising kingdom of Axum in Ethiopia.[1]

But historical memory had reserved for Kush an ironic twist of misinterpretation. In later times Nubia and Kush drifted into a remote and mythic position in the collective memory of the Mediterranean peoples. "Ethiopia" became an archetype of human society in its pristine innocence, divinely created and still close to the gods. The retention in the Sudan of forms of ancient Egyptian culture long after they had disappeared in Egypt proper deceived the observer into wrongly concluding that pharaonic society had originated in "Ethiopia." Forms of government, architecture, and the arts, even the very hieroglyphic script itself, all were claimed to have been invented by the Kushites and later adopted by the Egyptians. The close contact, moreover, between Egypt and Kush which would have been required to rectify these erroneous notions was lacking as the first millennium B.C. drew to a close. Political authority having passed even farther south, from Napata to Meroe, the region of the first two cataracts degenerated into a no-man's-land, dominated by marauding tribesmen. Only the ruined temples remained as a silent witness of the glories that once had been.

ABBREVIATIONS

AAAE   W. S. Smith and W. K. Simpson. *The Art and Architecture of Ancient Egypt.* 3d ed. New Haven, 1998.

ABL   Assyrian and Babylonian Letters. R. F. Harper, Assyrian and Babylonian Letters belonging to the Kouyunjik collection(s) of the British Museum. Chicago, 1892–1914.

AEO   Sir A. H. Gardiner. *Ancient Egyptian Onomastica.* 3 vols. Oxford, 1947.

AEPHE   *Annuaire de l'Ecole Pratique des Hautes Etudes.*

AfO   *Archiv für Orientforschung.*

AION   *Annali dell'Istituto Universitario Orientale di Napoli.*

AJSL   *American Journal of Semitic Languages and Literatures.*

ANET²   J. B. Pritchard, ed. *Ancient Near Eastern Texts Relating to the Old Testament,* 2d ed. Princeton.

ASAE   *Annales du Service des Antiquites de l'Egypte.*

BA   *Biblical Archaeologist.*

BASOR   *Bulletin of the American Schools of Oriental Research.*

BIFAO   *Bulletin de l'Institut Français d'Archéologie Orientale.*

BM   British Museum.

BN   *Biblische Notizen.*

BSFE   *Bulletin de la Société française d'Egyptologie.*

CAD   *Chicago Assyrian Dictionary.*

CAH   *Cambridge Ancient History,* 3rd ed. Cambridge, 1975.

CCG   Cairo. Catalogue Générale.

CdÉ	*Chronique d'Égypt.*
CRIPEL	*Cahiers de Recherches de l'Institut de Papyrologie et d'Egyptologie de Lille.*
DG	H. Gauthier. *Dictionnaire des noms géographiques contenus dans les textes hiéroglyphiques.* 7 vols. Cairo, 1925–31.
EA	El-Amarna Tablets.
GM	*Göttinger Miszellen.*
HO	Sir A. H. Gardiner and J. Černy. *Hieratic Ostraca.* Oxford, 1956.
HSLN	B. G. Trigger. *History and Settlement of Lower Nubia.* New Haven, 1965.
HTR	*Harvard Theological Review.*
IEJ	*Israel Exploration Journal.*
JAOS	*Journal of the American Oriental Society.*
JARCE	*Journal of the American Research Center in Egypt.*
JCS	*Journal of Cuneiform Studies.*
JEA	*Journal of Egyptian Archeology.*
JESHO	*Journal of the Social and Economic History of the Orient.*
JNES	*Journal of Near Eastern Studies.*
JSSEA	*Journal of the Society for the Study of Egyptian Antiquities.*
Kawa	M. F. Laming MacAdam. *The Temples of Kawa.* Oxford, 1947.
KRI	K. A. Kitchen. *Ramesside Inscriptions.* 7 vols. Oxford, 1968–88.
LD	C. R. Lepsius. *Denkmaeler aus Aegypten und Nubien.* 6 vols. Berlin, 1849–59.
LdÄ	*Lexikon der Aegyptologie.*
LdR	H. Gauthier. *Le Livre des rois d'Egypte.* 5 vols. Cairo, 1916.
LRL	J. Černy. *Late Ramesside Letters.* Brussels, 1939.
MDAIK	*Mitteilungen des Deutschen Archaeologischen Instituts zu Kairo.*
MIOF	*Mitteilungen des Instituts für Orientforschung.*
NAWG	*Nachrichten von der Akademie der Wissenschaften in Goettingen.*
P-M	B. Porter and R. Moss. *Topographical Bibliography of Ancient Egyptian Texts, Reliefs and Paintings.* 7 vols. Oxford, 1927–99.
RA	*Revue Assyriologique.*

ABBREVIATIONS

RdÉ	*Revue d'Égyptologie.*
RIDA	*Revue Internationale des Droits d'Antiquite.*
RT	*Recueil de Travaux.*
SAK	*Studien zur Altaegyptischen Kultur.*
UF	*Ugaritische Forschungen.*
Urk.	G. Steindorff, K. Sethe, H. Grapow, and W. Helck. *Urkunden des aegyptischen Altertums.* Leipzig and Berlin, 1903–99.
Wb.	A. Erman and H. Grapow. *Woerterbuch der aegyptischen Sprache.* 5 vols. Leipzig, 1926–31.
ZA	*Zeitschrift für Assyriologie*
ZÄS	*Zeitschrift für aegyptischen Sprache und Altertumskunde.*

NOTES

INTRODUCTION

1. B. G. Trigger, in *Études Nubiennes* (Cairo, 1978), 317–18; idem, "Nubian, Negro, Black, Nilotic?" in S. Hochfield and E. Riefstahl, eds., *Africa in Antiquity* (Brooklyn, 1979), 1:26–35.

2. N. Grimal, *A History of Ancient Egypt* (Oxford, 1992), 21; cf. J. D. Clark, *Proceedings of the Prehistoric Society* 37 (1971): 34–79.

3. K. W. Butzer, *Environment and Archaeology* (Chicago, 1971), 547; J. M. Renfrew, "The Archaeological Evidence for the Domestication of Plants: Methods and Problems," in P. J. Ucko and G. D. Dimbleby, eds., *Domestication and Exploitation of Plants and Animals* (London, 1969), 149–72; J. K. Kozlowski and B. Ginter, in L. Krzyzaniak, ed., *Late Prehistory of the Nile Basin and Sahara* (Poznan, Poland, 1989), 176.

4. J. Eiwanger, "Die Archäologie der späten Vorgeschichte: Bestand und Perspektiven," in J. Assmann, ed., *Problems and Priorities in Egyptian Archaeology* (London, 1987), 83.

5. P. Červiček, "Notes on the Chronology of the Nubian Rock Art to the End of the Bronze Age," in *Études Nubiennes* (Cairo, 1978), 36–38; M. A. Berger, "Predynastic Animal-Headed Boats from Hierakonpolis and Southern Egypt," in R. Friedman and B. Adams, eds., *The Followers of Horus* (Oxford, 1991), 118. *HSLN,* 68–73; B. G. Trigger, "The Rise of Egyptian Civilization," in B. G. Trigger, B. Kemp, D. O'Connor, and A. B. Lloyd, *Ancient Egypt: A Social History* (Cambridge, 1983), 42–43.

6. Cf. the First Dynasty trapezoidal fort at Elephantine: J. Leclant, "Fouilles et travaux en Égypte et au Soudan, 1987–1988," *Orientalia* 58 (1989): 397.

7. A. Loprieno, *Topos und Mimesis: Zum Ausländer in der ägyptischen Literatur* (= Ägyptologische Abhandlungen 48) (Wiesbaden, 1988).

8. D. O'Connor, "Early States along the Nubian Nile," in W. V. Davies, ed., *Egypt and Africa* (London, 1993), 147.

9. On the A-group in general, see T. Säve-Söderbergh, "Preliminary Report of the Scandinavian Archaeological Investigations between Faras and Gemal, November 1962–March 1963," *Kush* 12 (1964): 24–27; H.-A. Nordström, *Neo-*

lithic and A-Group Sites (Uppsala, 1972); Trigger et al., *Ancient Egypt*, 42–43; H. Smith, "The Development of the 'A-group' in Northern Nubia," in Davies, *Egypt and Africa*, 92–111; D. A. Welsby, "Nubia," in D. B. Redford, ed., *The Oxford Encyclopedia of Ancient Egypt* (New York, 2001), 2:552–53.

10. Cf. W. Y. Adams and H.-A. Nördström, "The Archaeological Survey on the West Bank of the Nile: Third Season, 1961–62," *Kush* 11 (1963): 16–20.

11. W. B. Emery, *Archaic Egypt* (London, 1962), 47, fig. 6 (Narmer); W. K. Simpson, *Heka-nefer and the Dynastic Material from Toshke and Arminna* (New Haven, 1963), 48f, fig. 39 (Hor-aha); A. J. Arkell, "Varia Sudanica," *JEA* 36 (1950): 28–30; idem, *A History of the Sudan to 1821* (London, 1959), 39f, fig. 5 (Djer? But see now W. J. Murnane, *JNES* 46 [1987]: 282–85); Z. Žaba, *The Rock Inscriptions of Lower Nubia* (Prague, 1974). 240 (Wadji).

12. W. M. F. Petrie, *The Royal Tombs of the Earliest Dynasties* (London, 1901), vol. 2, pls. 3:2, 7:11, and 11:1.

13. See "The Products of the South" in Chapter 3.

1. EGYPTIANS AND NUBIANS

1. On the "Egyptocentricity" of native rationalization, and its implications, see S. Morenz, *Egyptian Religion* (Ithaca, N.Y., 1973), 44–49.

2. Cf. the great hymn to the Disc col. 8 (M. Sandman, *Texts from the Time of Akhenaten* [= *Bibl. Aeg.* 8] [Brussels, 1938], 94–95): "The foreign lands of Syria and Kush, as well as the land of Egypt, thou (the sun-god) has set every man in his place . . . their colours are different, since thou hast made foreigners different." Cf. *ANET²*, 365–66.

3. H. G. Fischer, "The Nubian Mercenaries of Gebelein during the First Intermediate Period," *Kush* 9 (1961): 56 (cf. also the bushy hair in the stelae herein referred to); Trigger, "Nubian, Negro, Black, Nilotic?" 1:31–33, and T. Säve-Söderbergh, "Te-khet, the Cultural and Socio-political Structure of a Nubian Princedom in Tuthmosid Times," in Davies, *Egypt and Africa*, 187.

4. E. H. Warmington, in *Oxford Classical Dictionary* (Oxford, 1970), 408.

5. Cf. the PN *P3-wrm*, "the Black": N.-C. Grimal, *La Stèle triomphale de Pi(ꜥankh)y au Musée du Caire* (Cairo, 1981), 22 n. 55.

6. The high-flown term for the script: *Wb.* II, 180:13; *HO*, pl. 6, 1:3.

7. Cf. Sinuhe, 31–32.

8. Cf. Sall. I, 8:1; L. H. Lesko, *A Dictionary of Late Egyptian* (Berkeley, 1982), 1:2.

9. Cf. D. B. Redford, "Egypt and Western Asia in the Old Kingdom," *JARCE* 23 (1986): 125–26.

10. A. H. Gardiner, "The Memphite Tomb of the General Ḥaremḥab," *JEA* 39 (1953): 7–8; W. Helck, "Die bedrohung Palästinas durch einwandernde Gruppe am ende der 18. und am anfang der 19. Dynastie," *Vetus Testamentum* 18 (1968): 475–76.

11. *Urk.* IV, 138:15–16.

12. Senwosret III's frontier stela, Berlin 1157; S. J. Seidlmayer, "Zu Fundort

und Aufstellungskontext der grossen Semna-Stela Sesostris III," *SAK* 28 (2000): 233–42. It is somewhat ironic that the speaker came from a line with Nubian blood on the distaff side! R. Morkot, *The Black Pharaohs: Egypt's Nubian Rulers* (London, 2000), 53.

13. On Nubian magicians' prowess, see M. Lichtheim, *Ancient Egyptian Literature* (Berkeley, 1980), 3:142–50.

14. D. Dunham and J. Janssen, *Second Cataract Forts,* vol. 1, *Semna-Kumma* (Boston, 1960), pl. 82; W. Helck, "Eine Stele des Vizekönigs Wśr-Śt.t," *JNES* 14 (1955): 22–31 and pl. II; idem, *Urk.* IV, 1343–44; S. Morschauser, "Approbation or Disapproval? The Conclusion of the Letter of Amenophis II to User-Satet, Viceroy of Kush . . . ," *SAK* 24 (1997): 203–22. The meaning seems to be that if no Egyptian official is present to inventory and physically transfer the taxes to Egypt, it will have to be left to the natives themselves, and inefficiency, losses, and excuses will be the result. That the content of the letter is, broadly speaking, instructional does not mark it formally as an exemplar of *sb3yt;* and in the present writer's view it should be taken for what it is, namely, the spontaneous obiter dicta of a monarch celebrating an anniversary.

15. H̱st: D. B. Redford, *Pharaonic King-lists, Annals, and Day-books* (Toronto, 1986), 242 n. 54.

16. E.g., *Urk.* VII, 5:17.

17. Ibid., IV, 83:6.

18. D. B. Redford, "The Tod Inscription of Senwosret I and Early Twelfth Dynasty Involvement in Nubia and the South," *JSSEA* 17 (1987): 42–43 (X+30).

19. *Urk.* IV, 84:1–11.

20. Cf., e.g., ibid., 140:5; Žaba, *Rock Inscriptions of Lower Nubia,* no. 73. D. Randall-MacIver and C. L. Woolley, *Buhen* (Philadelphia, 1911), 91.

21. Cf. Sinuhe B, 121–22: "Who plants papyrus on a mountain?"

22. Cf. H. Te Velde, *Seth, God of Confusion: A Study of His Role in Egyptian Mythology and Religion* (Leiden, 1967).

23. Cf. the expression (mineral x) ḥr ḫ3st.f, "in its ore": J. E. Harris, *Lexicographical Studies in Ancient Egyptian Minerals* (Berlin, 1961), 56.

24. K. Zibelius-Chen, *Die ägyptische Expansion nach Nubien* (Wiesbaden, 1988), 218.

25. Admittedly, the use of the term *Chaos* by Egyptologists may have more appropriate application when rendering the "Primordial Waters," the Nun, but only by recourse to Greek Χάος, "the Abyss, the Void," But even here, the terms do not coincide. Χάος in its original connotation is entirely negative, associated with Blackness, Night (Hesiod, *Theogony* ii, 116–25), and through Night with war, death, grief, and famine (ibid., iv, 211–14). That is certainly not the "Nun." Only with the Stoics was it identified with a primal ocean, inchoate and disordered (cf. Ovid, *Metamorphoses* i, 7), out of which came the universe. Since the term has undergone such an evolution and is apt by moderns to be misconstrued (cf., e.g., M. Görg, "Zur Ikonographie der Chaos," *BN* 14 [1981], 18), it is better to avoid its use altogether.

26. Cf. Ḥeka-nefer of Toshke: Simpson, *Heka-nefer and the Dynastic Material from Toshke and Arminna;* Säve-Söderbergh, "Te-khet, the Cultural and Socio-political Structure of a Nubian Princedom in Tuthmosid Times," 186–94; Amenemhet of Tekh-het: idem, "Preliminary Report of the Scandinavian Joint Expedition," *Kush* 11 (1963): fig. 3. See Chapter 6.

27. See Chapter 6.

28. Cf. G. Husson and D. Valbelle, *L'État et les institutions en Égypte* (Paris, 1992), 115–16; the best example attested archaeologically is that of the "pan-grave" people. On these, see now P. Lacovara, "Pan-grave People," in D. B. Redford, ed., *The Oxford Encyclopedia of Ancient Egypt* 3:20–22.

29. H. Fischer, *Dendera in the Old Kingdom and Its Aftermath* (Locust Valley, N.Y., 1968), 138 (foreigners residing in Dendera); idem, "Nubian Mercenaries of Gebelein during the First Intermediate Period," pl. X (Nubians and Sa'idis in the same town).

30. Cf. the will of Senimose: *Urk.* IV, 1066 (324) l. x+12.

31. On the Medjay, see K. Zibelius, *Afrikanische Orts- und Völkernamen in hieroglyphischen und hieratischen Texten* (Wiesbaden, 1972), 133–37; Zibelius-Chen, *Die ägyptische Expansion nach Nubien,* 59–63 and passim.

32. Cf. Anast. V.16.6; EA 287:33, 71–75.

33. Anast. IV.16.5.

34. P. Abbott, Docket A,16; B,16.

35. Cf. the family of Ḥek-reshu and Ḥekerneheḥ: B. Bryan, *The Reign of Tuthmosis IV* (Baltimore, 1991), 41–43; 259–61.

36. Generations of Hyksos, Libyans, and Greeks, though born in Egypt, were never considered "Egyptian" by the natives solely on the fact of their place of birth.

37. H. Goedicke, *Königliche Dokumente aus den Alten Reich* (Wiesbaden, 1967), Abb. 10.

38. BM 10326 vs. 5–6; Turin vs. 5–6; *LRL,* 19 and 32. It is possible, however, that the remarks here have more personal rather than racial reference.

39. Cf. *Urk.* IV, 1369. The document is a petition from the king's barber that such discrimination *not* be meted out to *his* foreign slave. See further D. B. Redford, *The Asiatic Wars of Thutmose III* (Leiden, 2003), pt. II, 3.1.

40. Cf. Morenz, *Egyptian Religion,* 53; P. Bremner-Rhind, colophon 33–38 (R. O. Faulkner, *The Papyrus Bremner-Rhind* [Brussels, 1933], 34) on the sacred books; *Dendera V,* 54, 60f, and pl. 361; J. Vercoutter, "Les Haou-Nebout," *BIFAO* 48 (1949): 172; S. Sauneron, "Un document égyptien relatif à la divinisation de la reine Arsinoé II—Les possédés," *BIFAO* 60 (1960): 111–12.

41. T. Säve-Söderbergh, "A Buhen Stela from the Second Intermediate Period," *JEA* 35 (1949): 50–54; W. Helck, *Historisch-biographische Texte der 2. Zwischenzeit und neue Texte der 18. Dynastie* (Wiesbaden, 1975), no. 116; D. B. Redford, "Textual Sources for the Hyksos Period," in E. Oren, ed., *The Hyksos: New Historical and Archaeological Perspectives* (Philadelphia, 1997), 5 no. 16.

2. THE PROBLEM OF FRONTIERS

1. See J. M. Galán, *Victory and Border. Terminology Related to Egyptian Imperialism in the XVIIIth Dynasty* (Hildesheim, 1995).

2. Ḥwdt: *Wb*. III, 355:12; A. De Buck, *Egyptian Readingbook* (Leiden, 1948), 70:11; this passage from Beni Hasan proves that not even a provincial governor could accede to his patrimony before the boundaries of his township had been resurveyed.

3. Cf. the "office of the granaries": A. H. Gardiner, *Late Egyptian Miscellanies* (Brussels, 1933), 87:15–16.

4. Nauri 24–25 (= KRI 1:50; cf. 231:16); cf. H. Gauthier, *La grande inscription dédicatoire d'Abydos* (Cairo, 1912), 84; T. E. Peet, *The Great Tomb-Robberies of the Twentieth Egyptian Dynasty* (Oxford, 1930), 1:134 n. 2; A. H. Gardiner, *The Wilbour Papyrus* II (Oxford, 1941–52), 78 n. 5. See, in general, S. L. D. Katary, *Land Tenure in the Ramesside Period* (London, 1989).

5. KRI 1:45:5 (lit. "which makes [or 'is made by'] inventory").

6. Cf. Amenemope vii 12–viii 10.

7. *mhwt*: D. Franke, *Altägyptische Verwandtschaftsbezeichnungen im Mittleren Reich* (Hamburg, 1983), 179 ff and 197–203.

8. Shipwrecked Sailor, 133–34 and 169.

9. Cf. the colorful description in Merikare. D. B. Redford, *Egypt, Canaan, and Israel in Ancient Times* (Princeton, 1992), 67.

10. Cf. Anast. VI. 4:11–5:5; H. Goedicke, "Papyrus Anastasi VI. 51–56," *SAK* 14 (1987): 83–98; Redford, *Egypt, Canaan, and Israel*, 228; the Semna Despatches indicate how closely the southern frontier was watched for movements of foreigners: P. C. Smither, "The Semnah Despatches," *JEA* 31 (1945): 3–10.

11. Berlin 14753: K. Sethe, *Ägyptische Lesestücke zum Gebrauch im Akademischen Unterricht. Texte des Mittleren Reiches* (Leipzig, 1928), 84–85. Cf. Morkot, *Black Pharaohs*, 57.

12. Berlin 1157: Sethe, *Ägyptische Lesestücke zum Gebrauch im Akademischen Unterricht*, 84.

13. W. A. Ward, *Index of Egyptian Administrative and Religious Titles of the Middle Kingdom* (Beirut, 1982), nos. 56–57; cf. *Wb*. I, 164:25–26; J. J. Clère and J. Vandier, *Textes de la première période intermédiaire* (Brussels, 1949), no. 13 (p. 8).

14. H. G. Fischer, *Dendera in the Third Millennium B.C., down to the Theban domination of Upper Egypt* (Locust Valley, N.Y., 1968), 12 n. 56.

15. *Urk*. I, 254:12 (Qar); cf. ibid., 123:14 (Harkhuf); P. Montet, *Kêmi* VI (1938), 100 (Tjarity).

16. On the significance of the cataract and first township (*T3 Zty*) as a great divide, see D. O'Connor, in Hochfield and Riefstahl, *Africa in Antiquity*, 1:53; R. Morkot, "Aswan," in Redford, *Oxford Encyclopedia of Ancient Egypt*, 1:151–54.

17. *Urk*. VII, 5:17–21.

18. L. Habachi, *Elephantine IV: The Sanctuary of Heqaib* (Mainz, 1985), pl. 25.

19. *Urk.* VII, 4.

20. Ibid., 9.

21. Habachi, *Elephantine IV.*

22. P. C. Smither, "An Old Kingdom Letter Concerning the Crimes of Count Sabni," *JEA* 28 (1942): 16–19.

23. *Urk.* IV, 814.

3. NUBIA

1. P-M 5:245–50.

2. H. Goedicke, "The Pharaoh Ny-Swth," *ZÄS* 81 (1956) 18–19; G. E. Kadish, "An Inscription from an Early Egyptian Fortress," *JNES* 29 (1970): 99–102; G. Goyon, "Les navires de transport de la chaussée monumentale d'Ounas," *BIFAO* 69 (1971): 13; *AEO* 2:14f (no. 325); P. Montet, *Géographie de l'Égypte ancienne,* vol. 2 (Paris, 1957), 49. Note the specific *mnw,* "fortress," applied to Elephantine: F. Gomàa, *Die Besiedlung Ägyptens während des Mittleren Reiches* I (Wiesbaden, 1986), 26.

3. *mšˁ,* "to march," *Wb.* II, 155–56; Coptic, W. Westendorf, *Koptisches Handwoerterbuch* (Heidelberg, 1977), 108; the derived noun denotes any large body of men recruited and assembled for a specific purpose, military or civil: thus "army, expeditionary force, quarry/mining/trading expedition." When the purpose is military, the term approximates the mediaeval *chevauchée,* "a raid which systematically devastated enemy territory": D. Seward, *The Hundred Years'·War: The English in France, 1337–1453* (New York, 1978), 38.

4. *Urk.* I, 236:10.

5. *Iry-ḫt-nsw,* originally "he who belongs to the extended family of the king": H. Kees, *ZÄS* 86 (1961): 118; (literature in D. Meeks, *Année lexicographique,* vol. 2 [Paris, 1981], 38f, and vol. 3 [Paris, 1982], 27); later "he who is assigned to the king's business." More than one royal chargé-d'affaires could be assigned to the townships: cf. P. Posener-Kriéger, *The Abusir Papyri* (London, 1968), pl. 83.

6. J. Lopez, *Las inscripciones rupestres faraonicas entre Korosko y Kasr Ibrim* (Madrid, 1966), nos. 27–28; W. Helck, "Die Bedeutung der Felseninschriften J. Lopez, *Inscripciones rupestres* Nr. 27 und 28," *SAK* 1 (1974): 215 ff.

7. Trigger's contention (B. G. Trigger, *Early Civilizations: Ancient Egypt in Context* [Cairo, 1993], 13) that "the Pharaohs who established the First Dynasty . . . sought to enhance the natural borders of Egypt by depopulating adjacent areas . . . (thus making it) more difficult for Egyptians who objected to the authority of these Pharaohs to avoid their rule" in fact identifies a concomitant as a conscious intent. Egypt is sufficiently isolated by natural geography: any dissident inhabitant would face a frightful and impossible task fleeing the country, even under the most favorable conditions. Surely the prospect of cheap labor loomed much larger.

8. Cf. H. Goedicke, *Re-used Blocks from the Pyramid of Amenemhet I at Lisht* (New York, 1971), 143–47 (all doubtful); for figurines ritually smashed, see G. Posener, *Cinq figurines d'envoûtement* (Cairo, 1987), 2.

9. H. Junker, *Giza* (Vienna, 1929–55), 2:172–74, pl. 28, fig. 16b; and 3:38.

10. *Urk.* I, 240:4.

11. See Redford, "Egypt and Western Asia in the Old Kingdom," 125–26 nn. 7–8. Zibelius (*Afrikanische Orts- und Völkernamen in hieroglyphischen und hieratischen Texten,* 4 n. 20) continues to render "Dolmetscher," but her interpretation is mistaken, it seems to me. Her evidence (F. Ll. Griffith and W. M. F. Petrie, *Two Hieroglyphic Papyri from Tanis* [London, 1889], 13, pt. 9, frag. 47) comes from a protocol governing the order of officials standing in the "Presence," on the "right and left," and is an ideal listing. Under a series of seated figures are the titles of officials: "throne-keeper(?), *ḵn*-placer, cup-giver, . . . doorkeepers, superintendent of petitions"; then in two boxes read horizontally: "[king's]-messengers who report on (*wḥm*) every foreign land." There is nothing here about interpreting.

12. Zibelius, *Afrikanische Orts- und Völkernamen in hieroglyphischen und hieratischen Texten,* 88–89 (west bank, around Tomas).

13. Undetermined location in Lower Nubia: ibid., 134–36.

14. Kerma? Cf. *HSLN,* 82; K. Zibelius, *LdÄ,* vol. 3 (Wiesbaden, 1980), 242; idem, *Die ägyptische Expansion nach Nubien,* 15; D. O'Connor, "The Locations of Yam and Kush and Their Historical Implications," *JARCE* 23 (1986): 27–50.

15. *Urk.* I, 101. See also Zibelius, *Afrikanische Orts- und Völkernamen in hieroglyphischen und hieratischen Texten,* 160–61.

16. H. G. Fischer,"A God and a General of the Oasis on a Stela of the Late Middle Kingdom," *JNES* 16 (1957): 227; idem, "Nubian Mercenaries of Gebelein during the First Intermediate Period," pl. X and passim; idem, *Dendera in the Old Kingdom,* 138. See the colorful model Nubian soldiers from Assiut: D. Wildung, *Sesostris und Amenemhet* (Munich, 1984), 175 Abb. 150.

17. *Inw n ḥkr-nsw: Urk.* I, 124:1; cf. 124:14; the translation "insignia" is wide of the mark (R. O. Faulkner, *Concise Dictionary of Middle Egyptian* [Oxford, 1962], 205).

18. *Urk.* I, 127:2, 137:10; *Urk.* IV, 329:5, 335:8, 373:7, 524:8, 949:4, 950:7, 983:16, 1099, 1237:3, 1375:14, 1442:8–11; P. Koller, 3:8; Shipwrecked Sailor, 164–65.

19. *Urk.* I, 127:1; IV, 329:5, 335:7, 423:17, 524:8, 948:5 (throw-sticks), 950:7, 983:16, 1237:3, 1346:8, 1375:14, 1442:8–11; P. Koller, 3:8.

20. *Urk.* IV, 695:16, 702:15, 709:1, 715:16, 720:15.

21. In Amenophis II's "theatrical" procession, it took 340 men to carry the ivory, 1,000 men to carry the ebony: ibid., 1346:7–8.

22. *Urk.* I, 127:1; IV, 329:10, 336–37, 373:8, 949, 1099, 696:1, 702:16, 1346:11, 1375:15; P. Koller, 4:2.

23. *Urk.* I, 126:17, 137:9; IV, 329:3, 8; 334:16, 524:7, 1375:16; Shipwrecked Sailor, 162.

24. *Urk.* IV, 329:2, 7; 1346:9; 1375:15.

25. Ḥs3yt: ibid., 329:7, 1375:16; Shipwrecked Sailor, 163: R. Germer, *Untersuchungen über Arzneimittelpflanzen im alten Ägypten* (Hamburg, 1979), 181; P. Koller, 4:2 (ḵmyt).

26. *Urk.* IV, 329:6, 948:17, 950:7, 983:16, 1099, 1236:19, 1346:5, 1375:14, 1442:8–11, 1654:14; P. Koller, 3:8.

27. *Urk.* IV, 335:4, 1099, 1442:8–11; P. Koller, 3:8.

28. *Urk.* IV, 1375:14, P. Koller, 4:2; A. Lucas, *Ancient Egyptian Materials and Industries,* 4th ed. (London, 1989), 397–98; B. Aston et al., "Stone," in P. T. Nicholson and I. Shaw, eds., *Ancient Egyptian Materials and Technologies* (Cambridge, 2000), 29.

29. *Urk.* IV, 1099.

30. Ibid.

31. P. Koller, 4:2. *Urk.* IV, 1099, 1346:6; K.-J. Seyfried, *Beiträge zu den Expeditionen des Mittleren Reiches in die Ostwüste* (Hildesheim, 1981), 7–151. Zibelius-Chen, *Die ägyptische Expansion nach Nubien,* 81–82.

32. *Urk.* IV, 1668:3; Zibelius-Chen, *Die ägyptische Expansion nach Nubien,* 84–86.

33. Shipwrecked Sailor, 163: *Urk.* IV, 329:8, 335:5; Zibelius-Chen, *Die ägyptische Expansion nach Nubien,* 88–91.

34. A. Rowe, *ASAE* 38 (1938): 393–96 (pl. 55:1–2: Khufu and Sahure); F. Hintze, "Preliminary Note on the Epigraphic Expedition to Sudanese Nubia," *Kush* 13 (1965), 13–14; Harris, *Lexicographical Studies in Ancient Egyptian Minerals,* 96–97; Zibelius, *Afrikanische Orts- und Völkernamen in hieroglyphischen und hieratischen Texten,* 74–75.

35. *Urk.* IV, 1237:4–8; 1442:11; Zibelius-Chen, *Die ägyptische Expansion nach Nubien,* 91–96.

36. *Urk.* I, 127:8, 134:7; IV, 696:8–10 (and passim in Thutmose III's annals); 1346:13, 1548:5, 1570:5; P. Koller, 3:5–6; goats: *Urk.* I, 134:9. This may have been one of the chief attractions for the Egyptians: cf. H.-A. Nordström, *Kush* 10 (1962): 40f and n. 33; Zibelius-Chen, *Die ägyptische Expansion nach Nubien,* 104–14.

37. *Urk.* I, 127:8; P. Koller, 3:6.

38. *Urk.* IV, 1570:6, 949:2 (eggs).

39. Monkeys: Shipwrecked Sailor, 165; *Urk.* IV, 329:9, 949:1,3; P. Koller, 4:3; dogs: Shipwrecked Sailor, 165; *Urk.* IV, 1346:12; giraffes: *Urk.* IV, 948:4, Shipwrecked Sailor, 163–64 (tails of); ostrich feathers: P. Koller, 4:1.

40. *Urk.* I, 127:1; IV, 696:12, 703:13, 709:3,12; 716:2,9; 720:17, 733:16; P. Koller, 4:1 (fruit).

41. E. Edel, *ZÄS* 97 (1971): 54 Abb. 1; *Urk.* I, 124, 132, 135, 141; A. Fakhry, "Stela of the Boat-captain Inikaf," *ASAE* 38 (1938): 35–39; Cairo 68916; Redford, "Egypt and Western Asia in the Old Kingdom," 125–43.

42. A. Weigall, *A Report on the Antiquities of Lower Nubia (the First Cataract to the Sudan Frontier) and Their Condition in 1906–7* (Oxford, 1907), pl. 58, no. 5; *Urk.* I, 126:3, 134:4, 136:13.

43. A. J. Spalinger, *Aspects of the Military Documents of the Ancient Egyptians* (New Haven, 1983), ch. 1.

44. KRI 7:10.

45. *Urk.* IV, 139:12–16.

46. Žaba, *Rock Inscriptions of Lower Nubia,* no. 73; Morkot, *Black Pharaohs,* 56.

47. *Urk.* I, 240:4.
48. *Urk.* IV, 1660:19.
49. KRI 7:11.
50. H. S. Smith, *The Fortress of Buhen. Part 2: The Inscriptions* (London, 1976), pl. LXXV.
51. KRI 2:193:7–8.

4. "PLOTTING IN THEIR VALLEYS"

1. Redford, *Egypt, Canaan, and Israel,* 63–64.
2. B. Bell, "The Oldest Records of the Nile Floods," *Geographical Journal* 136 (1970): 569–73; K. Butzer, "Perspectives on Irrigation in Pharaonic Egypt," in D. Schmandt-Besserat, ed., *Immortal Egypt* (Malibu, 1978), 17; F. Hassan, *Climate History, Periodicity and Predictability* (New York, 1987), 37–46.
3. The reign of Tety may be a *terminus post quem:* Weigall, *Report on the Antiquities of Lower Nubia,* pl. 57:4, 58, no. 9; all the names at Tomâs appear to be Elephantinian: cf. nos. 10 and 16; Žaba, *Rock Inscriptions of Lower Nubia,* no. 142.
4. *Urk.* I, 125:1. H. Goedicke ("Harkhuf's Travels," *JNES* 40 [1981]: 3–4) argues that the word means "ivory road" and indicates a tract via Kurkur and Dunkul. On the alleged "roads" of the Old Kingdom, see H. G. Fischer, "Sur les routes de l'ancien empire," in *Mélanges Jacques Jean Clère (CRIPEL* 13; Lille, 1991), 59–64.
5. Every harbor preserved the right to levy a fee on shipping in transit: cf. R. A. Caminos, *The Chronicle of Prince Osorkon* (Rome, 1958), 70.
6. J. Vercoutter, in *Colloque international du CNRS: Axes prioritaires des recherches égyptologiques,* vol. 1 (Grenoble, 1979); H. S. Smith and L. Giddy, "Nubia and Dakhla Oasis," in *Mélanges offerts à Jean Vercoutter* (Paris, 1985), 317–31; L. Giddy, *Egyptian Oases: Bahriya, Dakhla, Farafra and Kharga during Pharaonic Times* (Warminster, 1987). Execration texts from Balat in the Dakhleh oasis indicate a concern for the Nubian threat: N.-C. Grimal, "Les 'noyes' de Balat," in *Mélanges offerts à Jean Vercoutter,* 111–12.
7. *Urk.* I, 125:14. E. Edel ("Inschriften des Alten Reiches, VI, Die Reiseberichte des Ḥrw-hwjf (Herchuf)," in O. Firchow, ed., *Ägyptologische Studien Hermann Grapow zum 70. Geburtstag gewidmet* [Berlin, 1955], 62f) read the abraded sign as the glyph for the Thinite nome, but my personal collation and photograph would indicate the *nḏ.fyt*-tree (i.e., U.E. 13): F. Gomàa, *Die Besiedlung Ägyptens während des Mittleren Reiches* (Wiesbaden, 1986), 1:262–64.
8. Three hundred donkeys in one case: *Urk.* I, 126:17; one hundred in another: *Urk.* I, 136:4. Six days from Manfalūt to Dakhleh in the early nineteenth century: Sir Archibald Edmonstone, *A Journey to Two of the Oases of Upper Egypt* (London, 1822). The Nile leg of the trip would, of course, have been done by ship: *Urk.* I, 127:12.
9. *Urk.* I, 134:6–9.

10. Ibid., 127:4–6.

11. Ibid., 125:15–126:4 (Yamites vs. the land of Tjeme*ḫ*).

12. Note the frequent use of the verb *sḥtp*, always, however, with the implied threat of force: G. E. Kadish, "Old Kingdom Egyptian Activity in Nubia: Some Reconsiderations," *JEA* 52 (1966): 23–33; Helck, *Historisch-biographische Texte der 2. Zwischenzeit*, 25 (top line); Meeks, *Année lexicographique*, vol. 1 (Paris, 1980), 337.

13. The question as to whether in the high Old Kingdom the Egyptian king and court moved periodically from place to place must remain moot, but in the absence of evidence it is highly unlikely (the passages cited by Goedicke ["Harkhuf's Travels," 2 n. 11] do not by any means prove "periodic perambulations of the royal court"). The biennial royal progress, signified by *šmsw ḥr* (on the expression, see W. Kaiser, *ZÄS* 84 [1959]: 119 ff; 85 [1960]: 118 ff; W. Helck, *Untersuchungen zur Thinitenzeit* [Wiesbaden, 1987], 176), is no longer used to designate alternate years after the close of Dynasty 2.

14. P-M 5:246.

15. *Urk.* I, 133:9–10, 16.

16. Ibid., 134:6–10.

17. On Execration Texts in general, see Redford, *Egypt, Canaan, and Israel*, 87–93.

18. M. Bietak, *Studien zur Chronologie der nubischen C-gruppe. Ein Beitrage zur frühgeschichte Unternubiens* . . . (Wien, 1968), 142–45; cf. the caveat of J. Vercoutter, review of Bietak, *Studien zur Chronologie der nubischen C-gruppe*, in *RdÉ 23* (1971): 203; O'Connor, in Hochfield and Riefstahl, *Africa in Antiquity*, 1:55–56; T. Säve-Söderbergh, *Middle Nubian Sites: Scandinavian Joint Expedition to Nubia* (Uppsala, 1989), 6–14.

19. E. Edel, "Die Ländernamen Unternubiens und die Ausbreitung der C-Gruppe nach den Reiseberichten des Ḥrw-ḫwjf," *Orientalia* 36 (1967): 133–58; Y. Koenig, "Les textes d'envoûtement de Mirgissa," *RdÉ* 41 (1990): 105f; W. Y. Adams, *Nubia: Corridor to Africa* (London, 1977), 142–62; M. Bietak, "The C-group and Pan-grave Culture in Nubia," in T. Hagg, ed., *Nubian Culture Past and Present* (Stockholm, 1987), 113–28.

20. H. T. B. Hall, "A Note on the Cattle Skulls Excavated at Faras," *Kush* 10 (1962): 58 ff.

21. Säve-Söderbergh, "Preliminary Report of the Scandinavian Joint Expedition" (1963), 58.

22. E.g., *Kush* 10 (1962): 24f, 35, 39, 89f; G. R. Hughes, "Serra East: The University of Chicago Excavations, 1961–62: A Preliminary Report on the First Season's Work," *Kush* 11 (1963): 122; and M. Almagro, F. Presedo, and M. Pellicer, "Preliminary Report on the Spanish Excavations in the Sudan," *Kush* 11 (1963): 175; cf. also B. Gratien, "Les necropoles Kerma de l'isle de Sai," *CRIPEL* 3 (1975): 50–53; idem, "La grande necropole Kerma de l'isle de Sai," *CRIPEL* 5 (1981): 159–81.

23. L. Jourdan, "Campagnes 1976–1977 à l'isle de Sai: Offrandes animales dans les tombes de la nécropole Kerma," *CRIPEL* 6 (1981): 171–89.

24. G. J. Verwers, "The Survey from Faras to Gezira Dabarosa," *Kush* 10 (1962): 19–30.

25. Cf. ivory and mother-of-pearl hairclips, bracelets and rings, button seals, bronze mirrors, and so on.

26. See in particular K. Sethe, *Die Ächtung feindlicher Fürsten, Völker und Dinge auf altägyptischen Tongefässcherben des Mittleren Reiches* (Berlin, 1926), 32–43; G. Posener, *Princes et pays d'Asie et de Nubie* (Brussels, 1940), 48–62; A. M. Abu Bakr and J. Osing, "Ächtungstexte aus dem Alten Reich," *MDAIK* 29 (1973): 97–133; J. Osing, "Ächtungstexte aus dem Alten Reich (II)," *MDAIK* 32 (1976): 133–85; G. Posener, "Une nouvelle statuette d'envoutement," in *Studien zur Sprache und Religion Ägyptens* (Göttingen, 1984), 1:613–20; idem, *Cinq figurines d'envoûtement*, 17–25; Koenig, "Les textes d'envoûtement de Mirgissa," 101–25. As a generic *nḥsyw* is much more common in these texts, Medjay being much rarer and restricted to Weba-sepet and the eastern desert.

27. Ḥḳ3; *ḫ3swt* is occasionally added (Abu Bakr and Osing, "Ächtungstexte aus dem Alten Reich," 112) because *ḥḳ3* alone can be used for Pharaoh.

28. In some cases "born of his mother," which substitutes for a PN, might indicate that the mother's name was unknown: Posener, *Cinq figurines d'envoûtement*.

29. Osing, "Ächtungstexte aus dem Alten Reich (II)," 134f and 143f.

30. Abu Bakr and Osing, "Ächtungstexte aus dem Alten Reich," 111–12, 32, 142.

31. Cf. Tjay: Sethe, *Die Ächtung feindlicher Fürsten, Völker und Dinge auf altägyptischen Tongefässcherben des Mittleren Reiches*, a, 3.

32. Abu Bakr and Osing, "Ächtungstexte aus dem Alten Reich," 112, 32, 135.

33. Posener, *Cinq figurines d'envoûtement*, 29.

34. A standard list, used for both Nubian and Asiatic enclaves: Koenig, "Les textes d'envoûtement de Mirgissa," 114.

35. Posener, *Cinq figurines d'envoûtement*, 23–30.

36. *Sḳrw* is essentially a pejorative appellative, looking to a future state, rather than a present one (as Koenig, "Les textes d'envoûtement de Mirgissa," 103).

37. Posener, *Cinq figurines d'envoûtement*; relevant discussion on 20–21.

38. A2 through 6 are too fragmentary for connected translation.

39. The line drawing on pl. 6 of Posener, *Cinq figurines d'envoûtement*, supports a restoration of the second feminine singular suffix, *t*.

40. There is no need, however, to postulate a *kingdom* (Morkot, *Black Pharaohs*, 54–57): the cartouches in question belong to Egyptian kings.

41. Cf. Idy's assignment: Goedicke, *Königliche Dokumente aus den Alten Reich*, 187; the measures he was obliged to take seem to have been severe: cf. M. F. Mostafa, "Kom El-Koffar. Teil II: Datierung und Historische Interpretation des Textes B," *ASAE* 71 (1987): Taf. 1 (opp. p. 184).

42. L. Habachi, "God's-Fathers and the Role They Played in the History of the First Intermediate Period," *ASAE* 55 (1958): 178–80.

43. Grimal, *History of Ancient Egypt*, 143 (with a different arrangement of the individuals).

44. Strasbourg 345 (G. Daressy, "Inscriptions tentyrites," *ASAE* 18 [1918]:

186); Clère and Vandier, *Textes de la première période intermédiaire,* no. 13; Fischer, *Dendera in the Third Millennium,* 129.

45. Cf. Merikare P 76–78: "He (i.e., the Theban rebel) has no grain that he might give it: let it be a source of satisfaction that they are weakened for you, and sate yourself with your own bread and beer. Granite comes to you without restriction."

46. Habachi, *Elephantine IV.*

47. Clère and Vandier, *Textes de la première période intermédiaire,* no. 20.

48. The antecedent must be the name of a territory.

49. D. Arnold, *Gräber des Alten und Mittleren Reiches in El-Tarif* (Mainz-am-Rhein, 1976), Taf. 42, 52.

50. A foreign land is intended?

51. H. G. Fischer, *Inscriptions from the Coptite Nome* (Rome, 1964), 37; W. Schenkel, *Memphis—Herakleopolis—Theben: Die epigraphischen Zeugnisse der 7.–11. Dynastie Aegyptens* (Wiesbaden, 1965), 214–17.

52. Cf. the fascinating text of Tjehemau: G. Roeder, *Debod bis Bab Kalabscheh* (Cairo, 1911), pls. 107–8; Redford, "Egypt and Western Asia in the Old Kingdom," 129 n. 41; idem, *Egypt, Canaan, and Israel,* 70.

53. For the periodic raids, see Žaba, *Rock Inscriptions of Lower Nubia,* no. 10A (year 20), no. 4 (year 29) of Amenemhet I; no. 52 (year 7[?]), no. 74 (year 18); cf. Smith, *Fortress of Buhen. Part 2: The Inscriptions,* 39–41; Dunham and Janssen, *Second Cataract Forts,* vol. 1, pl. 90; Žaba, *Rock Inscriptions of Lower Nubia,* no. 73.

54. See, among others, S. T. Smith, *Askut in Nubia: The Economics and Ideology of Egyptian Imperialism in the Second Millennium B.C.* (London, 1995), 25–50; reports on Buhen by W. B. Emery, "A Preliminary Report on the Excavations of the Egypt Exploration Society at Buhen 1957–8," *Kush* 7 (1959): 7–14 and passim; A. W. Lawrence, "Ancient Egyptian Fortifications," *JEA* 51 (1965): 69–94; B. J. Kemp, "From Old Kingdom to Second Intermediate Period," in Trigger et al., *Ancient Egypt,* 130–34; B. G. Trigger, "The Reasons for the Construction of the Second Cataract Forts," *JSSEA* 12 (1982): 1–6; D. Dunham, *Second Cataract Forts,* vol. 2, *Uronarti, Shalfak, Mirgissa* (Boston, 1967); J. Vercoutter, *Mirgissa,* vol. 1 (Paris, 1970).

55. A. Vila, "L'armement de la forteresse de Mirgissa-Iken," *RdÉ* 22 (1970): 171–99.

56. It may be that the Nubian fortresses reflect the standard military fortifications of the time, developed farther north: Kemp, "From Old Kingdom to Second Intermediate Period," 131. It should be noted that rams (*iašibu*) and siege towers (*dimtu*) were Asiatic (Hurrian) inventions: J. R. Kupper, "Notes lexicographiques," *RA* 45 (1951): 125–27; A. Götze, "Warfare in Asia Minor," *Iraq* 25 (1963): 128; Y. Yadin, "Hyksos Fortifications and the Battering Ram," *BASOR* 137 (1955): 23–31; *CAD,* 3:144–47. On siege techniques in the Nile Valley, see Grimal, *La Stèle triomphale de Pi('ankh)y,* 48 n. 119 and 61 n. 135.

57. R. Wenke, "The Evolution of Early Egyptian Civilization: Issues and Evidence," *Journal of World Prehistory* 5 (1991): 315–17.

58. Cf. L. V. Žabkar, "The Egyptian Name of the Fortress of Semna South," *JEA* 58 (1972): 85 ff.

59. B. Gratien, *Prosopographie des nubiens et des égyptiens en Nubie avant le Nouvel Empire* (Lille, 1991); R. J. Leprohon, "Administrative Titles in Nubia in the Middle Kingdom," *JAOS* 113 (1993): 423–36.

60. ⸢w:⸣ see Redford, "Egypt and Western Asia in the Old Kingdom," 126 n. 8.

61. *Imy-r šnt:* "Upper Egyptian Settlers in Middle Kingdom Nubia," *Kush* 5 (1957): pl. XIV; Smither, "Semnah Despatches," 7; Leprohon, "Administrative Titles in Nubia in the Middle Kingdom," 432 nn. 156–57.

62. Lit. "follower." These constitute the all-purpose "bodyguards" and attendants seen in tomb scenes behind the figure of the tomb owner.

63. Žaba, *Rock Inscriptions of Lower Nubia*, no. 135.

64. Redford, *Egypt, Canaan, and Israel*, 80 n. 54.

65. For gold production in the Middle Kingdom, see T. Säve-Söderbergh, *Ägypten und Nubien. Ein Beitrage zur Geschichte altägyptischer Aussenpolitik* (Lund, 1941), 73; J. Vercoutter, "The Gold of Kush: Two Gold-Washing Stations at Faras East," *Kush* 7 (1959): 133; Zibelius-Chen, *Die ägyptische Expansion nach Nubien*, 73–80.

66. *Smsw-h3yt*, lit. "elder of the porch."

67. Simpson, *Heka-nefer and the Dynastic Material from Toshke and Arminna*, 50–53; cf. also Weigall, *Report on the Antiquities of Lower Nubia*, pl. 18:10–11.

68. Dunham and Janssen, *Second Cataract Forts*, 1:131, pl. 93A; 132, pl. 93D; Žaba, *Rock Inscriptions of Lower Nubia*, 75, no. 53; 85, no. 58. On the *phrt* see G. P. F. van den Boorn, *The Duties of the Vizier* (London, 1988), 205; D. B. Redford, *Egypt and Canaan in the New Kingdom* (Beersheba, Israel, 1990), 35.

5. FROM CHIEFDOM TO STATE AND BACK AGAIN

1. Kemp, "From Old Kingdom to Second Intermediate Period," 131–35.

2. On the conquests of Senwosret III, see Zibelius-Chen, *Die ägyptische Expansion nach Nubien*, 201–2.

3. Sethe, *Ägyptische Lesestücke zum Gebrauch im Akademischen Unterricht*, 65–66.

4. See O'Connor, "Early States along the Nubian Nile," 153–56.

5. The earliest settlement dates from the early third millennium, but the real beginnings must be set around 2400 B.C. or later: C. Bonnet, "Upper Nubia from 3000–1000 B.C.," in Davies, *Egypt and Africa*, 112–13.

6. I am indebted to Dr. K. Grzymski for the correct form of this place-name. Kerma ware is now attested in Dr. Grzymski's area of concession around Hambukol: B. Gratien, *Bulletin de Liaison du Groupe International d'Étude de la Céramique Égyptienne* 18 (1994): 68–71; see also J. Leclant and G. Clerc, "Fouilles et travaux en Égypte et au Soudan, 1991–1992," *Orientalia* 62 (1993): 278.

7. Koenig, "Les textes d'envoûtement de Mirgissa," 103. On Kerma, see,

among others, G. A. Reisner, *Excavations at Kerma*, vols. 1–3 (Cambridge, Mass., 1923); Adams, *Nubia*, 189–211; B. Gratien, *Les Cultures de Kerma: Essai de classification* (Lille, 1978); Kemp, "From Old Kingdom to Second Intermediate Period," 128–29 and 163–68; Zibelius-Chen, *Die ägyptische Expansion nach Nubien*, 64–67; C. Bonnet et al., *Kerma, Royaume de Nubie* (Geneva, 1990); O'Connor, "Locations of Yam and Kush and Their Historical Implications," 39–42; Leclant and Clerc, "Fouilles et travaux en Égypte et au Soudan, 1991–1992," 275–77, and idem, "Fouilles et travaux en Égypte et au Soudan, 1992–1993," *Orientalia* 63 (1994): 452–54; D. O'Connor, *Ancient Nubia: Egypt's Rival in Africa* (Philadelphia, 1993), ch. 4; T. Kendall, *Kerma and the Kingdom of Kush, 2500–1500 B.C.: The Archaeological Discovery of an Ancient Nubian Empire* (Washington, 1997); C. Bonnet, "Kerma," in Redford, *Oxford Encyclopedia of Ancient Egypt*, 2:227–28.

8. S. Wenig, *LdÄ*, 3:409–11; J. Vercoutter, *Livre de centennaire d'IFAO* (Cairo, 1980), 157–78; D. O'Connor, "The Location of Irem," *JEA* 73 (1987): 99–136. Kush, as a chiefdom rather than a monarchy, is attested in the Twelfth and Thirteenth Dynasties: Posener, *Princes et pays d'Asie et de Nubie*, 48; idem, *Cinq figurines d'envotement*, 46. Similarity of name, *I3trs*, might suggest roots in the late Old Kingdom: Abu Bakr and Osing, "Ächtungstexte aus dem Alten Reich," 112.

9. Morkot, *Black Pharaohs*, 63.

10. C. Bonnet, "Remarques sur la ville de Kerma," in *Hommages Sauneron*, vol. 1 (Cairo, 1979), 3–10. Idem, *Kerma: Territoire et metropole* (Cairo, 1986); J. Leclant, *Orientalia* 69 (2000): 146–47.

11. Gereg, Towef, Khant-ib-re, Kakare In, whose names are found written in hieroglyphs and cartouches at Abu Hor, Tomas, Gerf Hussein, Amada, and Toshka (cf. Weigall, *Report on the Antiquities of Lower Nubia*, pls. 32:1, 34:1, 44:1, 3, 4, 6; 50:1; Žaba, *Rock Inscriptions of Lower Nubia*, nos. 141, 149; Simpson, *Heka-nefer and the Dynastic Material from Toshke and Arminna*, pl. 18a,b), are scarcely to be identified as Kerma rulers (cf. B. Williams, "A Prospectus for Exploring the Historical Essence of Ancient Nubia," in Davies, *Egypt and Africa*, 90–91 n. 73). The name forms point to the Second Intermediate Period and may be ephemeral rulers of the Thirteenth or Sixteenth Dynasties. Cf. O'Connor, *Ancient Nubia*, 57.

12. On "chiefdom" and "state," see E. M. Brumfiel, *American Anthropologist* 85 (1983): 261–84; R. Cohen and E. R. Service, *The Anthropology of Political Evolution* (Philadelphia, 1978); R. L. Carneiro, *Science* 169 (1970): 733–38; E. R. Service, *Origins of the State and Civilization* (New York, 1975); F. S. Frick, *The Formation of the State in Ancient Israel* (Sheffield, 1985); T. Earle, *Annual Review of Anthropology* 16 (1987): 279–308; A. W. Johnson and T. Earle, *The Evolution of Human Societies* (Stanford, 1987); W. Heimpel, "Herrentum und Königtum im vor-und frügeschichlichen Alten Orient," *ZA 82 (1992): 4–21.*

13. Säve-Söderbergh, "Buhen Stela from the Second Intermediate Period," 50–56; Smith, *Fortress at Buhen. Part 2: The Inscriptions*, 41; Redford, "Textual Sources for the Hyksos Period," 5 nos. 15–16.

14. Meeks, *Année lexicographique*, 1:259f and 2:203; the root is rendered in

Greek by Βασιλευς/Βασίλισσα: F. Daumas, *Les Moyens d'expression du grec et de l'égyptien, comparés dans les décrets de Canope et de Memphis* (Cairo, 1952), 219.

15. Kamose II, line 20; R. Stadelmann, "Ein Beitrag zum Brief des Hyksos Apophis," *MDAIK* 20 (1965): 62–69.

16. ꜥḥꜥ: cf. *Wb.* I, 219:1–5. For related expressions, see H. Fischer-Elfert, "Das Textmuster von Spruch R im magischen Papyrus Harris," *GM* 166 (1998): 105–6.

17. Cf. T. Säve-Söderbergh, "The Nubian Kingdom of the Second Intermediate Period," *Kush* 4 (1956): 54–61.

18. See F. Geus, "Burial Customs in the Upper Main Nile: An Overview," in Davies, *Egypt and Africa*, 64–65; Williams, "Prospectus for Exploring the Historical Essence of Ancient Nubia," 80.

19. For this period, see J. von Beckerath, *Untersuchen zur politischen Geschichte der zweiten Zwischenzeit in Ägypten* (Glückstadt, 1964); S. Quirke, *The Administration of Egypt in the Late Middle Kingdom* (Whitstable, 1990); Grimal, *History of Ancient Egypt*, 182–85.

20. See Smith, *Askut in Nubia*, 69–80; Sealings-Mirgissa: Dunham, *Second Cataract Forts*, 2:171 no. 120 (cf. von Beckerath, *Untersuchen zur politischen Geschichte*, 237 no. 8): Sobekḥotpe III); Uronarti: Dunham, *Second Cataract Forts*, 2:167; statuary: Dunham and Janssen, *Second Cataract Forts*, 1:28, fig. 3; von Beckerath, *Untersuchen zur politischen Geschichte*, 58 n. 1; burials: von Beckerath, *Untersuchen zur politischen Geschichte*, 245 no. 18; officials are difficult to date, but those with Sobek-names *a fortiori* are to be assigned to the Thirteenth Dynasty. O'Connor has suggested (in Hochfield and Riefstahl, *Africa in Antiquity*, 1:56) that in the Thirteenth Dynasty the garrisons ceased to rotate and became permanent communities.

21. Year 3 of Sobekḥotpe II, second day of the third month (= early November): two Medjay chiefs and their retainers visited the king's court at Thebes: Boulaq XVIII, 29:1; 43:3 (= A. Scharff, "Ein Rechnungsbuch des koeniglichen Hofes aus der 13. Dynastie [Papyrus Boulaq Nr. 18]," *ZÄS* 56 [1920]: 51–68).

22. *Hieroglyphic Texts from Egyptian Stelae etc. in the British Museum*, vol. 4, pl. 23 (1060).

23. Smith, *Fortress of Buhen. Part 2: The Inscriptions*, 80–82; Adams, *Nubia*, 189–91. But see S. T. Smith (*Askut in Nubia*, 107–36), who argues a peaceful takeover.

24. Helck, *Historisch-biographische Texte der 2. Zwischenzeit*, 45f no. 62; P. Vernus, "La stèle du pharaon Mntw-ḥtpi à Karnak: Un nouveau témoignage sur la situation politique et militaire au début de la D.P.I.," *RdÉ* 40 (1989): 145–61; Redford, "Textual Sources for the Hyksos Period," nos. 4, 50.

25. The Hyksos were clearly doing the same thing to Memphis, Itj-towy, and Heliopolis to provide a monumental backdrop to their own settlements: W. Helck, "Ägyptische Statuen im Ausland—ein chronologisches Problem," *UF* 8 (1976): 101–14; for the deposit of Old Kingdom stone vases, see P. Lacovara, "The Stone Vase Deposit at Kerma," in Davies, *Egypt and Africa*, 118–28.

26. On the Egyptian freebooters who turn up in the staff of the rulers of Kush, see Smith, *Fortress at Buhen. Part 2: The Inscriptions*, 80–85; Adams,

Nubia, 202; S. Tyson Smith, *Sixth International Congress of Egyptology* (Turin, 1991), 368–69.

27. Adams, *Nubia,* 201 (brickwork and timber bonding).

28. O'Connor, *Ancient Nubia,* 51.

29. C. Bonnet, in C. Berger and N. Grimal, eds., *Hommages à Jean Leclant* (Cairo, 1994), 2:55–57.

30. Specifically the "Lisht" type: R. S. Merrilees, *Levant* 10 (1978): 75–98; on Hyksos pottery in general, see now P. E. McGovern, *The Foreign Relations of the Hyksos* (Oxford, 2000).

31. Reisner, *Excavations at Kerma,* 2:75, fig. 168, nos. 57–58, 61–62; fig. 168, no. 56; M. Bietak, "Egypt and Canaan during the Middle Bronze Age," *BASOR* 281 (1991): 59–60; Verwers, "Survey from Faras to Gezira Dabarosa," pl. 6(b); H.-A. Nordström, *Kush* 10 (1962): 39; T. Säve-Söderbergh, "Preliminary Report of the Scandinavian Joint Expedition," *Kush* 10 (1962): pls. 21(b) and 23(b); idem, "Preliminary Report of the Scandinavian Joint Expedition" (1963), 56 and pl. 7(c); Hughes, "Serra East," 122; Almagro, Presedo, and Pellicer, "Preliminary Report on the Spanish Excavations in the Sudan," 178; Säve-Söderbergh, "Preliminary Report of the Scandinavian Archaeological Investigations between Faras and Gemal," 30, pl. 5(a); Gratien, "Les necropoles Kerma de l'isle de Sai," 50–53; Kemp, "From Old Kingdom to Second Intermediate Period," 167.

32. There is little point, beyond explicating Manetho, of retaining "Dynasty 14" and "Dynasty 16." The former arises out of a misreading of Turin Canon ix,13, to x,11 (Redford, *King-lists, Annals, and Day-books,* 199–201) and the latter out of Manetho's "linear" perception of history (the Hyksos were contemporary with a Theban group different from the independent Itj-Towy kings and the Taʕo family). Building history on continued acceptance of "14" and "16" results in unnecessary distortion (cf., e.g., Grimal, *History of Ancient Egypt,* 187–89).

33. D. B. Redford, *History and Chronology of the Eighteenth Dynasty of Egypt: Seven Studies* (Toronto, 1967), ch. 2; J. E. Harris and K. R. Weeks, *X-raying the Pharaohs* (New York, 1973), 123–24. I see no purpose served in continuing to inflate Dynasty 17 (A. Dodson, "On the Internal Chronology of the Seventeenth Dynasty," *GM* 120 [1991]: 33–38; N. Dautzenberg, "SeneferibRe Sesostris IV.— ein König der 17. Dynastie?" *GM* 129 [1992]: 43–48): the first Taʕo represents a new line (C. Blankenberg-van Delden, "A Genealogical Reconstruction of the Kings and Queens of the Late Seventeenth and Early Eighteenth Dynasties," *GM* 54 [1982]: 36), and it seems to be most logical to begin Dynasty 17 with him: cf. W. Helck, "Der Aufstand des Tetian," *SAK* 13 (1986): 126.

34. Kemp, "From Old Kingdom to Second Intermediate Period," 169–70.

35. Helck, *Historisch-biographische Texte der 2. Zwischenzeit,* 88.

36. O'Connor, in Hochfield and Riefstahl, *Africa in Antiquity,* 1:51. While showing some affinities with Kerma ware, pan-grave pottery is markedly different from C-group ceramics. This poses problems for the identification of C-group with *Mdȝy,* unless the Egyptians used the term loosely or applied it to more than one related group: see M. Bietak, *Society for Nubian Studies. Sixth International Conference* (Bergen, 1986), 1–17.

37. Kamose II, 21–22.

38. Redford, "Textual Sources for the Hyksos Period," no. 61; A. Grimm, "Calembour, Trommelwettstreit oder Kampf auf Leben und Tod in der Autobiographischen Steleninschriften des Emheb," *JEA* 75(1989), 220–24; C. Vandersleyen, "Emheb le prince Nubien qui jouyait du tambour," in Berger and Grimal, *Hommages à Jean Leclant*, 2:399–402.

39. Redford, "Textual Sources for the Hyksos Period," no. 64.

40. On Miu, see Zibelius, *Afrikanische Orts- und Völkernamen in hieroglyphischen und hieratischen Texten*, 118–20; Zibelius-Chen, *Die ägyptische Expansion nach Nubien*, 79, 165, 192. The expedition might have taken the desert route from Karosko to Abu Hamed, bypassing Kerma, but there is little evidence this route was used at this time: D. A. Berg, "Early Eighteenth Dynasty Expansion into Nubia," *JSSEA* 17 (1987): 1–2.

41. Smith, *Fortress of Buhen. Part 2: The Inscriptions*, pls. II and LVIII; Smith, *Askut in Nubia*, 137.

42. Lit. "the forefront of the ultimate buttress" (imagery derived from the pillars of the world?), an unspecified and vaguely understood southern extremity: H. Gauthier, *Dictionnaire des noms géographiques contenus dans les textes hiéroglyphiques* (Cairo, 1929), 4:182–83; H. Goedicke, "The Location of Ḥnt-ḥn-nfr," *Kush* 13 (1965): 102–5; C. Vandersleyen, *Les guerres d'Amosis* (Brussels, 1972), 64–68; F.-G. Schmitz, *Amenophis I* (Hildesheim, 1978), 177–78.

43. *Urk.* IV, 5:4–6.

44. Undoubtedly a Nubian name or title: cf. such names as *3yt* (Abu Bakr and Osing, "Ächtungstexte aus dem Alten Reich," no. 101), *i-y3-ṯi* (ibid., no. 24), *y-ṯi* (ibid., no. 56 [called a *Nḥsy*]), *iy3ti* (ibid., no. 94), and related writings. Vandersleyen (*Les guerres d'Amosis*, 75–76) draws attention to the title *ata* in II Khamois.

45. *Urk.* IV, 5:16–6:6; Vandersleyen, *Les guerres d'Amosis*, 79–80.

46. *Urk.* IV; Schmitz, *Amenophis I*, 194–97.

47. Berg, "Early Eighteenth Dynasty Expansion into Nubia," 6–7.

48. Although some items of Aḥmose are found on Saï, it seems that they were brought to the site (cf. Säve-Söderbergh, *Ägypten und Nubien*, 145); for monuments of Amenophis I, see *Kush* 4 (1956): 75, no. 14; 77, nos. 19, 21, 22; 79, no. 25; Berg, "Early Eighteenth Dynasty Expansion into Nubia," 4, for additional sources and discussion. Amenophis I was commemorated on Saï by Thutmose III, a fact of possible significance: Vercoutter, *BSFE* 58 (1970): 28.

49. The vague excuse was "to eliminate uproar throughout the foreign lands and to put down the rebellion of foreign parts" (*Urk.* IV, 8:6–7).

50. Ibid., 89–90. The texts are dated to the return of the expedition in the third year, but the dredging makes sense only if it was a preparatory move.

51. Based on an accession date of vii, 21: W. Helck,"Bemerkungen zu den Thronbesteigungsdaten im Neuen Reich," in *Studia Biblica et Orientalia*, vol. 3 (Rome, 1959), 115; D. B. Redford, "On the Chronology of the Eighteenth Dynasty," *JNES* 25 (1966): 116.

52. *Urk.* IV, 8:8–9. The date, year 2, viii [?], is given by the graffito of the army scribe who counted ships at the delicate moment when they negotiated the rap-

ids: *LdR* 2:214; Säve-Söderbergh, *Ägypten und Nubien,* 147; Hintze, "Preliminary Note on the Epigraphic Expedition to Sudanese Nubia," 13 n. 6, 14 n. 10.

53. P-M 7:165.

54. Urk. IV, 8:13–9:6.

55. Morkot, *Black Pharaohs,* 71, fig. 33.

56. *Urk.* IV, 139:5.

57. As correctly divined by L. Bradbury, "The Tombos Inscription: A New Interpretation," *Serapis* 8 (1985): 20.

58. The text seems to be dated to the "first [month]": *akhet* should probably be restored: D. B. Redford, "A Gate Inscription from Karnak and Egyptian Involvement in Western Asia during the Early Eighteenth Dynasty," *JAOS* 99 (1979): 277; Bradbury, "Tombos Inscription," 4.

59. P-M 7:233; Arkell, "Varia Sudanica," 36 ff, fig. 4; J. Vercoutter, "New Egyptian Texts from the Sudan," *Kush* 4 (1956): 70, no. 7; Berg, "Early Eighteenth Dynasty Expansion into Nubia," 1–2, for literature and discussion. The retainer Iry and the steward Hory whose graffiti are close by (Vercoutter, "New Egyptian Texts from the Sudan," 68, nos. 2–3; 69, no. 5) were presumably members of the army.

60. O'Connor, in Trigger et al., *Ancient Egypt,* 255.

61. For the Tombos stela, see LD 3:5a; *Urk.* IV, 82–86; P-M 7:174f. There has been considerable discussion of this important text: cf. Säve-Söderbergh, *Ägypten und Nubien,* 154; Schmitz, *Amenophis* I, 184; Redford, "Gate Inscription from Karnak," 274–76; idem, "Egypt and Asia in the New Kingdom: Some Historical Notes," *JSSEA* 10 (1979): 68–69; Spalinger, *Aspects of the Military Documents of the Ancient Egyptians,* 45–47; Bradbury, "Tombos Inscription," 4 ff and passim; Berg, "Early Eighteenth Dynasty Expansion into Nubia," 1–14; Grimal, *History of Ancient Egypt,* 212; H. Goedicke, "The Thutmosis I Inscription near Tomas," *JNES* 55(1996): 161-76. The text is what is usually dubbed a "rhetorical" stela (infelicitous though the term is—the ancients would have called it a "song" [*ḥst*]), divided into five unequal stanzas concerned seriatim with (1) the king, his accession, and universal dominion; (2) his defeat of Kush; (3) his conquests as son of Amun; (4) his far-flung and unheralded fame; (5) the king as Horus. Paramount throughout the text is the insistence on a worldwide rule: this extends to the bedu, Asiatics, and Ḥau-nebu, to southerners and northerners, the limits and extent of the earth, the circumference of the sky, all lands, the islands of Okeanos, and so on. *Mwḳd,* therefore, must be sought at the northern reaches of Egypt's world, and that it should be construed as the "Euphrates" is natural (E. Edel, *BN* 11 [1980]: 72). That the expression is linked to the Red Sea (L. Störk, "'3 *jm* '3 *n mw ḳd*" zum dritten?" *GM* 9 [1974]: 39–40; Goedicke, "The Inverted Water," *GM* 10 [1974]: 13–17) is not at all at variance with ancient conceptualizing of the world. The "Euphrates" and the "Red Sea" are to the ancients inseparably linked (Strabo xi.14.7). To introduce into *this* context a parochial reference to the limits from Kurgus to Tombos of his southern conquest is meaningless (Bradbury, "Tombos Inscription," 6–8): when Thutmose I identifies "the northern (boundary)" (*Urk.* IV, 85:14), he is referring to the northern limit of his personal rule! For *Ḳd* has nothing to do with "turning someone into . . . " or with being "topsy-turvy": it means "to go around,

encircle." The content of the stela presupposes, in fact, Thutmose's having gained the banks of the Euphrates, which he did in his third or fourth year. The conclusion that the stela is backdated is inevitable.

62. See preceding note.

6. THE EGYPTIAN EMPIRE IN KUSH

1. *Urk.* IV, 139:2. Presumably this chief would be located in the region around the upper Second Cataract.

2. There is no need to conjure up any division into "5," since, as Posener has demonstrated ("Urk. IV, 139, 2–7," *RdÉ* 10 [1955]: 92–94) the text is to be read "3 parts (*dnyt*)." As Bradbury has clearly shown ("Tombos Inscription," 11 and n. 71), there is no justification for making the *Egyptians* the authors of the reorganization of territory: it was part of the act of rebellion!

3. *Urk.* IV, 138:15 to 139:1. Although unnamed, the fort may well have been at Saï: Berg, "Early Eighteenth Dynasty Expansion into Nubia," 14 n. 98; cf. Grimal, *History of Ancient Egypt*, 212.

4. E. Naville, *The Temple of Deir el-Bahari*, vol. 6 (London, 1908), pl. 165; Redford, *History and Chronology of the Eighteenth Dynasty of Egypt*, 57–59; S. Ratié, *La Reine Hatchepsout: Sources et problèmes* (Leiden, 1979), 219–21.

5. Early in Hatshepsut's reign: see O'Connor, "Location of Irem," 114 and n. 73.

6. L. Habachi, "Two Graffiti at Sehēl from the Reign of Queen Hatshepsut," *JNES* 16 (1957): 100, fig. 6.

7. *Urk.* IV, 1375; P-M 7:157; Hintze, "Preliminary Note on the Epigraphic Expedition to Sudanese Nubia," 14 n. 11; Helck, *Historische-biographische Texte der 2. Zwischenzeit*, nos. 141–42.

8. Säve-Söderbergh, *Ägypten und Nubien*, 207 ff, Abb. 16; P-M 7:175; *Urk.* IV, 1365–76. On the name of the viceroy, see J. H. Breasted, "Second Preliminary Report of the Egyptian Expedition," *AJSL* 25 (1908–9): 47; G. A. Reisner, "The Viceroys of Ethiopia," *JEA* 6 (1920): 30; Hintze, "Preliminary Note on the Epigraphic Expedition to Sudanese Nubia," 14 n. 12. The traces suit "Anebny" (Säve-Söderbergh, *Ägypten und Nubien*, 175–76, 208), who in fact boasts of service in the south; *Hieroglyphic Texts from Egyptian Stelae etc. in the British Museum*, vol. 5, pl. 34.

9. On the New Kingdom concept of "empire," see sources quoted in Redford, *Egypt and Canaan in the New Kingdom*, 79 n. 1.

10. *Urk.* IV, 70.

11. Ibid., 316: Naville, *Temple of Deir el-Bahari*, vol. 6, pl. 152; cf. pl. 154; Zibelius, *Afrikanische Orts- und Völkernamen in hieroglyphischen und hieratischen Texten*, 19–20; O'Connor, "Location of Irem," 112–15.

12. *Urk.* IV, 524.

13. Ibid., 947–49 (tomb of Yamu-nedjeḥ).

14. Ibid., 1375:14–16, 1442:8–11.

15. *b3kw*, that is, a tax on the products of one's labor; D. Meeks, *Année lexicographique*, vol. 3 (Paris, 1982), 84; J. Janssen, "Absence from Work by the

Necropolis Workmen of Thebes," *SAK* 8 (1975): 173–74; R. Müller-Wollermann, "Bemerkungen zu den sogenannten Tributen," *GM* 66 (1983): 81–83; W. Boochs, "Weitere Bemerkungen zu den sogenannten Tributen," *GM* 71 (1984): 61–64; Redford, *Egypt and Canaan in the New Kingdom,* 41 and 102 n. 297; E. Bleiberg, *The Official Gift in Ancient Egypt* (Norman, Okla., 1996). The term is used loosely, although it seems to have been capable of specific reference (cf. V. Condon, "Two Account Papyri of the Late Eighteenth Dynasty [Brooklyn 34.1453 A and B]," *RdÉ* 35 [1984]: 57–82; P. Brooklyn 35.1453B H/V pl. 7, line 4, 6; Turin Canon, recto iii.1; KRI 7:84; P. Pushkin, 4, 15). It could be directed to the temple (P. Harris, 12b, 2; 32b, 5; 51b, 10; 69, 4; etc.; *Urk.* IV, 186) or to the king (*Urk.* IV, 968; KRI 2:269:7).

16. On *ḥrwyt nt pr-nsw,* see D. B. Redford, *LdÄ,* vol. 6 (Wiesbaden, 1986), 151–53; idem, *King-lists, Annals, and Day-books,* 96–126. In no way can the "annals" be construed as a balanced reflection of the total tax structure or the complete range of *Handelsprodukte.*

17. *Urk.* IV, 526:11–12. At today's prices this would have the value of nearly $800 million.

18. Ibid., 1238:6; 1296:13–16 (display of executed chief).

19. Konosso stela of Thutmose IV: ibid., 1545–48; cf. B. Bryan, *The Reign of Thutmose IV* (Baltimore, 1990), 332–36 (who argues that the action took place in the Wady Mia; but cf. D. B. Redford, "A Bronze Age Itinerary in Transjordan [Nos. 89–101 of Thutmose III's List of Asiatic Toponyms]," *JSSEA* 12 [1982]: 58, and idem, *LdÄ,* 6:153). An engagement certainly took place, but it was in "remote valleys" and "over the hills" east of the Nile and sounds relatively minor.

20. R. A. Caminos, *The Shrines and Rock-inscriptions of Ibrim* (London, 1968), pls. 31–32; P. der Manuelian, *Studies in the Reign of Amenophis II* (Hildesheim, 1987), 92–95. This is the result of a "walk-about" to collect products in the Sudan: the material is *inw,* "tribute, products," rather than *ḥ3ḳ,* and *wrywt* means some kind of posts, not "chariots."

21. *Urk.* IV, 1661–66; D. Dehler, "*Mrj-msw* und der Nubienfeldzug Amenophis' III. im Jahre 5," *SAK* 11 (1984): 77–83; R. Gundlach, in J. Osing and G. Dreyer, eds., *Form und Mass* (Wiesbaden, 1987), 180–217; Z. Topozada, "Les deux campagnes d'Amenhotep III en Nubie," *BIFAO* 88 (1988): 153–64; this campaign is dealt with *in extenso* by the present author in a forthcoming book on the New Kingdom.

22. Not "30,000": cf. Dehler, "*Mrj-msw* und der Nubienfeldzug Amenophis' III. im Jahre 5," 78.

23. It may have taken place near Saï.

24. *Urk.* IV, 814; P-M 5:251; Säve-Söderbergh, *Aegypten und Nubien,* 153; J. Leclant, "Fouilles et travaux en Égypte et au Soudan 1990–1991," *Orientalia* 61 (1992): 288. The fact that this inscription is a verbatim copy of an earlier text of Thutmose I (*Urk.* IV, 89–90) makes its historical value suspect. On the other hand, Minmose, who participated in Thutmose III's eighth campaign and lived on under Amenophis II, says, "I saw (how) he overthrew the land of Nubia" (*Urk.* IV, 1441:18), surely a reference to a campaign later than that of year 20.

25. G. T. Martin, *The Memphite Tomb of Horemheb, Commander-in-Chief of Tut'ankhamun* (London, 1989), pls. 81–84, 92–93.

26. KRI 1:102–4; 7:9–11.

27. H. Ricke et al., *The Beit el-Wali Temple of Ramesses II* (Chicago, 1967), pls. 7–8.

28. J. Barns, "Four Khartoum Stelae," *Kush* 2 (1954): fig. on p. 19; Säve-Söderbergh, "Buhen Stela from the Second Intermediate Period," 50–55; Smith, *Fortress of Buhen. Part 2: The Inscriptions,* 72–85.

29. A *tsw* usually commands an army (Sinuhe, 99–101; Piankhy, ll. 8 and 15; *Hieroglyphic Texts from Egyptian Stelae etc. in the British Museum,* vol. 4, pl. 3), a frontier fort (*Urk.* IV, 1120:13; Dunham and Janssen, *Second Cataract Forts,* vol. 1, fig. 3, no. 69, pl. 93B), or a hamlet (*AEO* 1:31; cf. also *tsw n ḫ3st:* H. Gauthier, "Les 'Fils royaux de Kouch' et le personnel administratif de l'Éthiopie," *RT* 39 [1921]: 236; Simpson, *Heka-nefer and the Dynastic Material from Toshke,* pl. 17A): cf. A. R. Schulman, *Egyptian Military Rank, Title, and Organization in the Egyptian New Kingdom* (New Haven, 1982), 72.

30. Randall-MacIver and Woolley, *Buhen,* 79.

31. B. Schmitz, *Untersuchungen zum Titel S3-njśwt "Königssohn"* (Bonn, 1976), 203–57; S. Donadoni, "Sulla situazione giuridica della Nubia nell' impero egiziano," in S. I. Hodjacke and O. D. Berlev, eds., *Ägypten und Kusch* (Berlin, 1977), 133–37; I. Hafemann, *Altorientalische Forschungen* 19 (1992): 212–18.

32. Weigall, *Report on the Antiquities of Lower Nubia,* pl. 65:4; Säve-Söderbergh, *Ägypten und Nubien,* 141–42; Simpson, *Heka-nefer and the Dynastic Material from Toshke,* pl. 17B, fig. 27, and p. 34.

33. So he is called on the statue of his son Turo (L. Habachi, "Four Objects Belonging to Viceroys of Kush and Officials Associated with Them," *Kush* 9 [1961]: 212f, pl. 27a,b, and figs. 1–2), apparently with reference to his primary function before appointment. For the title, see G. Lefebvre, *Histoire des grands-prêtres d'Amon de Karnak jusqu'à la XXIe Dynastie* (Paris, 1929), 44; on its importance in the *cursus honorum* of New Kingdom officialdom, see H. Kees, *Das Priestertum im ägyptischen Staat vom neuen Reich bis zur Spätzeit* (Leiden, 1953), 1:74–75.

34. L. Habachi, "The First Two Viceroys of Kush and Their Family," *Kush* 7 (1959): 57; Säve-Söderbergh, *Ägypten und Nubien,* 144.

35. Cf. Merimose (cattle of Amun and construction): Z. Žaba, "Un nouveau fragment du sarcophage de Merymôsé," *ASAE* 50 (1950): 512f; Setau (chancery of vizier, stewardship of Amun): Cairo 41395 (KRI 3:92); Seni (granary of Amun): *Urk.* IV, 39–41.

36. Cf. Nehi (herald and court superintendent): Berlin 17895 (*Aegyptische Inschriften,* 2:598; P-M 7:165); Usersatet (herald and child of the nursery): *Urk.* IV, 1486:2.

37. Reisner, "Viceroys of Ethiopia," 38 ff.

38. The explicit reference to Kush falls under Thutmose IV: Bryan, *Reign of Tuthmosis IV,* 315f.

39. I. Müller, "Der Vizekoenig Merimose," in Hodjacke and Berlev, *Ägypten und Kusch,* 325–30; from the reign of Thutmose III until the Twentieth Dynasty

the title "king's-scribe" denoted the highest officials immediately under the king (with the exception of the vizier).

40. Säve-Söderbergh, *Ägypten und Nubien*, 180–81.

41. *Urk.* IV, 77.

42. *Urk.* IV, 76–77.

43. G. Steindorff, *Aniba*, 2 vols. (Glückstadt, 1935–37).

44. Listed in Koller 3,3 to 5,4: Gardiner, *Late Egyptian Miscellanies*, 118–20.

45. Vercoutter, "Gold of Kush," 147; Adams, *Nubia*, 232–35; G. Posener, "L'or de Pount," in Hodjacke and Berlev, *Ägypten und Kusch*, 337–42; Y. Koenig, in *Hommages Sauneron* (Cairo, 1979), 185 ff.

46. Reisner, "Viceroys of Ethiopia," 86; KRI 3:120.

47. Säve-Söderbergh, *Ägypten und Nubien*, 192; Žaba, *Rock Inscriptions of Lower Nubia*, 226, 232; Adams, *Nubia*, 233.

48. Reisner, "Viceroys of Ethiopia," 86.

49. N. de G. Davies, *The Tomb of Huy, Viceroy of Nubia* (London, 1926), pls. 16–17.

50. Reisner, "Viceroys of Ethiopia," 85; Davies, *Tomb of Huy*, 16f. The latter's headquarters were at first at Soleb; after the reign of Sety I, at Amarna West, about 50 miles south of Semna: A. Fouquet, "Deux hauts fonctionnaires du Nouvel Empire en Haute-Nubie," *CRIPEL* 3 (1975): 138; sometimes sacerdotal or ambassadorial functions were combined with the purely administrative: Vercoutter, "New Egyptian Texts from the Sudan," 76; Fouquet, "Deux hauts fonctionnaires du Nouvel Empire en Haute-Nubie," 135.

51. KRI 4:282f.

52. The treasurers in question were often buried at Aniba: Vercoutter, "Gold of Kush," 148f.

53. KRI 3:124.

54. Ibid., 104; Reisner, "Viceroys of Ethiopia," 86.

55. Davies, *Tomb of Huy*, pls. 14–15.

56. *Rwdw:* KRI 3:104 (for the running of farms and estates); these are sometimes qualified as "bailiffs of the king's-house," sometimes as "bailiffs of the Land of Kush": KRI 1:51 (ll. 36, 38).

57. *Urk.* IV, 1237:4–7.

58. Naville, *Temple of Deir el-Bahari*, vol. 6, pl. 165. The term is *iwʿyt* (*Wb.* I, 51:11), which indicates a unit of full-time soldiers (*wʿw:* Redford, *Egypt and Canaan in the New Kingdom*, 30–31; 94–95 nn. 204–11); see also A. H. Gardiner, "Some Reflections on the Nauri Decree," *JEA* 38 (1952): 31; M. Guilmot, *ZÄS* 99 (1973): 101.

59. *Imy-r iwʿyt nt K3š: Kawa* I, no. 23; LD *Texte* 5:157; KRI 3:262:11–12.

60. Reisner, "Viceroys of Ethiopia," 73–75; KRI 3:113 ff.

61. Ḥry-iḥw: Cairo 34098.

62. KRI 3:104.

63. J. Wilson, "The Oath in Ancient Egypt," *JNES* 7 (1948): 138.

64. Cf. *Hieroglyphic Texts from Egyptian Stelae etc. in the British Museum*, vol. 8, pl. 20; *Urk.* IV, 1659–61 (restoring *iwʿyt* in l. x+4).

65. About year 44 of Ramesses II: KRI 2:222; 3:92 ff.

66. KRI 4:1–2.

67. Cf. ibid., 302, 315, 335, 408. All these references are contained in the obiter dicta of litigants. In years 1, 3, and 6 of Siptah a treasurer, envoys, and charioteers, all from Egypt, are found in Buhen with the expressed intent of collecting taxes: Randall-MacIver and Woolley, *Buhen*, pls. 11–12 and 15; KRI 4:362–65. Had the internal civil service failed to function?

68. KRI 5:357:5–10. A battalion commander of the garrison of Kush had been prevailed upon by his sister, an inmate of the royal harem, "to stir up strife and make rebellion" against the king. Cf. S. Redford, *The Harem Conspiracy: The Murder of Ramesses III* (De Kalb, Ill., 2002).

69. Cf. BM 10052, 4:27 and 8:25.

70. See below.

71. B. J. Kemp, "Temple and Town in Ancient Egypt," in P. J. Ucko, R. Tringham, and G. W. Dimbledy, eds., *Man, Settlement and Urbanism* (London, 1972), 651–54; cf. Smith (*Askut in Nubia*, 178–80), who stresses the closeness of the administrative link between Egypt and Nubia.

72. *ASAE* 8 (1907): 53–54 (Aḥmose, mayor of Saï).

73. Cf. "trusted of the king in the towns of the South": W. M. F. Petrie, *A Season in Egypt 1887,* pl. 10, no. 274; "overseer of the towns of Kush"; A. Mariette, *Monuments divers receuillis en Egypte et en Nubie* (Paris, 1871–77), no. 1169; "letter-scribe of the town": Žaba, *Rock Inscriptions of Lower Nubia,* no. 233.

74. *Urk.* IV, 1659:15.

75. *Wb.* II, 82:3.

76. Reisner, "Viceroys of Ethiopia," 87; *Urk.* IV, 196:7; Dunham and Janssen, *Second Cataract Forts,* 1:47 n. 1; KRI 3:104, 118, etc.; Smith, *Fortress of Buhen. Part 2: The Inscriptions,* 118. Mayors could convene with the viceroy for official purposes (KRI 3:104: honoring the king at the jubilee).

77. Cf. KRI 2:636:9, "the towns and their townships." It will remain moot whether the demography of Nubia was "never precisely 'urban,'" as Adams maintains: *Nubia,* 225.

78. Adams, *Nubia,* 227.

79. Cf. ibid., 235–45; P. J. Frandsen, in M. T. Larsen, ed., *Power and Propaganda* (Copenhagen, 1979), 183 n. 13; O'Connor, *Ancient Nubia,* 56–66; Smith, *Askut in Nubia,* 148–54. Population figures are difficult to assess: cf. L. Török, *The Kingdom of Kush: Handbook of the Napatan-Meroitic Civilization* (Leiden, 1997), 44–49.

80. Adams, *Nubia,* 235.

81. Säve-Söderbergh, "Preliminary Report of the Scandinavian Joint Expedition" (1962), 96; Adams, *Nubia,* 236; cf. the brick or stone pyramids at Soleb: Säve-Söderbergh, "Preliminary Report of the Scandinavian Joint Expedition" (1962), 134f; idem, "Preliminary Report of the Scandinavian Joint Expedition" (1963), 159 ff; and idem, "Preliminary Report of the Scandinavian Archaeological Investigations between Faras and Gemal," 31–34; Geus, "Burial Customs in the Upper Main Nile," 65; Williams, "Prospectus for Exploring the Historical Essence of Ancient Nubia," 84; P. J. J. Sinclair and L. Troy, in Davies, *Egypt and Africa,* 166–85.

82. Cf. Heka-nefer: J. Leclant, *Orientalia* 31 (1962): 218; Simpson, *Heka-nefer and the Dynastic Material from Toshka and Arminna*; HSLN, 107–8; cf. also Ruya and his son Thuthotpe, chiefs of Teḫkhet: T. Säve-Söderbergh, "The Paintings in the Tomb of Djehuty-hetep at Debeira," *Kush* 8 (1960): 25 ff, and idem, "Preliminary Report of the Scandinavian Joint Expedition" (1963), 170 ff; Leclant, *Orientalia* 31, 124; E. Edel, "Zur Familie des Sn-msjj nach seinen Grabinschriften auf der Qubet el-Hawa bei Assuan," *ZÄS* 90 (1963): 28–31; Hodjacke and Berlev, *Äegypten und Kusch*, 183 ff; Säve-Söderbergh, "Te-khet, the Cultural and Socio-political Structure of a Nubian Princedom in Tuthmosid Times," 186–94; possibly Aḥmose-Antef: H. Junker, *Erminne* (Vienna, 1925), 34–35; Resu and his son the scribe Amenemhet: Randall-MacIver and Woolley, *Buhen*, 110, pl. 37; Hormose: Leclant, *Orientalia* 31, 124; Amenemhet at Dabiera: T. Säve-Söderbergh and L. Troy, *New Kingdom Pharaonic Sites: The Finds and The Sites* (Uppsala, 1991), 182–211.

83. The chiefs of Teḫkhet no more exercised independent rule over the district from which they derived their title than the duke of Kent does over that county. The numbers of chiefs depicted in Huy's tomb (temp. Tutankhamun)— three for Wawat and six for Kush—convey the notion of plurality and relative importance and are not to be taken seriously.

84. Adams, *Nubia*, 231. Whether we can maintain that, under the empire, Nubia enjoyed a self-sufficient, redistributive economy similar to Egypt's (R. Morkot, "Studies in New Kingdom Nubia I. Politics, Economics and Ideology: Egyptian Imperialism in Nubia," *Wepwawet* 3 [1987]: 29, 43–47; idem, "*Nb-M3ʿt-Rʿ*-United with Ptah," *JNES* 49 [1990]: 323–27) is difficult to say. It seems to me that temple towns and any other type of settlement in the south existed for one purpose: to exploit the land, its produce, and manpower to the full and ship as much as possible back to Egypt. What was left was used locally to support the exploiters. Cf. Smith, *Askut in Nubia*, 166–70 (with interesting estimates as to what and how much Nubian revenues would support).

85. Adams, *Nubia*, 239.

86. A. M. Blackman, *The Temple of Derr* (Cairo, 1913), 7–8 and pl. V; L. Habachi, "Five Stelae from the Temple of Amenophis III at Es-Sebuaʿ now in the Aswan Museum," *Kush* 8 (1960): 45–51 and figs. 4–5; Redford, *Egypt, Canaan, and Israel*, 203 and 223 and n. 33.

87. F. Ll. Griffith, "The Abydos Decree of Seti I at Nauri," *JEA* 13 (1927): 193–208; KRI 1:45–58; Morkot, "Studies in New Kingdom Nubia I," 44.

88. Frandsen, in *Power and Propaganda*, 174, albeit remaining illiterate! Cf. Säve-Söderbergh, "Te-khet, the Cultural and Socio-political Structure of a Nubian Princedom in Tuthmosid Times," 189. The utter contempt at an official level in which the Egyptians held Canaanites and Nubians needs no stressing. Amenophis II (Chapter 1, n. 13) encapsulates in his letter to the viceroy the common attitude: Canaanites are good for nothing; Nubians at least have good magicians, see to the taxes of the serfs, and don't meddle in their affairs. In light of this, elite emulation appears to be a far better explanation of what is happening in Nubia than any conscious policy on Egypt's part.

89. The principal exception is the native god, Dedwen, whose cult and tem-

ple at Buhen were refurbished by Thutmose III: R. A. Caminos, *The New King-dom Temples at Buhen* (London, 1974); Dedwen, however, had long since been accepted into the Egyptian pantheon as a sort of divine "march-lord" on the southern frontier, and in this capacity he appears in the Pyramid Texts: Morenz, *Egyptian Religion*, 234; Zibelius-Chen, *Die ägyptische Expansion nach Nubien*, 98 and n. 287; D. Silverman, in B. Shafer, ed., *Religion in Ancient Egypt* (Ithaca, N.Y., 1991), 58.

90. Horus, lord of Buhen: Smith, *Fortress of Buhen. Part 2: The Inscriptions*, 237; H. Gauthier, *Le Temple de Ouâdi es-Sebouâ* (Cairo, 1912), 1:30, 37; Horus of Miam (Aniba): C. Desroches-Noblecourt, *Le petit temple d'Abou Simbel* (Cairo, 1968), 1:199 n. 313; Horus, lord of Baky (Kubban): Desroches-Noblecourt, *Temple d'Abou Simbel*, 200 n. 318; these correspond to the three major regions of settlement: Desroches-Noblecourt, *Temple d'Abou Simbel*, 207f n. 363; cf. also L. Christophe, *Revue de Caire* 47 (1961): 303–33; *HSLN*, 110. Cf. also "Horus the Bull, Lord of Nubia" at Saï: Vercoutter, "New Egyptian Texts from the Sudan," 73.

91. Säve-Söderbergh, "Paintings in the Tomb of Djehuty-hetep at Debeira," pl. 15.

92. At Soleb, where a moon-god is associated with the king as "Lord of Nubia": cf. Morkot in n. 84 above, "*nb-m3⟨t-r⟨* lord of Nubia."

93. Cf. Sobek, lord of Su-menu, at the Second Cataract: Vercoutter, "Upper Egyptian Settlers in Middle Kingdom Nubia," *Kush* 5 (1957): 64–69; Khnum at Kumma: Dunham and Janssen, *Second Cataract Forts*, 1:27, 44, pls. 39(c), 86(c), and 52(447), Khnum at Semna: *Kush* 5 (1957), 6.

94. Desroches-Noblecourt, *Temple d'Abou Simbel*, 162f n. 152. On the appearance of the related Isis in Nubia, see J. Leclant, "Isis au pays de Koush," *AEPHE* 90 (1981–82): 47–48.

95. In general, see Adams, *Nubia*, 220–23.

96. Dakkeh: P-M 7:41; Aniba: P-M 7:81; Kubban: P-M 7:83; Faras: J. Karkowski, *Faras*, vol. 5, *The Pharaonic Inscriptions from Faras* (Warsaw, 1981), 140–277; Semna: Dunham and Janssen, *Second Cataract Forts*, 1:8–9; Saï: Vercoutter, "New Egyptian Texts from the Sudan," 75f (nos. 15–16); M. Azim, "Quatres campagnes de fouilles sur la forteresse de Sai, 1970–1973. Iere partie: L'installation pharaonique," *CRIPEL* 3 (1975): 93, 116; Argo-island: H. Jacquet-Gordon et al., "Pnubs and the Temple of Tabo on Argo Island," *JEA* 55 (1969): 107–8, 110; the cult of "Menkheperre" continued to function into Ramesside times in Nubia: KRI 3:120.

97. Complete listing and bibliography in der Manuelian, *Studies in the Reign of Amenophis II*, 254–67.

98. Soleb: *Kush* 10 (1962): 152 ff, 12 (1964): 88, fig. 1; M. S. Giorgini, *Soleb*, vols. 1 and 2 (Florence, 1971); J. Leclant, *NAWG* (1965): 205–16; idem, "Fouilles et travaux en Égypte et au Soudan," *Orientalia* 34 (1965): 219–20; idem, "Le Temple funéraire d'Aménophis III à Soleb (Soudan)," in *Annuaire de la Collège de France* (Paris, 1980–81), 471–77; idem, "Soleb," in B. Gratien and F. Le Saout, eds., *Nubia: Les cultures antiques du Soudan* (Lille, 1994), 197–202; J.-L. de Cénival and G. Haeny, "Rapport préliminaire sur la troisième campagne de fouilles à Ouadi es-Sebouâ, Novembre-Décembre 1961," *BIFAO* 62 (1964):

224 ff; Sedeinga: P-M 7:166; Leclant, "Fouilles et travaux en Égypte et au Soudan," *Orientalia* 34 (1965): 215–17; 62 (1993): 273–74; 63 (1994): 451; construction at Saï: Vercoutter, "New Egyptian Texts from the Sudan," 74, 80; P-M 7:164–65; on Argo-island: Jacquet-Gordon et al., "Pnubs and the Temple of Tabo on Argo Island," 107–8, 110; at Aniba: P-M 7:81; at Kawa: P-M 7:181–91; at Gebel Barkal, P-M 7:220.

99. Sesebi: P-M 7:172–74; I. Hein, *Die Ramessidische Bautätigkeit in Nubien* (Wiesbaden, 1991), 61; Kawa: P-M 7:180. These presumably belong early in the reign, and one wonders whether they were ever finished; cf. Adams, *Nubia*, 222 and 228.

100. The "Fortress (called) 'Nebkheprure-is-propitiator-of-the-gods'": Karkowski, *Faras*, 5:115–40.

101. In general: Adams, *Nubia*, 222, 225; J. Leclant, "An Introduction to the Civilization of Nubia: From the Earliest Times to the New Kingdom," in Hochfield and Riefstahl, *Africa in Antiquity* (Brooklyn, 1979), 1:72–73; K. A. Kitchen, *Pharaoh Triumphant* (Warminster, 1982), 177–78. Abu Simbel: P-M 7:95–119; J. Černý, *Chapelle de Rê-Harakhty: Textes hiéroglyphiques* (Cairo, 1964); Gerf Hussein: P-M 7:33–37; H. Jacquet-Gordon, "Graffiti from the Region of Gerf Hussein," *MDAIK* 37 (1981): 224 ff; Aksha: see bibliography in J. Leclant, "Fouilles et travaux en Égypte et au Soudan 1990–1991," 304; Derr: Blackman, *Temple of Derr*; Beit el-Wali: H. Ricke et al., *The Beit el-Wali Temple of Ramesses II* (Chicago, 1969); Hein, *Die Ramessidische Bautätigkeit in Nubien*.

102. Cf. Morkot in n. 84 above.

103. One might mention Galan, *Victory and Border*; M. G. Hasel, *Domination and Resistance: Egyptian Military Activity in the Southern Levant, 1300–1185 B.C.* (Leiden, 1998); G. Mumford, "International Relations between Egypt, Sinai and Syria-Palestine during the Late Bronze Age to Early Persian Period" (Ph.D. diss., University of Toronto, 1998); Smith, *Askut in Nubia*; C. R. Higginbotham, *Egyptianization and Elite Emulation in Ramesside* (Leiden, 2000); one should also note the excellent dissertation on the subject proffered by E. Morris, "The Architecture of Imperialism" (Ph.D. diss., University of Pennsylvania, 2001).

104. Cf. *Economist*, Dec. 18–30, 1999, 63.

105. *Urk.* IV, 1229:5, 1333:13, and frequently.

106. Ibid., 1546:6

107. Ibid., 1230:13.

108. Ibid., 1254:9.

109. Ibid., 647:15, 758:7, 1545:12.

110. Ibid., 8:4–6.

111. Ibid., 1545:12.

112. Ibid., 138:15–139:7; cf. 685:5. The kernel of the oath of allegiance was a foreswearing of fomenting such uprisings in the future: ibid., 1235:2.

113. "for they (certain Egyptians) had forsaken Egypt, their mistress": W. Helck, *Historisch-biographische Texte der 2. Zwischenzeit*, 94.

114. Ibid., 84.

115. *Urk.* IV, 1230:14.

116. Ibid., 102:12–15.

117. Author's own copy. As expected, the text is composed metrically.

118. On this phrase, redolent of the Egyptian concept of empire, see Redford, *Egypt and Canaan in the New Kingdom,* 80 n. 6; Galan, *Victory and Border,* 117–20; in general, M. Liverani, *Prestige and Interest: International Relations in the Near East ca. 1600–1100 B.C.* (Padua, 1990), 51f, 79.

119. *Urk.* IV, 138:9, 140:17, 1236:15, and passim; sources and a slightly different interpretation in Bleiberg, *Official Gift in Ancient Egypt,* 98–99.

120. For Kamose, see Helck, *Historisch-biographische Texte der 2. Zwischenzeit,* 84; for Amenophis II, see *Urk.* IV, 1343–44; for Akhenaten, see EA 162 and W. Moran, *The Amarna Letters* (Baltimore, 1992), 249 and n. 10. This last passage must be rendered on the basis of an Egyptian original, something like *iw.k rh.ti gr ntk ntt nn ib n hm.f r p3 t3 n Kncn r dr.f iw.f dndw,* "you yourself know that H.M.'s intent is not hostile to the whole land of Canaan," in which the Akkadian *ki ira'ub* renders an Egyptian stative in verb-qualifier position.

121. See the dissertation alluded to in n. 103 above, and also for the concept, T. C. Champion, ed., *Centre and Periphery* (London, 1989).

122. Cf. *Medinet Habu,* vol. *1, Earlier Historical Records of Ramses III* (Chicago, 1930), pls. 11:8, 23:55, 28:42, 46:30; H. Goedicke and E. F. Wente, *Ostraka Michaelides* (Wiesbaden, 1962), taf. xciii, line 3.

123. D. B. Redford, "The Ancient Egyptian City: Figment or Reality?" in W. E. Aufrecht, ed., *Aspects of Urbanism in Antiquity* (Sheffield, 1997), 216–17.

124. That is, those in which Pharaoh had put his name (cartouche) on either a stela or a gate.

125. Little, however, is known from Egyptian sources about foreign trade in the New Kingdom: cf. C. J. Eyre, "Work and the Organization of Work in the Old Kingdom," in M. A. Powell, ed., *Labor in the Ancient Near East* (New Haven, 1987), 200; W. Helck, in R. Hagg and N. Marinatos, eds., *The Function of the Minoan Palaces* (Stockholm, 1987), 17–19.

126. J. J. Janssen, *Commodity Prices from the Ramessid Period* (Leiden, 1975), 540.

127. R. Wenke, "The Evolution of Early Egyptian Civilization: Issues and Evidence," *Journal of World Prehistory* 5, no. 3 (1991): 315–16.

128. Cf. Smith, *Askut in Nubia,* 22.

129. LL *financia* indicates, like its semantic predecessor *vectigal,* the generation of money revenue through fines and taxes *in coin.*

130. Cf. Goedicke, *Re-used Blocks from the Pyramid of Amenemhet I at Lisht,* 18–19; *Egyptian Art in the Age of the Pyramids* (New York, 1999), 222–23.

131. The implication of P. Harris, 57.8–9.

132. H.-W. Fischer-Elefert, *Die satirische Streitschrift des Papyrus Anastasi I* (Wiesbaden, 1986), 148–57.

133. Redford, *Egypt, Canaan and Israel,* 192–213,

134. Liverani, *Prestige and Interest,* 218–19.

135. See especially the work of A. Thijs, "Reconsidering the End of the Twentieth Dynasty," in *GM* 184 (2001): 65 and n. 1 for bibliography; also the useful summary in Török, *Kingdom of Kush,* 104–7.

136. Reisner, "Viceroys of Ethiopia," 51.

137. Steindorf, *Aniba*, 2:240–41.

138. Caminos, *New Kingdom Temples of Buhen*, 2:109–10, pl. 89 (surely a poor writing of "Paynehsi" and not an otherwise unknown).

139. A. H. Gardiner, *Ramesside Administrative Documents* (London, 1948), 36:4–5.

140. M. Bierbrier, *The Late New Kingdom in Egypt* (Warminster, 1985), 10–13. See also the insightful observations of D. Polz, "The Ramsesnakht Dynasty and the Fall of the Old Kingdom: A New Monument in Thebes," *SAK* 25 (1998): 257–93.

141. KRI 4:455:11–12.

142. Ibid., 456:5–6.

143. Presumably the rebuilding of the high priest's house was one of the "monuments" for which he was praised: S. Sauneron, "La restauration d'un portique à Karnak par le grand prêtre Amenhotpe," *BIFAO* 64 (1966): pl. II.

144. M. L. Bierbrier, "A Second High Priest Ramessesnakht," *JEA* 58 (1972): 195–99; but cf. L. Bell, "Only One High-priest Ramessesnakht and the Second Prophet Nesamun His Son," *Serapis* 6 (1980): 7–14; Grimal, *History of Ancient Egypt*, 292.

145. E. F. Wente, "The Suppression of the High Priest Amenhotep," *JNES* 25 (1966): 73–87. Wente argues for this identity of the speaker, and it is hard to see who else it can be.

146. Peet, *Great Tomb-Robberies of the Twentieth Egyptian Dynasty*.

147. Mayer A 6, 4–8.

148. Mayer A 2, 19–20.

149. BM 10383, 2:5.

150. Ibid. 15:12.

151. Mayer B 3.

152. Revealing examples are Ptahhotpe 18, 50; 27, 207; 32, 292; d'Orbiney 8, 6; *Urk.* IV, 1379:14, 1381:6; CCG 42208 c, 17; d, 5 (ignoring a will); J. Černý, "A Stone with an Appeal to the Finder," in *Studi in onore G. Botti* (Rome, 1967), pl. 16:5, p. 49 n. f (effacing a text); J. Leclant, *Montouemhât, quatrième prophète d'Amon, prince de la ville* (Cairo, 1961), 68 [7] (removing a statue).

153. BM 10383 13, 24–25. The word *hrwyw* means all-out conflict: *Wb.* III, 326:1–4; A. H. Gardiner, *JEA* 19 (1933): 19–22; C. Theodorides, "Les ouvriers 'magistrats' en Egypte à l'époque ramesside (XIXe–XXe dynastie 13e–10e s. av. J-C)," *RIDA* 16 (1969): 129 n. 104; Meeks, *Année lexicographique*, 3:223.

154. BM 10383, 10, 18.

155. Mayer B 2.

156. P. Pushkin, 127.2.11. Cf. R. A. Caminos, *A Tale of Woe* (Oxford, 1977), 30–31.

157. Cf. KRI 6:689:15, 691:4–6, 694:6–12; 698:1–2 (all Ramesses X year 3).

158. Was Ramesses XI a minor at his accession? He was a grandson of Ramesses IX, who had died less than a decade before (K. A. Kitchen, "Family Relationships of Ramesses IX and the Late Twentieth Dynasty," *SAK* 11 [1984]: 131–32); and the high-sounding titles of his mother, Queen Tity (KRI 6:732–33), might suggest she acted as regent.

159. Cf. Bierbrier, "Second High Priest Ramessesnakht," 195–99; Bell, "Only One High-priest Ramessesnakht," 7–27.

160. KRI 6:734–35..

161. M. Römer, *Gottes- und Priesterherrschaft in Ägypten am Ende des Neuen Reiches* (Wiesbaden, 1994), 3–34. On Ḥeriḥor's arrival in year 12 or shortly after, see Bell, "Only One High-priest Ramessesnakht," 18 n. 131.

162. That Ḥeriḥor was of Libyan descent is doubtful on the basis of the names of "offspring": *The Temple of Khonsu*, vol. 1 (Chicago, 1979), pl. 26. It remains to be shown that *any* of these "king's-sons" are really blood progeny of Ḥeriḥor.

163. *Temple of Khonsu*, 1:35–44.

164. *LdR* 3:233.

165. Römer, *Gottes- und Priesterherrschaft in Ägypten*, 37.

166. *Temple of Khonsu*, vol.2, pl. 132 (also personal copy, collated). This text, of which only half is preserved, promises "many good things" to Ḥeriḥor as well as twenty years in excess of his allotted life span; see Bell, "Only One High-priest Ramessesnakht," 18 n. 131.

167. Wenamun 2, 35. The word, as written, is a hapax. Solutions have been to emend to *snnw*, "(chariot)-officer" (*AEO* 1:28*; A. R. Schulman, "The Egyptian Chariotry: A Reexamination," *JARCE* 2 [1963]: 87–88; Meeks, *Année lexicographique*, 2:332–33, 3:258), or *snt-t3*, "foundations" (Römer, *Gottes- und Priesterherrschaft in Ägypten*, 75). My own suggestion would be to read *ḥn.tyw*, "commanding officers": *Wb.* III, 122:4–6; P. Harris, 77, 9; KRI 2:912:2.

168. See Chapter 13.

169. BM 10383, 1, 10.

170. Cf. ibid., 3, 3–6. Note how the mayor of Thebes refused to act without Pharaoh's authorization! That Ramesses XI was a "shrewd and tactically apt politician" (A. Thijs, *GM* 184 [2001]: 73) is, however, beyond anyone's power to verify. Debunking conventional views may be gratifying but does not necessarily point the way to the truth.

171. Wenamun 1, 52; 2, 61.

172. Ibid., 15–16; 2, 26.

173. M.-A. Bonhême, *Le Livre des rois de la Troisième Période intermédiaire*, vol. 1, XXIe Dynastie (Cairo, 1987).

174. Cf. E. F. Wente, *Late Ramesside Letters* (Chicago, 1966); idem, *Letters from Ancient Egypt* (Atlanta, 1990), 171–204; A. Thijs, "Piankh's Second Nubian Campaign," *GM* 165 (1998): 99–103; idem, "Reconsidering the End of the Twentieth Dynasty I: The Fisherman Pnekhtemope and the Date of BM 10054," *GM* 167 (1998): 95–108; idem, "Reconsidering the End of the Twentieth Dynasty, Part II," *GM* 170 (1999): 83–100.

7. THE SILENT YEARS

1. *LdR* 3:233; occasionally the title turns up in the Third Intermediate Period (cf. Osorkon-onkh: Reisner, "Viceroys of Ethiopia," 75), but by this time it was obsolete.

2. *Kawa* I, 84–86.

3. Randall-MacIver and Woolley, *Buhen*, 86.

4. Reisner, "Inscribed Monuments from Gebel Barkal," *ZÄS* 66 (1931): 84.

5. KRI 7:396:15–16.

6. See Chapter 6.

7. Cf. the chilling passage in the trial transcript of BM 1052:11, 7–8, "in the year of the jackal, when people were hungry I sold it for corn" (Ramesses XI, year 19); cf. Gardiner, *Ramesside Administrative Documents*, 68:2. A "hydrological crisis" (Török, *Kingdom of Kush*, 31) seems very much in evidence during the late Twentieth through early Twenty-second Dynasties.

8. Archaeological Survey of Nubia, 1908–9, 29; Säve-Söderbergh, "Preliminary Report of the Scandinavian Archaeological Investigations between Faras and Gemal," 37; Adams, *Nubia*, 241–42; J. Leclant, in *General History of Africa*, vol. 2, *Ancient Civilizations of Africa* (Paris, 1981), 278; O'Connor (*Ancient Nubia*, 58) puts the Nubian withdrawal down to "hostilities with Egypt." Assertions to the contrary rest largely on an *argumentum e silentio*.

9. *HSLN*, 112–14.

10. But cf. M. Horton, "Egypt in Africa: New Evidence from Qasr Ibrim," in Davies, *Egypt and Africa*, 264–77. Alleged references to Kushites in Egyptian armed forces in the contexts of the tenth and ninth centuries B.C. come from demonstrably late and unreliable sources (II Chron. 12:3; 14:8–11).

11. P. Rowley-Conwy, "The Camel in the Nile Valley: New Radiocarbon Accelerator (AMS) Dates from Qaṣr Ibrîm," *JEA* 74 (1988): 246.

12. D. Dunham, *The Barkal Temples* (Boston, 1970), pls. 3–4.

13. Leclant, "Fouilles et travaux en Égypte et au Soudan, 1987–1988," 417.

14. T. Kendall, "The Origin of the Napatan State: El-Kurru and the Evidence for the Royal Ancestors," in *Seventh International Conference for Meroitic Studies* (Berlin, 1992); Török, *Kingdom of Kush*, 115–23.

15. Geus, "Burial Customs in the Upper Main Nile," 65.

16. *HSLN*, 117 ff; Arkell, *History of the Sudan to 1821*, 116; W. B. Emery, *Egypt in Nubia* (London, 1965), 208; O'Connor, in Trigger et al, *Ancient Egypt*, 269–70.

17. Caminos, *Chronicle of Prince Osorkon*, 125f.

18. On the inadequacy of our sources for the early Napatan period, see K.-H. Priese, "The Napatan Period," in Hochfield and Riefstahl, *Africa in Antiquity*, 1:75.

19. For a resumé, see E. Drioton and J. Vandier, *L'Égypte*, 4th ed. (Paris, 1962), suppl. 675; Kees, *Das Priestertum im ägyptischen Staat*, 1:265; Reisner, "Viceroys of Ethiopia," 54.

20. Reisner's denial (*HTR* 13 [1920]: 30) belongs to a forgotten mind-set; cf. Leclant, *Recherches sur les monuments thébains de la XXVe dynastie dite éthiopienne* (Cairo, 1965), 1:331f. Although the Napatan community belonged, broadly speaking, to the same *culture* group as the Nubians of the third and second millennia B.C., there is little or no *political* continuum between Kerma and the incipient Napatan kingdom. Kerma had been completely swept away in the Egyptian imperial expansion, and those Nubians and Kushites who had not been

killed, deported, or put to flight had been marginalized in the provincial admin-istration. Kerma and Napata, apart from exhibiting the aboriginal capacity of translating a chiefdom into a state, share little in common: cf. O'Connor, *Ancient Nubia*, 58–59.

21. R. A. Parker, *A Saite Oracle Papyrus from Thebes in the Brooklyn Museum* (Providence, 1962), pl. I.

22. K.-H. Priese, "Napatan Period," 89–95; A. Lohwasser, "Queenship in Kush: Status, Role and Ideology of Royal Women," *JARCE* 38 (2001): 61–76.

23. On the possibility that Alara was an outsider with respect to the Napatan community, having been born elsewhere, see Priese, "Napatan Period," 76–77; cf. Török, *Kingdom of Kush*, 123–24.

24. On the distinctive orthography, grammar, and dialect of "Kushite" Egyp-tian, see Leclant and Yoyotte, "Notes d'histoire et de civilisation éthiopiennes. A propros 'un ouvrage récent,'" *BIFAO* 51 (1952): 7.

25. *AAAE*, 225 and 236; Redford, *Egypt, Canaan, and Israel*, 344 and nn. 116–17.

26. R. A. Fazzini, "Some Egyptian Reliefs in Brooklyn," *Miscellanea Wilbouriana* 1 (1972): 65, fig. 36.

27. For the probable palace of the Twenty-fifth Dynasty kings, see T. Kendall, "The Napatan Palace at Gebel Barkal: A First Look at B 1200," in Davies, *Egypt and Africa*, 302–13. Further: idem, *National Geographic Magazine* 178, no. 5 (1990): 96–125.

28. Leclant, *Recherches*, 230; *Orientalia* 59 (1990): fig. 92; for devotion to the area, cf. the queenly title *Mr.s Npt*, "She-loves-Napata": A. Leahy, "Kushite Monuments at Abydos," in C. Eyre et al., eds., *The Unbroken Reed: Studies in the Culture and Heritage of Ancient Egypt* (London, 1994), 182 and 191 n. 17.

29. See Chapter 13.

30. E. Russman, *Representations of the King in the Twenty-fifth Dynasty*, 25f; on the so-called Kushite cap, see idem, "Some Reflections on the Regalia of the Kushite Kings of Egypt," *Meroitica* 5 (1979): 49–51.

31. *Kawa* I, 16 (stela IV, 13–20); Leclant and Yoyotte, "Notes d'histoire et de civilisation éthiopiennes," 15.

32. Priese, "Napatan Period," 86; that some military tactics, that is, cavalry warfare, were developed "in Kush long before this tactic was employed in Egypt" (L. Török, in Davies, *Egypt and Africa*, 197) simply ignores the prior evolution of this military arm among the Assyrians and the overriding probability that the proximity of the Delta to the Assyrian empire would mean that Egypt received its influences first.

33. On the Kushite military establishment, see A. J. Spalinger, "The Military Background of the Campaign of Piye (Piankhy)," *SAK* 7 (1979): 273–301; the non-native origin of siege techniques is hinted at by the use of loanwords to des-ignate techniques and construction (cf. Piankhy, 32; J. Hoch, *Semitic Words in Egyptian Texts of the New Kingdom and Third Intermediate Period* [Princeton, 1994], 368 no. 548). Interestingly, remains of an Egyptian(?) siege mound, prob-ably temp. Sheshonk I, have now been recovered at Megiddo: B. Halpern oral communication.

34. P-M 5:227; *LdR* 4:5 (2, 1), n. 2; J. Leclant, "Kashta, Pharaon, en Egypte," *ZÄS* 90 (1963): 74–81, fig. 1.

35. The bibliography on the "Sea Peoples" is enormous. One might consult the following recent additions to the corpus: J. F. Brug, *Literary and Archaeological Study of the Philistines* (Oxford, 1985); R. Drews, *The End of the Bronze Age* (Princeton, 1993); P. W. Haider, *Griechenland-Nordafrika* (Darmstadt, 1988); O. Margalith, *The Sea Peoples in the Bible* (Wiesbaden, 1994); F. Schachermayer, *Mykene und das Hethiterreich* (Wien, 1986); W. A. Ward and M. Joukowsky, *The Crisis Years: The Twelfth Century B.C.* (Dubuque, Iowa, 1992); F. Woudhuizen, *The Language of the Sea Peoples* (Amsterdam, 1992); an excellent bibliography is amassed in B. Eder, *Staat, Herrschaft, Gesellschaft in frühgriechischer Zeit* (Vienna, 1994); E. Oren, ed., *The Sea Peoples and Their World: A Reassessment* (Philadelphia, 2000).

36. For concern by the authorities, cf. P. Louvre, 3169 (G. Maspero, *Mémoire sur quelque papyrus du Louvre* [Paris, 1875], 110–11); for disturbances in the Thebaid by Libyans and "foreigners," see KRI 6:687:14–688; cf. 643, 871:4; also P. Mayer A, 8:14.

37. Redford, *Egypt, Canaan, and Israel*, 299; cf. the "Stronghold of Ramesses-ruler-of-Heliopolis" and the contingent of *Thr* troops stationed there under Ramesses III: D. Kessler, *SAK* 2 (1975): 103 ff, pl. 2; KRI 5:270; cf. also KRI 3:59, 63. The chief agent of Herihor had been one Peri-Arsaphes (KRI 7:387), who, as his name implies, probably hailed from Herakleopolis.

38. In general, see A. Leahy, ed., *Libya and Egypt c. 1300–750 BC* (London, 1987).

39. Cf. E. Naville, *The Festival Hall of Osorkon II in the Great Temple of Bubastis* (London, 1892), pl. 6 lines 10–11.

40. Cf. *LdR* 3:232–35.

41. Cf. Nakhtefmut (Cairo 42208), who mentions "the king whom I served in my time. . . . I served the kings, and was unscathed by their rages"; also Dkedkhonsefankh (Cairo 42211), who was "a solitary voice speaking when (other) voices are silent, calming the sovereign down in (his) rages." Harsiese (Philadelphia, UM E 16025): "with unrestricted movement permitted by the king, pacifying H.M. in his moment (scil. of anger)."

42. Naville, *Festival Hall*, pl. 6.

43. On the Theban rebellion, see Caminos, *Chronicle of Prince Osorkon*.

44. Cf. Osorkon's autobiography (cf. ibid.): "the sky not having swallowed the moon," that is, there had not been a lunar eclipse.

45. Admittedly this was the usual legal punishment for treason: A. B. Lloyd, *Herodotus, Book II. A Commentary* (Leiden, 1988), 2:214.

46. Memphis, Saïs, Sebennytos, Mendes, Busiris, Parbaëthos, and Pisapti.

47. Bubastis, Leontopolis, Herakleopolis, and Hermopolis.

48. See for this period J. Yoyotte, *Les Principautés du Delta au temps de l'anarchie libyennes, études d'histoire politique* (Cairo, 1961); K. A. Kitchen, *The Third Intermediate Period in Egypt (1100–650 B.C.)* (Warminster, 1973); F. Gomàa, *Die libyschen Fürstentümer des Deltas* (Wiesbaden, 1974).

49. For the concept and hierarchy of authority in the eighth century, see Chapter 13.

8. THE SUDAN INVADES EGYPT

1. On the reading of the name, see Priese, "Nichtaegyptische Namen und Woerter in den aegyptischen Inschriften der Könige von Kusch," *MIOF* 14 (1968): 166–91; J. von Beckerath, "Zu den Namen des kuschitischen Königs Pi(anchy," *MDAIK* 24 (1969): 58–62; G. Vittman, *Orientalia* 43 (1974): 12–16. Although I realize the difficulties, I have chosen to retain the traditional reading.

2. Unfortunately, no artistic representations of any size have been preserved for Piankhy. On his reign as transitional in the confluence of a "Kushite style" with native Egyptian traits, see K. Myśliwiec, *Royal Portraiture of the Dynasties XXI–XXX* (Mainz am Rhein, 1988), 34–35.

3. Cf. Neskhons, singer of Amun, daughter of the great chief of the Me, Horwadj: Berlin 7478; Nebyammehi, daughter of the great chief of Labu, Ankhhor: J. Yoyotte, "Les Principautés du Delta au temps de l'anarchie Lybienne," in *Mélanges Maspero* (Cairo, 1961), 4:117.

4. On the quay graffiti from Karnak, recording the height of the annual inundations, see J. von Beckerath, "The Nile Level Records at Karnak and Their Importance for the History of the Libyan Period (Dyn. XXII and XXIII)," *JARCE* 5 (1965): 43–55.

5. P. Barguet, *Le Temple d'Amon-rê à Karnak* (Paris, 1962), 92.

6. Pedibast's ancestry is in doubt. There is no proof that he was a son of Sheshonq III or of the high priest of Amun Harsiese II (*LdR* 4:349, 380). Moreover, the very *number* of kings called by the name is not certain, since several prenomina are found coupled with the name *P3-di-b3stt*: A. R. Schulman, "A Problem of Pedubast," *JARCE* 5 (1966): 33 ff; L. Habachi, "Three Monuments of the Unknown King Sehetepibre Pedubastis," *ZÄS* 93 (1966): 69–75. Still, the eventuality of changes of prenomina is not without parallel.

7. W. G. Waddell, *Manetho* (London, 1940), 160–62.

8. P. Montet, *Le Lac sacré de Tanis* (Paris, 1966), pl. 30 (with prenomen "Sehetep-ib-re").

9. Scarab distribution of the Twenty-third Dynasty includes the northwestern Delta (Naukratis) and the western Mediterranean (Carthage, Spain, and Portugal): J. Leclant, *Orientalia* 48 (1979): 407; but in the present quest this is weak evidence.

10. P-M 4:39.

11. G. Daressy, "Trois stèles de la Période Bubastite," *ASAE* 15 (1915): 144. It is clear now that Pemiu's authority continued to extend as far as Heliopolis: S. Bickel, M. Gabolde, and P. Tallet, "Des annales heliopolitaines de la Troisieme Periode Intermediaire," *BIFAO* 98 (1998): 31–56.

12. Stela of Horkheby, dated as from year 23 of "Usermare Setepen-amun, Pedibast son-of-Bastet, maiamun," a donation stela: S. Bosticco, *Le stele egiziane (Firenze)*, vol. 3 (Rome, 1972), no. 3 (7207). The cartouches of Pedibast and the

date are very lightly incised at the feet of the gods depicted in the vignette, in contrast to the boldness of the rest of the cutting. They are not part of the main text and look for all the world like an afterthought!

13. There is a school of thought which would assign Thebes as a place of origin and residence of the Twenty-third Dynasty: cf. for discussion and literature A. Dodson, "The Third Intermediate Period," in *The Oxford Encyclopedia of Ancient Egypt*, 3:388–94. If the dynasty ever in fact resided in Thebes, it must have shortly abandoned it: Piankhy, always precise in recording names and bailiwicks, mentions no member of that dynasty in Thebes, even though he must have belonged to the generation of Takelot III.

14. Von Beckerath, "Nile Level Records at Karnak," 52.

15. *ASAE* 14 (1914): 39–40.

16. *Karnak* 6 (1980): pl. XIIIb.

17. G. E. Kadish and D. B. Redford, *The Temple of Osiris Heqa Djet at Karnak* (Toronto, forthcoming).

18. CCG 42226c; K. Jansen-Winkeln, *Aegyptologische Biographien der 22. und 23. Dynastie* (Wiesbaden, 1985), pl. 30–34.

19. CCG 42226h.

20. CCG 42226k.

21. CCG 42211.

22. CCG 42210.

23. Cf. the tomb of King Userton; F. Ll. Griffiths, *Catalogue of the Demotic Papyri in the John Rylands Library, Manchester* (Manchester, 1909), 3:19 n. 2; M. Malinine, *Choix de textes juridiques* (Paris, 1953), no. XI; Redford, *King-lists, Annals, and Day-books*, 313 and n. 112.

24. Cf. his epithets: "the holy likeness of Amunre, his living image upon earth," CCG 42197; his Horus-name was "appearing in Thebes" (*LdR* 3:382–84), his kingship was written "upon the august [*ished*]-tree of Upper Egypt" (P-M 2^2:206 [22]); var. "the august *ished*-tree in Karnak": he was "master of the cultus in Karnak" (*LdR* 3:383), and he more frequently wears the white crown in the temple of Osiris (D. B. Redford, "An Interim Report on the Second Season of Work at the Temple of Osiris Ruler of Eternity, Karnak," *JEA* 59 [1973]: pl. 21).

25. On the role of Amun, the supernal king, as a unifying element during the Third Intermediate Period, see Török, *Kingdom of Kush*, 145.

26. For detail, see Chapter 13.

27. Leclant, *Recherches*, 356 n. 2.

28. Cf. Berlin stela 14995; cf. also Berlin 2278 and 303–5, 323–25, 964, 966 (shawabtis), 2105, 2106 (canopics).

29. P-M 2^2:205(9).

30. Ibid., 205–6; Redford, "Interim Report on the Second Season of Work at the Temple of Osiris," 21–23; Török, *Kingdom of Kush*, 148.

31. Redford, "Interim Report on the Second Season of Work at the Temple of Osiris."

32. Redford, *King-lists, Annals, and Day-books*, 312–15.

33. P-M 3:787–88.

34. Redford, *King-lists, Annals, and Day-books*, 340 n. 120.

35. Sources and discussion in Redford, *Egypt, Canaan, and Israel*, 340–43; W. Pitard, *Ancient Damascus* (Winona Lake, Ind., 1987), 185–87; H. Tadmor, *The Inscriptions of Tiglath Pileser III, King of Assyria* (Jerusalem, 1994).

36. Tadmor, *Inscriptions of Tiglath Pileser III*, 168–69; idem, "Philistia under Assyrian Rule," *BA* 29 (1966): 88–89; B. Oded, in *Israelite and Judaean History* (1977), 425; N. Na'aman, "The Brook of Egypt and Assyrian Policy on the Border of Egypt," *Tel Aviv* 6 (1979): 68–70; idem, "Tiglath Pileser III's Campaigns against Tyre and Israel (734–732 B.C.E.)," *Tel Aviv* 22 (1995): 268–78; H. Klengel, *Syria 3000–300 B.C.* (Berlin, 1992), 224.

37. H. W. Saggs, "The Nimrud Letters 1952, Part II. Relations with the West," *Iraq* 17 (1955): 127–54; A. Lemaire, *Studia Phoenicia*, vol. 5 (Louvain, 1987), 53f n. 28.

38. The chronology followed here is based on D. B. Redford, "Saïs and the Kushite Invasions of the Eighth Century B.C.," *JARCE* 22 (1985): 5–15. Note, however, that a new stela of Sargon, dated as probably being from 705 B.C., mentions Shebitku as king of Egypt (I am indebted to my colleague Dr. Grant Frame for this information: see "The Inscription of Sargon II at Tang-i Var," *Orientalia* 68 [1999]: 31–57; D. B. Redford, "A Note on the Chronology of Dynasty 25 and the Inscription of Sargon II at Tang-i Var," *Orientalia* 68 [1999]: 58–60). The implications for Egyptian chronology have yet to be articulated. At the very least a long co-regency between Shabaka and Shebitku seems called for.

39. Ankh-hor fled to Memphis: J. Yoyotte, *Les Principautés*, 153 n. 2.

40. On this homogeneity, see H. de Meulenaere, "Cultes et sacerdoces à Imaou (Kôm El-Hisn) au temps des dynasties Saïte et perse," *BIFAO* 62 (1964): 167.

41. Yoyotte, *Les Principautés*, 153.

42. The famous "Athens" stela (*LdR* 3:409) is dated in his eighth year, which would fall, on the basis of the chronological system promoted herein, in 717 B.C., the very year of Piankhy's invasion and the last of Tefnakhte's reign. Those who wish to conjure up a *second* Tefnakhte reigning after Bocchoris and before Necho I (cf. Redford, *King-lists, Annals, and Day-books*, 326–27) will have to counter not only the arguments presented in the last cited work but also the improbability of the historical situation, for they will have to assume that the rule of Saïs, terminated by the execution of Bocchoris at the hands of Sabaco, mysteriously reappeared under a conquering Sudanese dynasty whose control of the Delta was complete and whose antipathy towards Saïs implacable! They will also have to assume that a triumphant Sabaco, who had just put Bocchoris to death, allowed a successor to call himself king!

43. Piankhy stela, lines 2–4.

44. Ibid., lines 99 and 115: Yoyotte, *Les Principautés*, 159 ff.

45. Piankhy stela, line 18; Yoyotte, *Les Principautés*, 165 ff.

46. Piankhy stela, line 18; F. Gomàa, *Die libyschen Fürstentümer*, or his predecessor Hornakht, cf. *Brooklyn Museum Annual* 9 (1967–68): 55.

47. Piankhy stela, line 19; Yoyotte, *Les Principautés*, 163f.

48. A. Leahy, *Libya and Egypt* (London, 1987), 183–85.

49. Redford, *King-lists, Annals, and Day-books*, 314–25. Although I had ear-

lier suggested Osorkon IV was another son of Osorkon III (ibid., 317 n. 126), it is tempting to see in this Osorkon a son of Takelot III, and grandson of Osorkon III, thus exemplifying the principle of papponymy in the family. On the district of Ra-noufe, see ibid., 317 n. 127: clearly Osorkon IV controlled the entire eastern tract as far as Tanis, where he had supplanted the defunct Twenty-second Dynasty.

50. Cf. Isa. 19:11–14; Hos. 7:11, 16; 9:3, 6.

51. The *So'* of II Kings 17:4. The secret of this passage was long ago revealed by H. Goedicke, "The End of 'So King of Egypt,'" *BASOR* 171 (1963): 64–66; but that has not prevented every new generation from turning a blind eye to what Goedicke has done and trying its own hand: see Redford, *Egypt, Canaan, and Israel,* 346 n. 132, for literature. Possibly this trend has now ended: cf. J. Day, *Vetus Testamentum* 42 (1992): 289 ff.

52. On the siege of Samaria and the end of Israel, see M. Cogan and H. Tadmor, *II Kings,* Anchor Bible 11 (New York, 1988), 195–201.

53. W. H. Hallo, "From Qarqar to Carchemish: Assyria and Israel in the Light of New Discoveries," *BA* 23 (1960): 51; B. Oded, *Mass Deportations and Deportees in the Neo-Assyrian Empire* (Wiesbaden, 1979), 52, 66.

54. Tadmor, *Inscriptions of Tiglath Pileser III,* 141, 171, 189.

55. Tadmor, "Philistia under Assyrian Rule," 91.

56. That is, a hypocoristicon of a PN compounded with *Re';* the name is entirely appropriate within the Egyptian onomasticon, although the individual is yet unknown.

57. Although Tefnakhte is not mentioned, it seems likely that he initiated this countermove: see the discussion in Redford, *Egypt, Canaan, and Israel,* 347 and n. 136. On the tradition of Plutarch and Diodorus, see A. Burton, *Diodorus Siculus Book I. A Commentary* (Leiden, 1972), 144f, who suggests that it originated in a misinterpretation of Tefnakhte's letter to Piankhy in the Piankhy stela.

58. *ANET*[2], 285. For possible relief material illustrating this campaign, see N. Na'aman, "Hezekia and the Kings of Assyria," *Tel Aviv* 21 (1994): 241–42. For the possibility that, on this campaign, Sargon posed a threat to Jerusalem, see M. A. Sweeney, *Biblica* 75 (1994): 457–70; K. L. Younger, *Biblica* 77 (1996): 108–10.

9. THE INVASION OF PIANKHY

1. On this king, see Kitchen, *Third Intermediate Period in Egypt,* 358; E. R. Russmann, "An Egyptian Royal Statuette of the Eighth Century B.C.," in *Dunham FS,* 149–55.

2. The list is given in the Piankhy stela, lines 3–4: see Grimal, *La Stèle triomphale de Pi('ankh)y au Musée du Caire,* 8–14; the list extends from Hnes (Kom el-Aḥmar), five kilometers south of Sharuna (*AEO* 2:106f), to Atfiḥ including the Fayum (Pi-sekhemkheperre; Caminos, *Chronicle of Prince Osorkon,* 147; Yoyotte, *Les Principautés,* 135 n. 1), "the Temple of Sobek" = Crocodilopolis (*DG* 4:102), and thus encompasses townships U.E. 18 to 22, probably inclusive. It is most likely that this represents the northern and southern limits of Peftjawabast's hegemony.

3. Cf. the "Tomb of king Userton" in Demotic contracts: Griffiths, *Catalogue of the Demotic Papyri*, 3:19 n. 2; Malinine, *Choix de textes juridiques*, 85–89, no. 11. It remains a possibility that Osorkon I is here referred to: cf. P-M vol. 1, pt. 2, p. 850 s.v. "Osorkon I."

4. Painted cartouches in the third room of the Temple of Osiris-Ruler-of-Eternity at Karnak: G. Legrain, *RT* 22 (1900): 134, 136; G. E. Kadish and D. B. Redford, *The Temple of Osiris Hk3 Dt at Karnak* (forthcoming), which are clearly later additions to the chapel; cartouche from Medinet Habu: J. Leclant, *Recherches*, 268 n. 2; A. Leahy, *SAK* 7 (1979): 146–47; Kitchen, *Third Intermediate Period in Egypt*, sec. 322.

5. LD 3:Bl. 284:a; *LdR* 3:393; M. G. el-Din Mokhtar, *Ihnâsya el-Medina* (Cairo, 1983), 131.

6. V. Hölscher, *The Excavations of Medinet Habu*, vol. 5 (Chicago, 1954), 32 nn. 102–3, fig. 21; P-M 2(2)^2:773, no. 21.

7. The absolute chronology is unknown. In the fortieth year of an unknown king Piankhy was acknowledged in Thebes, a sure sign that he controlled the region. If this was Sheshonq V of the Twenty-second Dynasty (Redford, "Saïs and the Kushite Invasions," 5–15), the date would be 725/724 B.C.

8. Perhaps in his fourth year: Török, *Kingdom of Kush*, 155–56.

9. Cf. the family of Montuemhet: Leclant, *Montouemhât*; the family of Ata contemporary with Sabaco which could trace service in the Theban priesthood of Amun through five generations: J. Leclant, *Enquêtes sur les sacerdoces et les sanctuaires égyptiens à l'époque dite "éthiopienne"* (Cairo, 1954), 16–17, 26; similarly the family of Bakenptaḥ, chief of document scribes of Amun: Leclant, *Enquêtes*, 8, and E. Graefe, *Untersuchungen zur Verwaltung und Geschichte des Institution der Gottesgemahlin des Amun vom Beginn des Neuen Reiches bis zum Spaetzeit* (Wiesbaden, 1981), 7–10; the family of the "chief of the scribes of the divine adoratress and chamberlain Tjaw-Amun-ewēse," who was probably functioning under Shepenwepet I (Graefe, *Verwaltung und Geschichte*, 80); the descendants of Takelot III are found still functioning under the Twenty-fifth and Twenty-sixth Dynasties: Redford, *King-lists, Annals, and Day-books*, 314 and n. 120.

10. Kees, *Das Priestertum im ägyptischen Staat*, 1:266.

11. Cf. Nesnebneteru, "chamberlain of the god's-wife, messenger of the Divine Worshipper to the Land of Nubia": R. Moss, *Kush* 8 (1960): 269 ff.

12. Grimal, *La Stèle triomphale de Pi($^(nkh$)y au Musée du Caire* for full bibliography.

13. One wonders whether our choice ought not to fall on the chief lector-priest Padi-amun-nebnesuttowy (stela, line 140), whom Piankhy used as a trusted ambassador. The name suggests a Theban origin, and it is not difficult to imagine this worthy as an intimate of the king from the early years of Napata's hegemony over the Thebaid. As chief lector-priest he will have been familiar with both religious and secular compositions.

14. There are lapses into the "Day-book style" at 31 to 32 and 100 to 106, but these do not seem sufficient to justify the postulate of a king's journal as one of the composer's sources.

15. The surprising success that Tefnakhte enjoyed in amassing a following is a good indication of the judgment of the moment: the northerner was the clear "odds-on" favorite. Who was this southern barbarian?

16. Attempts to locate Per-pega farther north seem to disregard the spatial sequence of events: Grimal, *La Stèle triomphale de Pi(ʿankh)y au Musée du Caire*, 38f n. 90.

17. Piankhy stela, line 27: "they took it like a cloudburst."

18. Ten miles north of modern Minya, on the east bank.

19. That Piankhy's tirade should be explained solely on the basis of economic value or the tradition of the "sportsman" king (A. J. Spalinger, "Military Background of the Campaign of Piye," 283; Török, in Davies, *Egypt and Africa*, 197) seems a trifle superficial. Whether sincere or not, Piankhy is surely intent on creating an atmosphere of righteous indignation and political correctness.

20. Piankhy stela, lines 77–78.

21. Ibid., line 82.

22. The "dry air," emanation of the "All-inclusive": S. Quirke, *Ancient Egyptian Religion* (London, 1992), 25–26.

23. Plutarch, *Agesilaus* xxxviii.1.

24. T. B. Macaulay, *The History of England* (New York, n.d.), 3:212.

25. Piankhy stela, line 89.

26. This must have been the old harbor of Peru-nefer ("The-Fair-Embarcation"), founded seven hundred years earlier in the Eighteenth Dynasty as a mustering point for expeditions into Canaan: P. Petersburg 1116A, vs.42. Precisely where it lay in the late eighth century is difficult to determine. In Piankhy's time the city was arguably smaller than in Ptolemaic times, so that the harbor may well have lain as far south as Kom el-Nawa: D. J. Thompson, *Memphis under the Ptolemies* (Princeton, 1988), 13–14, 59.

27. Piankhy stela, lines 95–96.

28. Ibid., line 96.

29. Ibid., line 99.

30. Cf. G. Daressy, "Le Fils Aîné de Chéchanq III," *ASAE* 16 (1916): 61–62; L. Habachi, "A Statue of Bakennifi, Nomarch of Athribis during the Invasion of Egypt by Assurbanipal," *MDAIK* 15 (1957): 68–77; J. Yoyotte, *Mélanges Maspero*, 4:161 ff; Gomaà, *Die libyschen Fürstentümer*, 153–54; P. Vernus, *Athribis, textes et documents* (Cairo, 1976), 74–76.

31. To nullify their pretensions to the royal office.

32. Cf. the Esarhaddon treaties: *ANET²*, 534–41.

33. Could it be that a chapter has been left out, perhaps intentionally omitted by the Nubian conqueror? Reliefs at Napata probably dating from Piankhy's floruit show battle with an enemy in Assyrian helmets (A. J. Spalinger, "Notes on the Military in Egypt during the XXVth Dynasty," *JSSEA* 11 [1981]: 48), and the name of the king's chariot, "Awe-of-His-Majesty-shall-attack-the-Asiatics," seems to presage, or commemorate, an engagement with northerners. One wonders whether at some point shortly after the reduction of Memphis and the visit to Heliopolis and Athribis Piankhy was faced by a threat from an Assyrian force.

For battle scenes from the Amun temple at Napata, see T. Kendall, *Gebel Barkal Epigraphic Survey: 1986 Preliminary Report of First Season's Activity* (Boston, 1986), figs. 9, 10; idem, *Nubian Letters* 9 (Aug. 1987): 7–10.

34. J. J. Janssen, "The Smaller Dâkhla Stela," *JEA* 54 (1968): pl. XXV.

35. R. A. Parker, "King Py: A Historical Problem," *ZÄS* 93 (1966): 111 ff.

36. Redford, *King-lists, Annals, and Day-books*, 297–302.

10. THE TWENTY-FOURTH DYNASTY

1. R. el-Sayed, *La déesse Neith de Saïs* (Cairo, 1982), 2:405.

2. Redford, *Egypt, Canaan, and Israel*, 419.

3. Not his nomen, pace G. Möller, *ZÄS* 56 (1920): 76f.; Fecht, *Wortakszent und Silbenstruktar*, sec. 139 n. 231. On the reign, see J. Krall, in *Festgaben zu Ehren Max Büdingers* (Innsbruck, 1898), 3–11; A. Moret, *De Bocchori Rege* (Paris, 1903); J. M. Janssen, in *Mélanges A. W. Byvanck* (Leiden, 1954), 17–29; D. Gill and M. Vickers, "Bocchoris the Wise and Absolute Chronology," *Mitteilungen des deutschen archaeologischen Instituts, Roemisch Abteilung* 103 (1996): 1–9.

4. Diodorus, i.65.1; i.94.5.

5. Cf. J. Hoch, "The Grotesque in Egyptian Literature and Art" (unpublished paper).

6. Cf. the description of Horus in the mouth of Re-Harakhte, *Contendings of Horus and Seth*, 3.7–8, or the array of scrawny master scribes in *Anastasi I*, 9.4–10.5; H.-W. Fischer-Elfert, *Die satirische Streitschrift des Papyrus Anastasi I* (Wiesbaden, 1986), 80–92.

7. Fazzini, "Some Egyptian Reliefs in Brooklyn," 65, fig. 36.

8. On the motif of the wise king, see Lloyd, *Herodotus*, 3:89.

9. Diodorus, i.94.5.

10. Ibid., i.79. There is no reason to give the sequence of seven Egyptian "lawgivers" any credence. The pattern is wholly Hellenic, not Egyptian. Folkloristic memory as well as misinterpreted archives lie at the root of the characterization: cf. P. Frei, "Die persische Reichsautorisation, Ein Uberblick," *Zeitschrift fur altorientalische und biblische Rechtsgeschichte* 1 (1995): 1–6.

11. For these reforms in practice, see B. Menu, *Recherches sur l'histoire juridique, économique et sociale de l'ancienne Égypte* (Paris, 1982), 272–75, 282f.

12. E. Seidl (in *Ägyptische Rechtsgeschichte der Saïten- und Perserzeit* [Berlin, 1956], 53f) thinks the reforms better fit the Twenty-first Dynasty; but A. Theodorides ("The Conception of Law in Ancient Egypt," in J. R. Harris, ed., *The Legacy of Egypt*, 2d ed. [Oxford, 1971], 319) seems to accept them; see also J. H. Johnson, "The Persians and the Continuity of Egyptian Culture," in *Achaemenid History*, vol. 8 (Leiden, 1994), 157; D. B. Redford, "The So-called 'Codification' of Egyptian Law under Darius I," in J .W. Watts, ed., *Persia and Torah: The Theory of Imperial Authorization of the Pentateuch* (Atlanta, 2001), 137–38.

13. Psammetichos III: W. W. How and J. Wells, *A Commentary on Herodotus* (Oxford, 1912; reprint, 1967), 1:iii.13–14; Mycerinos: ibid., ii.129–35; Amasis is referred to in the context of the codification of Egyptian law. Diodorus, i.95.1; E. Bresciani, "La satrapia d'Egitto," *SCO* 7 (1958): 153–55; on the memory of a census, see Pliny, *Historia naturalis*, v. 11; Amasis may also have authorized a major redaction of sacred books: E. A. E. Reymond, *From Ancient Egyptian Hermetic Writings* (Vienna, 1977), 30f; cf. P.D. 6319 x+iii, 1–2, 5–6.

14. Cf., for example, the doings of one Ikeni in the forty-ninth year of Sheshonq III: Parker, *Saite Oracle Papyrus from Thebes*, 49–51.

15. See Piankhy's brief but pithy disquisition on kingship, Chapter 13.

16. See further below.

17. Redford, *King-lists, Annals, and Day-books*, 327.

18. See ibid., 276–96.

19. See P-M 4:46–49; R. Lepsius, *Denkmäler aus Ägypten und Nubien* (Berlin, 1849), 1:56.

20. Inexplicably the possibility has been entertained that Piankhy's campaign had terminated the kingships of Auput and Osorkon, leaving Saïs with the field (Yoyotte, *Les Principautés*, 172), even though the Piankhy stela says nothing of the sort. Although the fate of Auput remains unknown, Osorkon is undoubtedly the Shilkanni of Sargon's records (see below).

21. J. Leclant, "Découvertes de monuments égyptiens ou égyptisants hors de la vallée du Nil, 1955–1960," *Orientalia* 30 (1961): 404.

22. Eusebius, *Hieron. Chronicon* (ed. Schöne II, 81): A. Bernard, *Le Delta égyptien d'après les Textes grecs* (Cairo, 1970), 603.

23. H. Tadmor, "The Campaigns of Sargon II of Assur: A Chronological-Historical Study," *JCS* 12 (1958): 77–78; the strategic advantage of controlling Wady el-Arish was that it controlled the route to Egypt, which bifurcated at that point: J. Clédat, "Fouilles à Cheikh Zouède (Janvier-Février 1913)," *ASAE* 15 (1915): 16.

24. N. Na'aman and R. Zadok, "Sargon II's Deportations to Israel and Philistia (716–708 BC)," *JCS* 40 (1988): 36–46.

25. Tadmor, "Philistia under Assyrian Rule," 92; M. Elat, "The Economic Relations of the Neo-Assyrian Empire with Egypt," *JAOS* 98 (1978): 87f; R. Reich, "The Identification of the 'Sealed *kāru* of Egypt,'" *IEJ* 34 (1984): 32–38; on the nature of Sargon's overall policy, see A. Alt, *Kleine Schriften zur Geschichte des Volkes Israel* (Munich, 1953), 2:141–46; Na'aman, "Brook of Egypt and Assyrian Policy," 71 n. 7.

26. E. F. Weidner, "Silka(ḫe)ni, König von Muṣri, ein Zeitgenosse Sargons II," *AfO* 14 (1941–44): 40–53; Tadmor, "Campaigns of Sargon II of Assur," 78; N. Na'aman, "Population Changes in Palestine Following Assyrian Deportations," *Tel Aviv* 20 (1993): 109; for tribute about the same time from Gaza, Judah, Moab, and Ammon, see H. Saggs, "Nimrud Letters 1952, Part II," 134; five horses from Egypt are mentioned in ABL no. 1427

27. W. F. Albright, "Further Light on Sychronisms between Egypt and Asia in the Period 935–685 B.C.," *BASOR* 141 (1956): 24.

28. Redford, *King-lists, Annals, and Day-books*, 315.

29. A Philistine, according to H. Tadmor: cf. "Campaigns of Sargon II of Assur," 80 n. 217; on the alleged (Greek) Cypriot origin of Yamani, see Z. J. Kapera, "Biblical Reflections of the Struggle for Philistia at the End of the Eighth Century B.C.," *Folia Orientalia* 14 (1972–73): 207–18.

30. N. Na'aman, "Sennacherib's 'Letter To God' on His Campaign to Judah," *BASOR* 214 (1974): 32.

31. Redford, "Egypt and Western Asia in the Old Kingdom," 11–15; Z. J. Kapera, "The Oldest Account of Sargon II's Campaign against Ashdod," *Folia Orientalia* 24 (1987): 29–39.

32. In fairness the sources represent Pir(u as being bribed and cajoled and do not suggest that there was an Egyptian initiative. Note that chapter 20 of Isaiah, which records the prophets' reaction to the events of 712, suggests that help had been expected from Egypt but had not arrived.

33. How and Wells, *Commentary on Herodotus,*1:ii.137.1.

34. Ibid.

35. Plausibly identified with Herakleopolis Parva (*Ḥwt-nn-nsw*) near Tanis: Lloyd, *Herodotus*, 3:91.

36. *Sub.* "Sabacon": Waddell, *Manetho*, 166–68; Lloyd, *Herodotus*, 3:94, regards this tradition as implausible. Cf. also the Sothis-book (Waddell, *Manetho*, 246).

37. Redford, *King-lists, Annals, and Day-books*, 229–30.

38. Akhenaten threatens Aziru with death by fire for his treasonous acts: EA 162; Sesostris I consigns rebellious subjects and invaders to the flames: Redford, "Tod Inscription of Senwosret I," 92–93; the high priest Osorkon executes the Theban rebels by fire: *Bubastite Portal*, col. 36; Caminos, *Chronicle of Prince Osorkon*, 48; on the common motif in Ptolemaic times of throwing the rebellious Seth and his accomplices into the flames, see J. Vandier, *Le papyrus Jumilhac* (Paris, 1953), 147; in Onkhsheshonqy iv.4–5 the king burns in a copper furnace those who had conspired against his life; see in general A. Leahy, "Death by Fire in Ancient Egypt," *JESHO* 27 (1984): 200–206; of course the ultimate act of treason, that is, against the almighty, was punishable by fire in the Underworld: cf. the cauldron in the eleventh hour of the Am-duat, J.-C. Goyon, *Confirmation du pouvoir royal au nouvel an* (Cairo, 1972), 105 n. 210; E. Hornung, *Höllenvorstellungen* (Berlin, 1968), pl. V; on the river or lake of fire in the Underworld, cf. J. Zandee, *Death as an Enemy* (Leiden, 1963), 309; W. F. von Bissing, "Tombeaux d'époque romaine à Akhmîm," *ASAE* 50 (1950): 573f (cf. pl. 1, where the Soul burns in a cauldron in anticipation of the early Christian "hell"); in general see L. Kakósy, *ZÄS* 97 (1971): 95–106. For the erroneous notion of the ceremonial execution of the king, see J. G. Griffiths, *Plutarch: De Iside et Osiride* (Cardiff, 1970), 551–53.

39. Adultery: Westcar IV, 15–17; murder: Rylands, IX and XIII, 10–11.

40. The point is developed in Redford, *King-lists, Annals, and Day-books*, 315–17.

41. Survived, perhaps, by his great royal wife, Peksater: Leahy, "Kushite Monuments at Abydos," 176–82.

42. Redford, "Saïs and the Kushite Invasions," 7–8.

11. THE RESISTANCE TO ASSYRIAN EXPANSION

1. On the conquest, see Leclant, "Les inscriptions 'éthiopienne' sur la porte du IVᵉ pylone du grand temple d'Amon à Karnak," *RdÉ* 8 (1951): 111 n. 1; the conventional scene on the pylon at Medinet Habu of Sabaco slaying his enemies, both Asiatic and African (Leclant, *Recherches.* vol. 2, pl. 82B) can scarcely be accepted as evidence: Leclant, *Recherches*, 1:339 n. 4. On the representation of Sabaco in art, see Myśliwiec, *Royal Portraiture*, 35–38.

2. Leclant, *Recherches*, 1:323–25; E. K. Lillesø, "Two Wooden Uraei," *JEA* 61 (1975): 139.

3. Leclant, *Recherches*, 1:335–36.

4. For the southern limit of Twenty-fifth Dynasty hegemony, see Arkell, *History of the Sudan to 1821*, 136–37.

5. On the Kushite failure to solve the "problem" of the Delta dynasts, see Chapter 13.

6. The new stela from Tang-i Var (G. Frame, "The Inscription of Sargon II at Tang-i Var," *Orientalia* 68 [1999]: 31–57) has complicated our former understanding of the chronology of the Twenty-fifth Dynasty. If Shebitku was already in power in 705 B.C., and if Sabaco enjoyed fifteen years on the throne (BM 24429: Leclant, *Enquêtes*, pl. V), then the latter's accession would have come about, barring a co-regency, in 721–720 B.C. Not only, however, is there no mention of him between 721 and 712, but the references we do have to magnates and kings of Egypt during this time span (Re'u, Silkanni, Pir⟨u) weigh heavily against a Kushite presence. Solutions that might be tendered include the following: (1) The BM text recording year 15 is a forgery (cf., e.g., the anomalous writing of the month name). Year 12 is in fact Sabaco's highest year. (2) Sabaco and Shebitku reigned jointly for at least three years and possibly longer, the latter, however, exercising principal authority. (3) Sabaco had indeed conquered Egypt in 720 B.C. but had exercised such loose hegemony that, for the first nine years, the Assyrians mistook Delta dynasts as independent rulers of Egypt. (4) Sabaco eliminated Bocchoris in 712–711, but his regnal years had been recognized in some quarters as early as his second year, perhaps in consequence of a Kushite claim already in place.

Sealings of Sabaco from the palace of Sennacherib (see n. 8 below) prove that he was still alive after 705 B.C. and make solution number 2 obligatory. Solutions 3 and 4 may be ruled out; the issue of number 1 remains moot.

7. Redford, "Saïs and the Kushite Invasions," 6–7; idem, *Orientalia* 68 (1999): 58–60.

8. A. H. Layard, *Discoveries in Nineveh and Babylon* (London, 1853), 1:156–59; H. R. Hall, *Catalogue of Egyptian Scarabs etc. in the British Museum* (London, 1913), 1:290f.

9. Cf. the paltry one thousand troops Osorkon II sent to the Battle of Qarqar. Lemaire ("Joas de Samarie, Barhadad de Damas, Zakkur de Hamat: La Syrie-Palestine vers 800 av. J.-C.," in S. Ahituv and B. A. Levine, eds., *Eretz Israel* 24: Avraham Malamat Volume [Jerusalem, 1993], 152*) has ingeniously tried to argue that *Musri* here is a mistake for *Simirra*, ancient Sumur, the erstwhile head-

quarters of the Egyptian empire. But it is that very longstanding attachment to Sumur as a conduit for Egyptian influence which could militate as well in favor of the accuracy of Shalmaneser's record. Osorkon's very titulary, in fact, indicates the will to get involved militarily in western Asia: cf. his title "smiting the Asiatics," *LdR* 3:237–39; cf. (probably), I. E. S. Edwards, *Hieratic Papyri in the British Museum. Fourth Series* (London, 1960), L. 7:34–37.

10. On Phoenicia as Egypt's trading partner in the Late Period, see Redford, *Egypt, Canaan, and Israel,* 334f; on the dominance of Tyre as a commercial and trading power, see E. Lipínska, in *Studia Phoenicia,* vol. 3 (Louvain, 1985), 213–20; I. M. Diakonoff, "The Naval Power and Trade of Tyre," *IEJ* 42 (1992): 168–93.

11. After the fall of Samaria the policy of Assyria was to isolate Judah by concentrating on the coastal plain (N. Na'aman, "Brook of Egypt and Assyrian Policy," 71 n. 7; L. D. Levine, "Sennacherib's Southern Front," *JCS* 34 [1982]: 28–58) and strengthening Transjordan. For Assyrian influence in Moab and Edom, see C. M. Bennett, "Neo-Assyrian Influences in Transjordan," in A. Hadidi, ed., *Studies in the History and Archaeology of Jordan,*vol. 1 (Amman, 1982), 181–88; idem, in J. F. A. Sawyer and D. J. A. Clives, *Midian, Moab and Edom* (Sheffield, 1983), 16; M. M. Ibrahim, "Sahab and Its Foreign Relations," in A. Hadidi, ed., *Studies in the History and Archaeology of Jordan,* vol. 3 (Amman, 1987), 79; U. Worschek, *The Near East in Antiquity* 3 (1992): 12.

12. On the campaign of 701, see in general J. M. Miller and J. H. Hayes, *A History of Ancient Israel and Judah* (Philadelphia, 1986), 353–63; Cogan and Tadmor, *II Kings,* 223–51; Redford, *Egypt, Canaan, and Israel,* 351–54 and n. 165.

13. Cf., in general, Tadmor, "Philistia under Assyrian Rule," 95 ff; Na'aman, "Hezekia and the Kings of Assyria," 235–54.

14. The seal of the Kingdom of Judah: A. D. Tushingham, "A Royal Israelite Seal(?) and the Royal Jar Handle Stamps," *BASOR* 200 (1970): 71-78; 201 (1971): 23–35.

15. A. F. Rainey, "Wine from the Royal Vineyards," *BASOR* 245 (1982): 61; N. Na'aman, "Hezekiah's Fortified Cities and the *LMLK* Stamp," *BASOR* 261 (1986): 5–21.

16. Cf. II Kings 20:12–13.

17. B. Oded, in Miller and Hayes, *History of Ancient Israel and Judah,* 445–47; on the geopolitical commonality of Tyre, Sidon, and the Philistine coast, see M. Haran, "Observations on the Historical Background of Am. 1.2–2.6," *IEJ* 18 (1968): 202; N. Na'aman, in *Ah Assyria! . . . Studies in Assyrian History Presented to Hayim Tadmor* (Jerusalem, 1991), 80–89.

18. Cf. II Kings 18:24; Isa. 18:1–2 (referring to Kushite emissaries), usually dated between 705 and 701; H. Donner, *Israel unter der Völkern* (Leiden, 1964), 124.

19. His courage was nonetheless ill advised. Upon later reinstatement he still had to pay one talent of silver to Assyria: A. Sachs, "The Late Assyrian Royal Seal Type," *Iraq* 15 (1953): 169 and n. 21, pl. 19; A. R. Millard, *Iraq* 27 (1965): 16 no. 21.

20. S. Mittmann, "Hiskia und die Philister," *Journal of North West Semitic Language* 16 (1990): 91–106.

21. M. Elayi, "Les Relations entre les cités phéniciennes et l'empire assyrien sous le règne de Sennacherib," *Semitica* 35 (1985): 19–26.

22. R. D. Barnett, *Archaeology* 9 (1956): 87–92.

23. Cf. *ANET²*, 287b.

24. Ten years later he and some Egyptians turn up in a Ninevite document: C. H. W. Johns, *Assyrian Deeds and Documents* (Cambridge, 1898), 324.

25. D. D. Luckenbill, *The Annals of Sennacherib* (Chicago, 1924), 30:63–64.

26. On the siege of Lachish, see D. Ussishkin, *The Conquest of Lachish by Sennacherib* (Tel Aviv, 1982); R. Jacoby, "The Representation and Identification of Cities on Assyrian Reliefs," *IEJ* 41 (1991): 122–31.

27. II Kings 18:13–16.

28. It was apparently the prospect of imminent reprisals against Ekron which prompted the final call for help to Egypt (*ANET²*, 287), but as we have seen, Egypt was probably involved in the anti-Assyrian coalition from the beginning.

29. On the location of Eltekeh, see W. F. Albright, *Archaeology and the Religion of Israel* (Baltimore, 1956), 209 n. 82.

30. *ANET²*, 287.

31. On the implications for Egyptian "kingship," see Chapter 13, section entitled "The Twenty-fifth Dynasty versus the Delta Dynasts."

32. Cf. Exod. 16:4; Judg. 4:15, 5:21.

33. Leclant, *Recherches,* 1:339 n. 4; vol. 2, pl. 82B.

34. An archaic term for the West Semitic–speaking peoples north of the Sinai Peninsula.

35. Von Beckerath, "Nile Level Records," 53, no. 33.

36. II Kings 19:35.

37. A. de Selincourt and A. R. Burn, *Herodotus: The Histories* (New York, 1971), 185–86; Lloyd, *Herodotus,* 3:98–105.

38. Josephus, *Ant. Jud.,* X.1.5.

39. Cf. the abortive Assyrian attempt at the eastern Delta in 674 B.C.(?): *ANET²*, 303; Nebuchadrezzar's defeat at "Migdol" in 600 B.C.: D. J. Wiseman, *Chronicles of Chaldaean Kings* (London, 1956), 71; E. Lipínska, "The Egypto-Babylonian War of the Winter 601–600 B.C.," *AION* 22 (1972): 235–41; Cambyses's victory over Psammetichus III: How and Wells, *Commentary on Herodotus,* 1:ii.10–12. On the Persian invasions, see Diodorus, xv.41-43; xvi.46.4–47.7.

40. I Sam. 6:5.

41. R. A. S. MacAlister, *The Philistines, Their History and Civilization* (Chicago, 1965), 47.

42. How and Wells, *Commentary on Herodotus,*1:i.105. Not very convincingly construed as pederasty or impotence (How and Wells, *Commentary on Herodotus,* 107). On Aphrodite Ourania, see MacAlister, *Philistines, Their History and Civilization,* 94; K.-H. Bernhardt, *MIOF* 13 (1967): 173 n. 53; V. Pirenne, in *Studia Phoenicia,* 5:148–53; D. B. Redford, "The Sea and the God-

dess," in S. Israelit-Groll, ed., *Studies in Egyptology (FS Lichtheim)* (Jerusalem, 1990), 824–35; on Astarte *nbt pt* see R. Stadelmann, *Syrisch-Pal. Göttheiten in Ägypten* (Leiden, 1967), 106–8; Griffiths, *Plutarch*, 560.

43. It is very difficult to subscribe to such statements as "Sennacherib completely succeeded in consolidating the Syro-Palestinian region" and that "he defeated the Egyptians": so J. Pečírtová, *Archiv Orientalni* 61 (1993): 3–4.

12. "TAHARQA THE CONQUEROR"

1. BM 24429 (collated): *LdR* 4:14; J. Černy, "Philological and Etymological Notes, III," *ASAE* 51 (1952): 441f; Leclant, *Enquêtes,* 15ff; idem, "Taharqa," *LdÄ* 6:156–84.

2. "Lo, His Majesty appeared (*ḫ⁽y*) in the Temple of Amun, who caused him to appear in (?) the 'Two Flourishers' (the double uraeus), like Horus on the Throne of Re": J. von Beckerath, *JARCE* 5 (1966): 53. The problem turns on whether *ḫ⁽y,* "to appear," here is used in the technical sense "to come to the throne": Redford, *History and Chronology of the Eighteenth Dynasty of Egypt,* 3–27. On the co-regency, see W. Murnane, *Ancient Egyptian Coregencies* (Chicago, 1977), 189–90.

3. Redford, *Orientalia* 68 (1999): 58–60.

4. Cf. J. von Beckerath, "Die Nilstandinschrift vom 3. Jahr Schebitkus am Kai von Karnak," *GM* 136 (1993): 7–9; the wording of *Kawa* IV, 7–9, implies that Shebitku was residing in Thebes when he sent for the siblings of the royal house. There is some evidence in the early seventh century of an erstwhile royal secretariat in Thebes: cf. the "letter-scribe of Pharaoh" Ḥor, B. V. Bothmer, *Egyptian Sculpture of the Late Period* (Brooklyn, 1960), pl. 5 (12).

5. Leclant and Yoyotte, "Notes d'histoire et de civilisation éthiopiennes," 18 n. 3; Török, *Kingdom of Kush,* 170. On the subsequent defacement of Taharqa's cartouches (which may, however, have had another rationale), see Leclant, "Découvertes de monuments égyptiens ou égyptisants," 100 and n. 7.

6. *Kawa* I, 17 nn. 17 and 19.

7. *Kawa* IV, 7–9; the last line, a "second" form (modal nominalization), lays stress on the fact that Taharqa remained with the king in Thebes and did not return home.

8. Cf. *Kawa,* V, 16–17, where, speaking of his mother, Taharqa says: "Now in fact I had left her as a youth of 20 years, when I came with His Majesty to Lower Egypt." Unless "Lower Egypt" is a loose characterization of Egypt in general, one might postulate a further trip to the Delta shortly after Taharqa's initial arrival in Thebes. On "20 years" as the age of the draft, see Merikare, P VI, l.

9. *Kawa* V, 13–14.

10. See Chapter 13.

11. Ibid. and n. 30 for the translation.

12. Karnak Room VI, cols. 17–18.

13. Ibid., col. 17.

14. For the chronology of the period, see R. A. Parker, "The Length of Reign

of Amasis and the Beginning of the Twenty-Sixth Dynasty," *MDAIK* 15 (1957): 208f; idem, *ZÄS* 92 (1965): 38f.

15. Tanis stela, line 15.

16. February 690 B.C.

17. Tanis stela, lines 1–4.

18. *LdR* 4:31 (I); Leclant, *Recherches,* 1:347.

19. *LdR* 4:32 (V).

20. D. Kessler, *Historische Topographie der Region zwischen Mallawi und Samalut* (Wiesbaden, 1981), 16; K. Butzer, *Quaternary Stratigraphy and Climate in the Near East* (Bonn, 1958), 105–22.

21. That is, the waters did not quickly subside.

22. A common cliché always used to stress the uniqueness of an event: see D. B. Redford, in *Studien zur Sprache und Religion Aegyptens,* 1:327–43; idem, *King-lists, Annals, and Day-books,* 65–96.

23. Tanis stela, lines 4–13.

24. Leclant and Yoyotte, "Notes d'histoire et de civilisation éthiopiennes," 16; for scarabs commemorating the high Nile, see idem, *RdÉ* 8 (1951): 37 ff.

25. *LdR* 5:29 (II).

26. Myśliwiec, *Royal Portraiture,* 38–39.

27. Ḥḳ3 ḫ3swt.

28. *Kawa* I, 5 ff, 33 ff. In the light of the new evidence from Tell Miqne, Onasch's doubt is quite unfounded: H.-U. Onasch, *Die assyrischen Eroberungen Ägyptens I* (Wiesbaden, 1994), 12.

29. Leclant, *Montouemhât,* 197 (2), 213 (11).

30. J. Simons, *Handbook for the Study of Egyptian Topographical Lists Relating to Western Asia* (Leiden, 1937), 187.

31. D. B. Redford, "Taharqa in Western Asia and Libya," in Ahituv and Levine, *Eretz Israel,* 188–91.*

32. J. A. Knudtzon, *Assyrische Gebete an den Sonnengott für Staat und königliches Haus aus der Zeit Asarhaddons und Asurbanipals,* vol. 2 (Leipzig, 1893), nos. 69 and 70; Tadmor, "Philistia under Assyrian Rule," 100; R. Borger, *Die Inschriften Asarhaddons Königs von Assyrien* (Osnabrück, 1967), 102; Elat, "Economic Relations of the Neo-Assyrian Empire with Egypt," 33.

33. *ANET*² *Suppl.,* 533–34; H. J. Katzenstein, *The History of Tyre, from the Beginning of the Second Millennium B.C.E. until the Fall of the Neo-Babylonian Empire in 538 B.C.E.* (Jerusalem, 1973), 267–73; in general, Redford, *Egypt, Canaan, and Israel,* 354–57; on the size and importance of the kingdom of Sidon, see E. Lipínski, in Ahituv and Levine, *Eretz Israel,* 158*–63*.

34. Na'aman, "Brook of Egypt and Assyrian Policy," 71 n. 7; Levine, "Sennacherib's Southern Front," 28–58.

35. Bennett, "Neo-Assyrian Influences in Transjordan," 1:181–87; idem, in Sawyer and Clives, *Midian, Moab and Edom,* 16; Ibrahim, "Sahab and Its Foreign Relations," 3:79; V. Worscheck, *The Near East in Antiquity* 3 (1992): 12.

36. Török, *Kingdom of Kush,* 172–73.

37. Lit. "the army of trust," that is, the royal bodyguard.

38. A. M. Moussa, "A Stela of Taharqa from the Desert Road at Dahshur," *MDAIK* 37 (1981): 332.

39. Ibid.

40. Note the "good name" of a Kushite commander in chief Pagetrer: "The-Living-One-shall-fight-for-Him": Leahy, "Kushite Monuments at Abydos," pl. XXVIa (possibly temp. Taharqa).

41. Note the important role played by the Kushite army in slightly later times in choosing the next king: Priese, "Napatan Period," 85.

13. EGYPT OF THE "BLACK PHARAOHS"

1. Cf. the growing problem of *khato*-land under the Twentieth Dynasty. See S. L. D. Katary, *Land Tenure in the Ramesside Period* (New York, 1989), 169–72 and passim.

2. Amounts taken in revenue collection seem to be dropping off: A. Gasse, *Données nouvelles administratives et sacerdotales sur l'organization du domaine d'Amon (XXe–XXIe Dynasties)* (Cairo, 1988); the scarcity may find literary reflection in Caminos, *Tale of Woe*, 4,1–5,2.

3. D. J. Brewer, D. B. Redford, and S. Redford, *Domestic Plants and Animals: The Egyptian Origins* (Warminster, 1994), 78.

4. Population figures for pharaonic Egypt are extremely difficult to come by, and a total population of about 3.5 million in Ramesside times is based partly on the assumption (quite unfounded) that it is perhaps half the putative population of Roman Egypt, that is, 7 million to 8 million: see A. K. Bowman, *Egypt after the Pharaohs* (Berkeley, 1986), 17–18.

5. The difference between "magistrates" and "support staff" as totally disparate classes is made plain in Anastasi V, 26, 5–7.

6. W. Pleyte and F. Rossi, *Les papyrus de Turin* (Wiesbaden, 1981), pl. LXVI: Ramses XI is the bearer of this titulary.

7. LRL, 36; Wente, *Letters from Ancient Egypt*, 183, no. 301.

8. A good deal of water has passed under the bridge since Sethe doubted Maspero at the turn of the century in the matter of the identity of "Sesostris," yet his views essentially live on. Cf. C. Obsomer, *Les Campagnes de Sesostris dans Herodote* (Brussels, 1989); idem, *Sesostris Ier: Etude chronologique et historique du règne* (Brussels, 1995). Needless to say, the problem of identification is still with us.

9. Gardiner, *Late Egyptian Miscellanies*, 2.

10. KRI 5:244:10–12.

11. *LdR*, vol. 3; M.-A. Bonhême, *Les Noms royaux dans l'Égypte de la troisième période intermédiaire* (Cairo, 1987).

12. The Akkadian transcription *Waš-mu-a-ri-ya* proves that the adjective is in a bound construction with $m3^{(}t$, and therefore the translation ought to be "Powerful-of-Truth-is-Re."

13. Usually the god is Re; in the case of Ramesses XI it is Ptaḥ Siptaḥ employs $sḫ^{(}.n\ R^{(}$ "he whom Re caused to appear."

14. Redford, *King-lists, Annals, and Day-books,* 310–17.

15. Smendes: "beloved of Re, whose arm Amun has strengthened to raise up *ma⟨at*"; Psusennes I: "Horus, as one granted by Amun, made to accede (to the throne) in Thebes"; Siamun: "[eldest(?)] son of Amun who came forth from his flesh"; Sheshonq I: "beloved of Re whom he has made to accede (to the throne) to unite the Two Lands"; Osorkon I: "Atum has set him on his throne to (re)-establish the Two Lands"; Osorkon II: "Re has made him accede (to the throne) as king of the Two Lands."

16. Cf. Piankhy stela, line 33.

17. Reisner, "Inscribed Monuments from Gebel Barkal," 90 (#26, line 22).

18. Ibid., line 23 (read *ḥ3wtiw*).

19. For kingship in the Late Period, see P. Kaplony, *CdÉ* 46 (1971): 250–74; Török, *Kingdom of Kush,* 163.

20. Gebel Barkal #26, lines 17–18.

21. Ibid., lines 2–6; Reisner, "Inscribed Monuments from Gebel Barkal," 90.

22. Piankhy stela, lines 1–2.

23. Karnak Room VI (P. Vernus, "Inscriptions de la Troisième Période Intermédiaire I," *BIFAO* 75 [1975]: 29), line 8.

24. *Tit* (*Wb.* V, 239–40; E. Drioton, "Trois documents d'époque amarnéenne," *ASAE* 43 (1943): 38, 44, 153; cf. K. Sethe, *Dramatische Texte in altägyptischen Mysterienspielen* (Leipzig, 1964), 51; B. Ockinga, *Die Gottebenbildlichkeit im alten Aegypten und im alten Testament* (Wiesbaden, 1984), 101-22.

25. Karnak Room VI, col. 8; more banal statements in Piankhy stela, lines 68–69.

26. *Kawa* I (year 6 inscription), line 6.

27. Moussa, "Stela of Taharqa," 332, line 17.

28. Read *m?*

29. Gebel Barkal #26, lines 8–13.

30. Karnak Room VI, line 19.

31. Ibid., 14.

32. Ibid., 6.

33. Ibid., 20.

34. Gebel Barkal #26, lines 18–20.

35. Piankhy stela, lines 67–69; cf. 79.

36. Lines 114–17.

37. *ANET*[2], 294b; Onasch, *Die assyrischen Eroberungen Aegyptens,* 36.

38. On the extent of Ra-nofer, see Redford, *King-lists, Annals, and Day-books,* 317 n. 127.

39. On the Rekhty-water, the *pḥw* of the Mendesian nome, see Redford, "Textual Sources for the Hyksos Period," 21–23. Ta-remu, "land of fishes," must be connected with the Dakahlieh plain (= the Rekhty-water): cf. the title "mayor of Ta(*sic*)-remu" at Tell Tebilla: C. C. Edgar, *ASAE* 10 (1910): 29, and 13 (1913): 227f.

40. H. de Meulenaere, "Mendes," *LdÄ,* vol. 4 (Wiesbaden, 1982), 45.

41. Why the otherwise unknown "Granary of Re" (Dunham, *Barkal Temples,* pl. L:C) should be given such prominence is a mystery.

42. These occupy positions 9–11 in Ashurbanipal's list.

43. Yoyotte, *Les Principautés,* 132; K. A. Kitchen, "Two Donation Stelae in the Brooklyn Museum," *JARCE* 8 (1969–70): 59–63; Gomaà, *Die libyschen Fürstentümer,* 74–89.

44. H. de Meulenaere and P. Mackay, *Mendes* vol. 2 (Brooklyn, 1976), 191-93, pl. 9.

45. G. Fecht, "Zu den Namen ägyptischer Fürsten und Städte in den Annalen des Assurbanipal und der Chronik des Asarhaddon," *MDAIK* 16 (1958): 112f; H. Ranke, *Die altaegyptischen Personennamen* (Glueckstadt, 1939), 100:15.

46. Largely because of the papponymy exhibited by the family over the five generations in question.

47. Yoyotte, *Les Principautés,* 159–61; Gomaà, *Die libyschen Fürstentümer,* 68–73; the Harsiese of Ashurbanipal's list (no. 9) is probably his son, which would make the Akenosh contemporary with Psammetichus I (E. Otto, *Die biographischen Inschriften der ägyptischen Spätzeit* [Leiden, 1954], no. 34), his grandson, thus satisfying the postulate of papponymy.

48. Takelot, cf. Yoyotte, *Les Principautés,* 131.

49. Piankhy stela, line 18.

50. Ibid., 116.

51. Yoyotte, *Les Principautés,* 165f; Gomaà, *Die libyschen Fürstentümer,* 60–67.

52. Cf. P. Dem. 31169 *ad loc.;* Strabo xvii.1.26 (Phagroriopolis). The latter locates it near "the canals and lakes" in the (eastern end of) Wady Tumilat. It seems likely that it is to be identified with the *P-g(!)rw* of Pithom St. 10 (= *Urk.* III, 90:11–13), where it is associated with Pithom and the "canal of the east" and is localized as "in front of (*m-ḫnt*) its (the canal's) eastern highland." Cf. *DG* 2:149. There is no valid reason for declaring its site unknown: as W. Helck, "Phagroriopolis," *LdÄ* 4:1017.

53. Daressy, "Le Fils Aîné de Chéchanq III," 61f.

54. Yoyotte, *Les Principautés,* 161–63.

55. Ibid.

56. *Bukkunanni-'pi:* Ranke, *Die altaegyptischen Personennamen,* 27; on the associations, see Habachi, "Statue of Bakennifi, Nomarch of Athribis," 68 ff; Vernus, *Athribis, textes et documents,* 74–76. Athribis was to retain its political preeminence into the Twenty-sixth Dynasty: L. Habachi, "Athribis in the XXVIth Dynasty," *BIFAO* 82 (1982): 213–35.

57. Gomaà, *Die libyschen Fürstentümer,* 97f.

58. Ibid., 99.

59. Naḫtihuruʿansini: M. Streck, *Assurbanipal und die letzten assyrischen Koenige bis zum Untergang Niniveh's* (Leipzig, 1916), II i.104; H.-U. Onasch, *Die assyrischen Eroberungen Ägyptens,* 55.

60. Yoyotte (*RA* 46 [1952]: 214) following Sauneron (*Kêmi* 11, 117–19) identifies with *Pr-spdw nḫ i3ty.* Apart from the fact that *i3t* interchanges with *iw* (*Wb.* I, 47) and is sometimes written with "walking legs" (Meeks, *Année lexicographique,* 3:7), thus suggesting a vocalization) ī, the dual of *i3ty* would undoubtedly have preserved a *t:* cf. Sethe, *ZÄS* 47 (1906): 42f.

61. On the Saïte family and succession, see Redford, *King-lists, Annals, and Day-books*, 321–22.

62. On *Si'nu*, see A. H. Gardiner, "The Delta Residence of the Ramessides," *JEA* 5 (1918): 253; H.-J. Thiessen, "Pelusium," *LdÄ* 4:925; Montet, *Géographie de l'Égypte ancienne*, 1:199; this is *not* Sile, now identified with Tel-Hebwa, pace H. W. Helck, *Die altägyptischen Gaue* (Wiesbaden, 1974), 188.

63. For discussion of the problem of Natho, see Helck, *LdÄ* 4:354–55; Lloyd, *Herodotus*, 3:189. The doubling of personal names could have resulted from failure to appreciate a patronymic.

64. *AEO* 2:147 ff.

65. One is tempted to identify Pedibast (*Putubišti*) at Tanis with the Sehtepibre Pedibast known from the Sacred Lake at Tanis: Montet, *Le Lac sacré de Tanis*, pl. 30; Habachi, "Three Monuments of the Unknown King Sehetepibre Pedubastis," 69–74; Schulman, "Problem of Pedubast," 33–41.

66. Yoyotte, *RA* 46 (1952): 212f; P. Bremner-Rhind 20, 10 (Faulkner, *Papyrus Bremner-Rhind*, 39).

67. *AEO* 2:186*f; *DG* 1:31; Helck, *Die altägyptischen Gaue*, 151.

68. G. Daressy, "Les cercueils royaux de Gournah," *ASAE* 12 (1912): 200f.

69. *AEO* 2:160*-61*.

70. In P. Bremner-Rhind 20, 9 (Faulkner, *Papyrus Bremner-Rhind*, 39) it follows the Red Mountain and precedes Unubu.

71. Cf., for example, the prominence of the sacerdotal titles at Athribis: Vernus, *Athribis, textes et documents*, 76–80.

72. Only Athribis, it seems, is the exception: Leclant, *LdÄ*, vol. 6 (Wiesbaden, 1986), 178 n. 154; for Bubastis, see idem, *Mélanges Mariette* (Cairo, 1961), 277 n. 2.

73. L. Habachi, "Mentuhotp, the Vizier and Son-in-law of Taharqa," in Hodjacke and Berlev, *Ägypten und Kusch*, 165–70.

74. Cf. Kawa VI, 15: "there were appointed to him (Amun) gardeners . . . from the people of L.E. . . . 20 . . . he filled (the temple) with numerous servants, and he appointed maidservants to it, wives of the chieftains of Lower Egypt." On Egyptian artists in Kush, see Myśliwiec, *Royal Portraiture*, 43.

75. Lamintu of Hmunu, unless it is a grandson.

76. Cf. *Oriens Antiquus* 26 (1987): 65–71.

77. Fecht, "Zu den Namen ägyptischer Fürsten und Städte," 116 n. 1. *Ta-a-a-ni* should stand for a vocalization *$Tay(a)n^e$ = Tni*, Θινις; its position in Ashurbanipal's list, as well as the PN of its ruler, confirms an identification with U.E. 8.

78. A. Leahy, *GM* 35 (1979): 31-39; Onasch, *Die assyrischen Eroberungen Ägyptens*, 56–57.

79. H. Kees, *Die Hohenpriester des Amun von Karnak von Herihor bis zum Ende der Äthiopenzeit* (Leiden, 1964).

80. Though not necessarily by the chief queen: Leahy, "Kushite Monuments at Abydos," 186–87.

81. For the origins of the office, see above.

82. For what follows, see Graefe, *Verwaltung und Geschichte.*

83. Interestingly, in the description of Saïte Egypt in Rylands IX, the Theban priesthood is a shadowy, though amiable, body of individuals far to the south, who are incapable of influencing politics in the north.

84. Graefe, *Verwaltung und Geschichte,* 1:130 ff and 7 ff.

85. Leclant, *Montouemhât,* 275; H. Kees, *Die Hohenpriester des Amun von Karnak,* 163f; Cairo/CCG 42203.

86. Brooklyn Museum Papyri nos. 50, 50a.

87. Cairo/CCG 646.

88. Berlin 17271.

89. Mut Temple Inscr. I.B, 14.

90. Cairo/CCG 42241, C(a), 5.

91. Mut Temple Inscr. I.B, 21.

92. Ibid., 15.

93. Cairo/CCG 646, C(a), 4. "Filling in lacunae" (i.e., in old and worn inscriptions) is a feat many scribes in the Late Period boast of as a pious act: Redford, *King-lists, Annals, and Day-books,* 225 n. 84.

94. On temple libraries and the ancient texts they contained, see Redford, *King-lists, Annals, and Day-books,* 215–29.

95. On the "blue book" of cult prescriptions, see D. B. Redford, "A Royal Speech from the Blocks of the Tenth Pylon," *BES* 3 (1981): 92–94; S. Schott, *Bücher und Bibliotheken im alten Aegypten* (Wiesbaden, 1990), 343–44.

96. On this expression, see Leclant, *Montouemhât,* 211 and n. *bb;* for *stp,* perhaps better "gone to pieces," see the root meaning in V. E. Orel and O. V. Stolbova, *Hamito-Semitic Etymological Dictionary* (Leiden, 1995), 487.

97. Mut Temple Inscr. II.A, 21–25.

98. Cairo/CCG 646, C(a), 9–10.

99. *Sšm-ḥw:* M. Roemer, *Gottes- und Priesterherrschaft in Aegypten am Ende des Neuen Reiches* (Wiesbaden, 1994), 440.

100. Cf. BM 10053: Peet, *Great Tomb Robberies of the Twentieth Egyptian Dynasty,* pl. 19–21.

101. On Khemkhem, see Leclant, *Montouemhât,* 229–30.

102. P-M 5:165; J. Vandier, "Hémen et Taharqa," *RdÉ* 10 (1955): 73–79 and pl. 5.

14. THEBES UNDER THE TWENTY-FIFTH DYNASTY

1. Török, *Kingdom of Kush,* 139–42.

2. Barguet, *Le Temple d'Amon-rê à Karnak,* 17f.

3. Ibid., 90.

4. Leclant, "Découvertes de monuments égyptiens ou égyptisants," 180.

5. P-M 2²:305 (15).

6. Leclant, *Recherches,* vol. 2, pl. 82 (B).

7. P-M 2²:205.

8. Leclant, *Recherches,* 1:221, 337f.

9. Cairo JdE 44665: Leclant, *Enquêtes,* 31 ff, 35.

10. Medinet Habu.

11. Daressy, "Inscriptions tentyrites," 190; Leclant, *Recherches,* 2:347.

12. P-M 2^2:24–25; J. Lauffray, *Karnak* 5 (1975): 77–92; N. Strudwick and H. Strudwick, *Thebes in Egypt* (Ithaca, N.Y., 1999), 63–64; D. Arnold, *Temples of the Last Pharaohs* (New York, 1999), 51–54.

13. P-M 2^2:38.

14. Ibid., 189.

15. Ibid., 227.

16. A. Varille, *ASAE* 53 (1954): 79 ff; P-M 2^2:251.

17. P-M 2^2:5.

18. A. Varille et al., *Karnak-Nord,* vol. 1 (Cairo, 1943): 29f; idem, *Karnak-Nord,* vol. 4 (Cairo, 1951), 6 n. 1, 106–9.

19. P-M 2^2:7.

20. R. A. Parker et al., *The Edifice of Taharqa by the Sacred Lake of Karnak* (Providence, 1979), 1.

21. Vernus, "Inscriptions de la Troisième Période Intermédiaire I."

22. The remains of this wall were destroyed in Chevrier's clearance of the northeastern corner of Karnak.

23. This follows from the ritual described in P. Louvre 3176(S): P. Barguet, *Le Papyrus N. 3176(S) du Musée du Louvre* (Cairo, 1962), which makes use of both the Iseum (Namlot's shrine) and the Temple-of-Osiris-Ruler-of-Eternity in the fourth century B.C.; Redford, "New Light on Temple J at Karnak," *Orientalia* 55 (1986): 13.

24. See D. B. Redford, "Three Seasons in Egypt: II," *JSSEA* 18 (1992): 33–34.

25. H. Chevrier, *ASAE* 53 (1953): 12; A. F. Pirritano-Redford, *JSSEA* 11 (1981): 261, pl. 40.

26. Redford, "Interim Report on the Excavations of East Karnak, 1977–78," *JARCE* 18 (1981): 17.

27. Menkheperre says his wall was built of *bḫn:* P. Barguet, *Le Temple d'Amon-rê à Karnak,* pl. 32B.

28. The following description is based on the excavations of East Karnak undertaken by the Akhenaten Temple Project from 1975 to 1983 and from 1987 to 1991.

29. *Egypt's Golden Age: The Art of Living in the New Kingdom* (Boston, 1982), 35, figs. 1, 2.

30. W. Erickson, *Demotisches Glossar* (Copenhagen, 1954), 392; S. R. K. Glanville, *A Theban Archive of the Reign of Ptolemy Soter* (London, 1939), xxxiii; I also benefited from oral communication with Janet Johnson of the Oriental Institute.

31. Bibliography in Redford, "So-called 'Codification' of Egyptian Law under Darius I," 158 n. 166.

32. See Johnson, "Persians and the Continuity of Egyptian Culture," 8:157.

33. Herm. Code, vii.18 ff.

34. Ibid., viii.7–10 (it goes to whichever property it is closer to).

35. Ibid., 15–16.

36. Ibid., 4; cf. Hughes, "Serra East," 111.

37. Herm. Code, viii.20–24.

38. Ibid., 17–19.

39. Ibid., 24–26.

40. Ibid., vii.31–viii.5.

41. A small libation trough from square B, about eighty meters due east of the Nektanebo gate, preserves part of a PN that might be restored Padiamun-nebnesuttowy.

42. These professions may be elicited from the Theban documents treated by K.-T. Zauzich in *Die ägyptische Schreibertradition in Aufbau,* vol. 1 (Wiesbaden, 1968).

43. Arnold, *Temples of the Last Pharaohs,* 54–55, fig. 26.

44. P-M 2²:205; Leclant, *Recherches,* 47–54; D. B. Redford, "Report on the Third Season of Work at the Shrine of Osiris, Heqa-Djet Karnak," in *Annual Report of the SSEA* (Toronto, 1972).

45. Leclant, *Recherches,* 94–96.

46. P-M 2²:5–6, 14–15, and 17–18; Leclant, *Recherches,* 99–105.

47. Leclant, *Recherches,* 23–36.

48. Ibid., 41–47.

49. Ibid., 80–82, 110–13.

50. Ibid., 109.

51. D. B. Redford, H. Sternberg-el-Hotabi, and S. Redford, "Three Seasons in Egypt: I," *JSSEA* 18 (1989): 1–23.

52. Djed-hor, lines 167–71.

53. Imhotpe and Amenophis, son of Hapu, are the choice examples: D. Wildung, *Imhotep und Amenhotep* (Berlin, 1977); Thoth was efficacious against snakes: L. Kakosy, "Problems of the Thoth Cult in Roman Egypt," *Studia Aegyptiaca* 7 (1981): 43.

54. It has been assumed, largely on the basis of the Bentresh stela (see below), that the divine occupant of Temple C was Khonsu-the-One-That-Takes-Charge (*ir-shrw*, P-M 2²:254–55), but our excavation found no reference to this form of the god. One clay disk did, however, contain the name of *Hnsw-p3-hrd.*

55. M. Broze, *La princesse de Bakhtan* (Brussels, 1989).

15. THE END OF THE TWENTY-FIFTH DYNASTY IN EGYPT

1. For renewed trade with East Africa, see A. B. Lloyd, "Necho and the Red Sea: Some Considerations," *JEA* 63 (1977): 142–47; T. Braun, "The Greeks in Egypt," *CAH* III, 3, 49; C. Tuplin, "Darius's Suez Canal and Persian Imperialism," in *Achaemenid History,* vol. 6 (Leiden, 1991), 239–42.

2. For a settlement of Shasu at Atfih, see Caminos, *Chronicle of Prince Osorkon,* 142, 144; for one at Spermeru (U.E. 19), see Redford, *Egypt, Canaan, and Israel,* 274 n. 80; for Asiatics at El-Hibeh, see W. Spiegelberg, "Briefe der 21. Dynastie aus el-Hibe," *ZÄS* 53 (1922): 7 (P. Strasbourg 33, line 2).

3. Ashmolean stela, no. 1894: Janssen, "Smaller Dâkhla Stela," 25; Giddy, *Egyptian Oases,* 144.

4. A. Fakhry, *The Oases of Egypt,* vol. 2 (Cairo, 1974), 64 (Sabaco).

5. Herodotus, ii.161, iv.159; cf. Lloyd, *Herodotus,* 3:173–74.

6. Cf. the shrines to "Amun the Great God residing in *Dsds,*" Giddy, *Egyptian Oases,* 102 n. 52; Fakhry, *Oases of Egypt,* 2:64f, 79 ff; for Amasis's temple at Siwa, see A. Fakhry, *The Oases of Egypt,* vol. 1 (Cairo, 1973), 150 ff, and P-M 7:313.

7. Fakhry, "Stela of the Boat-captain Inikaf," 426; idem, *Oases of Egypt,* 2:80 ff, 85, 132.

8. H. Goedicke, "Psammetik I. und die Libyer," *MDAIK* 18 (1962): 1.

9. In general, see D. Valbelle, in J. Yoyotte, ed., *L'Egypte du Delta: Les capitales du nord,* Dossiers d'archéologie 213 (Dijon, 1996), 60–65.

10. Strabo, xvii.1.21; Diodorus, xvi.46.5. Investigation of Tel Qedwa, ten kilometers south of Pelusium, by the University of Toronto expedition revealed the phenomenal amount of beach sand and the extensive deposit of mollusca.

11. Egyptian "Ways of Horus"; Hebrew "way of the land of the Philistines."

12. Roughly the route now followed by the modern highway from Beluza via Qantara to Ṣalḫiya.

13. On these routes, see Redford, *Egypt, Canaan, and Israel,* 359 n. 194.

14. Cf. Merikare 99: F. Gomaà, *Die Besiedlung Ägyptens während des Mittleren Reiches* (Wiesbaden, 1987), 2:129–32 and the literature there cited; Redford, *Egypt and Canaan in the New Kingdom,* 30.

15. Gebel Murr and Gebel Abu Ḥassa: J. Clédat, *BIFAO* 16 (1919): 205–12; 17 (1920): 113–15; P-M 4:53; G. Goyon, *Kêmi* 7 (1938): pls. 18–23.

16. Tel Qedwa, no earlier than 610–600 B.C.: see E. Oren, "Midol: A New Fortress on the Edge of the Eastern Nile Delta," *BASOR* 256 (1984): 7–44; D. B. Redford, "A Report on the 1993 and 1997 Seasons at Tell Qedwa," *JARCE* 25 (1998): 45–60; Tel el-Ḥer, Saïte-Persian: D. Valbelle and M. Abd el-Maksoud, "La marche du nord-est," in Yoyotte, *L'Egypte du Delta,* 60–65; *T3-ḥwt-p3-nsw* (Daphnae), early Saïte: W. M. F. Petrie, *Tanis,* vol. 2 (London, 1888), pls. 22–23; J. Boardman, *The Greeks Overseas* (London, 1980), 133–34; Tel el-Maskhuta (Pithom), 610–600 B.C.: J. S. Holladay, *Cities of the Delta, 3. Tel el-Maskhuta* (Undena, 1982); D. B. Redford, "Pithom," *LdÄ* 4:1054–58; the canal through Wadi Tumilat also had its inception no earlier than Saïte times: C. A. Redmount, "The Wadi Tumilat and the 'Canal of the Pharaohs,'" *JNES* 54 (1995): 127–35.

17. P-M 4:1: ancient *Syn: DG* 5:14–15; P. Montet, *Géographie d'Égypte,* vol. 1 (Paris, 1957), 199. Though possibly derived from Syny, a district producing wine from the Old Kingdom through Ramesside times (KRI 7:68; K. Zibelius, *Ägyptische Siedlungen nach Texten des Alten Reiches* [Wiesbaden, 1978], 211–12; cf. Gomàa, *Die Besiedlung Ägyptens während des Mittleren Reiches,* 2:120–22), the town is not certainly attested before the Saïte period: Ezek. 30:15–16; cf. P. Cairo, 31169.3.26. It is difficult to link Assyrian Ṣiᵓnu (Onasch, *Die assyrischen Eroberungen Ägyptens,* 38–39) with Pelusium because of the sibilant.

18. See Chapter 11.

19. G. Roux, *Ancient Iraq* (Harmondsworth, 1971), 297.

20. Tadmor, "Philistia under Assyrian Rule," 92; Elat, "Economic Relations of the Neo-Assyrian Empire with Egypt," 27–28; E. Oren, "Ethnicity and Regional Archaeology: The Western Negev under Assyrian Rule," in *Biblical Ar-*

chaeology Today 1990 (Jerusalem, 1993), 103. An alternate location, and perhaps to be preferred, is Tell Abu Salima in the North Sinai, where an Assyrian temple and fortification are in evidence: R. Reich, "The Identification of the 'Sealed *karu* of Egypt,'" *IEJ* 34 (1984): 32–38; idem, *The New Encyclopedia of Archaeological Excavations in the Holy Land* (Jerusalem, 1994), 15.

21. Was it governed by a bilateral treaty or a suzerain-vassal oath?

22. *ANET*², 302a; S. Parpola, "The Murderer of Sennacherib," *Mesopotamia* 8 (1980): 171–82.

23. For Tel Jemmeh with its Assyrian residence, see G. van Beek, "Tel Gamma," *IEJ* 24 (1974): 139, 274; 27 (1977): 172; *National Geographic Research Reports* (Washington, 1984), 682–95; Na'aman, "Brook of Egypt and Assyrian Policy," 72–81; for Tel Haror and other sites, see Oren, *Biblical Archaeology Today 1990*, 102–105; Redford, *Egypt, Canaan, and Israel*, 358.

24. Redford, *Egypt, Canaan, and Israel*, 358; A. K. Grayson, "Assyria: Sennacherib and Esarhaddon (704–669 B.C.)," in *CAH* III, 2 (1991), 124.

25. On the size of Sidon at the time, see E. Lipínski, in Ahituv and Levine, *Eretz Israel*, 158*-63*.

26. Grayson, "Assyria," 125 (sources); H. Klengel, in Ahituv and Levine, *Eretz Israel*, 132*.

27. Ba'alu of Tyre benefited by his submission, receiving the southern part of Sidon's domain: Katzenstein, *History of Tyre*, 265.

28. *ANET*², 290b.

29. In general, Redford, *Egypt, Canaan, and Israel*, 359–61.

30. Onasch, *Die Assyrischen Eroberungen Ägyptens*, 18–23.

31. *ANET*², 292.

32. P. Dem. 31169 lists four: *Mktr* (iii, 20); *Mktr-t-s*(?) (iii, 21); *Mktr {pf}-Bcr zpn* (iii, 22), and *Mktr-ph-s3y(?)* (iii, 23). Of these only the third is identifiable as the shrine of Baal-saphon. One of the others may be Tel Kedwa, as E. Oren has suggested ("Migdol," *BASOR* 256 [1984]: 7–44), although not *the* Migdol of Jeremiah.

33. The name has been compared to *Wsr-ḥpr-rc* in P. Dem. 31169 ii, 22, and arbitrarily placed near Salhieh: G. Daressy, "La *Demeure royale* en Basse-Egypte," *ASAE* 17 (1917): 128–29. This would be the prenomen of Sety II of the Nineteenth Dynasty: Redford, *Egypt, Canaan, and Israel*, 360 n. 200.

34. Redford, *Egypt, Canaan, and Israel*, 359–60.

35. *ANET*², 293a.

EPILOGUE

1. See P. L. Shinnie, *Ancient Nubia* (London, 1996), 105–18.

INDEX